Fast Foods

Fast Foods
Eating In and Eating Out

Monte Florman and Marjorie Florman

and the Editors of
Consumer Reports

Consumers Union

Mount Vernon, New York

Copyright © 1990 by Consumers Union of United States, Inc.
Mount Vernon, New York 10553

Library of Congress Cataloging-in-Publication Data
Florman, Monte.
Fast foods—eating in and eating out / Monte Florman and Marjorie Florman and the
editors of Consumer Reports.
p.   cm.
ISBN 0-89043-353-4
1. Convenience foods—Composition.   2. Nutrition.   3. Fast food restaurants.
I. Florman, Marjorie.   II. Consumer Reports Books.   III. Consumer reports.
IV. Title.
TX370.F56   1990
613.2'8—dc20

90–33621
CIP

Design by Susan Hood

First printing, September 1990
Manufactured in the United States of America

Contents

Introduction

For many American families, the leisurely mealtime ritual now seems as old-fashioned as the trolley car. Family dinnertime has given way, much of the time, to eating on the run or before the television screen. The pressures of a fast-paced life-style, the TV habit, and the growing number of women in the workforce have all contributed to the demise of a valuable family tradition.

Fast-food restaurants, as a result, are prospering. Much of their appeal lies in the ready-made convenience of their products and services. There's no shopping, no preparation, no cleanup. Menu selection takes a minimum of decision making, and service is prompt. And it's a cheap way for a family to eat out.

But there's still something to be said for the "fast" meal at home, when the harried cook can look in the freezer or on the pantry shelf for a food item that can be prepared and presented with a minimum of fuss and bother. Indeed, fast and simple home dining is more popular now than ever before. Catering to this growing trend, many packaged, easy-to-prepare frozen and unfrozen foods are available in supermarkets, take-out shops, and specialty stores. And there are always the familiar canned and fresh standby foods that cook quickly, taste good, and are more nutritious and a lot cheaper than ordinary fast-food fare.

Manufacturers of kitchen appliances have cooperated in this culinary trend by perfecting a variety of microwave ovens that sell at a wide range of prices. These modern time-savers come in sizes that fit the smallest kitchen space and feature controls that vary from the simple and basic to the ultrasophisticated and complex.

About This Book

Fast Foods—Eating In and Eating Out contains updated reviews of popular fast-food places and many of the somewhat more upscale chain restaurants. These restaurants, although not recognized as particularly "fast," have captured a sizable share of the family dining-out market and so deserve to be featured here.

A large part of this book supplies detailed information about the nutrition and flavor of many "fast" foods that can be eaten at home, whether for breakfast, lunch, dinner, or as an occasional snack. Some of the foods may not seem particularly quick to prepare (chicken, for example), but these food items can be in the fast category if you cook and freeze them for use at a later time. You will also find helpful hints on food buying and preparation throughout, as well as a number of recipes for making some dishes from scratch.

The Ratings, covering some 1,300 individual brands, are based on Consumers Union's (CU) laboratory tests, controlled evaluations and/or judgments by expert tasters or panels of trained tasters. Although the Ratings are not an infallible guide, they do offer comparative buying information that can greatly increase the likelihood that you will receive value for your money.

Although you may be tempted to buy whatever brand appears at the top of Ratings order, it is best to begin by reading the full product report. In it you will find a general description of all the products in the test group. When products are listed in order of estimated quality, CU judged the brand listed first to be best, the next listed second best, and so on.

The order in which foods are listed in the Ratings is based on a combination of flavor, taste, texture, and appearance—often simply referred to as taste. (Occasionally, food Ratings are presented in order of nutritional quality.) Since preferences regarding taste are subjective, you may not always agree with the judgments of Consumers Union's specialists. Furthermore, food processing itself is variable: Manufacturers sometimes change their product formulations, depending on seasonal availability of foods and on marketing factors such as competition and regional differences in sensory preferences. So keep in mind that the Ratings information on flavor is meant to serve as a guide, not as the last word in gustatory pleasure. You are the final judge.

Ratings of appliances are generally listed in order of estimated quality in the same manner as stated above. However, appliance manufacturers commonly change their models every year or so. As a consequence, there is a good chance that the particular brand and model you select from one of the Ratings charts will not be in stock. But even if you substitute a more recent equivalent of an older model, Ratings information should help guide you through the maze of new features.

Each Ratings chart includes the month and year in which the test groups appeared in *Consumer Reports*. Any Ratings charts that appeared in the magazine more than three years ago are largely outdated and have been omitted.

Prices

Food prices are averages of what Consumers Union's shoppers paid at the time of the tests, although some of the cost information in the Ratings charts has been updated. In general, the prices have been rounded off for convenience. Because of inflation, seasonal changes, regional variations, and local sales competition, you are urged to use the prices only as a reference for comparing the relative cost of one brand with another.

The prices for food-preparation equipment are the list prices that existed at the time the article was originally published. Appliance prices vary substantially since these items are commonly discounted.

The editors of this book hope that this information, assembled from various issues of *Consumer Reports* magazine, will help you become more knowledgeable about the nutritional and sensory values of fast foods, both in the restaurant and at home. The overall intention of this book is to encourage and assist you in making mealtime a pleasant and enjoyable part of the day for you, your family, and your friends.

1

*E*ating Out

Fast-Food Restaurants

Fast food is better now than it was ten years ago.

It's the salads that have cut the grease. Wendy's introduced the salad bar to their fast-food customers more than a decade ago. But 1987 marked the year salad took off in a big way. After years of tossing (and market research), McDonald's finally came out with its own brand of boxed salads, practical and portable, and perfect for the drive-through and for take-out. Burger King, which had dabbled with salad bars in some of its outlets, quickly rushed out look-alike boxed salads. As a result, many big chains now offer a packaged salad or a salad bar.

Today, salads sell very well. Fast-food salads are said to be so successful that they've appreciably increased the national demand for lettuce, and farmers have had to plant more to keep up.

According to a 1987 Consumers Union survey, about one in seven respondents ate a salad the last time they visited a fast-food restaurant. They preferred Wendy's salad to Burger King's or McDonald's, awarding it significantly higher marks on freshness, variety, and dressings. (Since people's tastes change, as do restaurants themselves, respondents' preferences might differ somewhat if we were to conduct this survey today.)

Wendy's has expanded its salad bar to include hot and cold Mexican and Italian dishes. That salad-bar bounty may have helped

Wendy's win high marks from those who filled out CU's questionnaires. That chain's menu also rates highly compared with typical fast-food fare, getting high marks for the freshness and variety of its food, as well as for speed of service, and employee courtesy.

Many people eat at fast-food places more often than they did before salads were available. Salads thus have successfully expanded the "territory" of the fast-food restaurant. And they've done it without cutting into sales of other foods—important to the chains as they face more and more competition from one another and from new sources such as supermarket take-out counters.

Cynics say that salads and the like are intended mainly to lend chains a veneer of healthfulness, even as customers continue to devour burgers and fries. Some say that such dishes are calculated to win over the one nutrition-minded person in a group who might otherwise veto the group's eating at a fast-food place.

Many people, in fact, do seem to throw their nutritional caution to the winds when eating out. As a Wendy's spokesman put it, people view eating out "more as entertainment," reserving good nutrition for eating at home. His evidence: Wendy's customers showed little interest in its special "Light Menu" or multigrain burger bun. Those items were removed from the menu, as were several low-cal salad dressings at the salad bar. In addition, he said, few people ever write to Wendy's to ask for ingredients lists—just as at other chains.

Ingredients

That ingredients lists are offered at all is due in part to some bad publicity generated back in 1985, when the Center for Science in the Public Interest, a consumer group active in health issues, commissioned tests of the cooking oils the restaurants use. The results, widely reported at the time, revealed that many of the biggest chains—including Arby's, Burger King, Hardee's, McDonald's, and Wendy's—were frying potatoes, chicken nuggets, and other fare in beef fat.

The industry's response was positive. Burger King, McDonald's, and Wendy's switched to 100 percent vegetable oil for cooking everything but french fries. (Fries continued to be cooked in a fat that's a blend of beef fat and vegetable oil. Customers, the companies say, preferred the taste of potatoes cooked that way.)

McDonald's managed to turn the bad press into a marketing opportunity—"to neutralize the junk-food misconceptions about McDonald's good food," the company told its operators. It launched a multimillion-dollar advertising campaign stressing dietary "balance" and "variety" while extolling the good nutrition customers can glean at the Golden Arches—like calcium from calcium-enriched buns. The ads were so one-sidedly positive about the nutritional possibilities at McDonald's that the attorneys general of California, New York, and Texas asked the company to "cease and desist" or face charges of false advertising.

The cooking-oil revelation prompted health and consumer groups to press for ingredients labeling on fast-food wrappers, a move the industry opposed as unwieldy, given all the containers and food suppliers. A printed ingredients list, says a trade group, could even promote "undue anxiety" among consumers. (An ingredients list for, say, a *Wendy's Frosty* would have revealed the use of guar gum, carboxymethyl cellulose, monoglycerides, diglycerides, carrageenan, and disodium phosphate, among other items. None of those additives are known to be harmful, but they don't sound like milkshakes, either.)

In the compromise that was eventually reached, most big chains promised to offer booklets or brochures with ingredient and nutritional information.

More recently, the chains have had to cope with bad press over the mountains of trash they generate. Much of that trash is chlorofluorocarbon-based plastic foam. Not only is that type of plastic non-biodegradable, its manufacture uses chemicals that can harm the Earth's protective ozone layer. Environmentalists and public officials from New York City to Berkeley, California, have pressed the chains to abandon such packaging.

Fast-Food Nutrition

One way to evaluate a food's nutritional value is to consider what comes along with its calories. Does the food have a high per-calorie density of desirable nutrients such as protein, vitamins, and minerals? Do the calories carry excess baggage, such as too much sodium and fat? Are they empty calories, providing food energy but carrying no nutrients at all?

While you can't expect a single food or even a single meal to be perfectly balanced, too many badly balanced meals can add up to a poor diet. The profiles of these fast-food items show that, like the American diet, they are typically long on protein and fat. Most items, even the meat items, are comparatively low in calcium and iron, nutrients that are often short in women's diets. Vitamin A, typically supplied by milk and cheese, is scant.

The overall nutritional picture is summed up in the nutrient-density profiles on pages 8–11. Those profiles show the sort of nutritional load, good and bad, each calorie carries.

A perfectly balanced food would supply the same portion of a day's nutrient needs as it does calories; all the bars in its nutrient-density profile would be the same length as the calorie bar. If a *Big Mac* were so balanced, it would supply not only about one-quarter of the day's calories (as it does), but also one-quarter the protein, one-quarter the fat, one-quarter the vitamin C, and so on.

But no one food is perfectly balanced. The aim is to eat a well-balanced *diet,* day by day. So the most telling example of fast-food nutrition might be the profile of the "*Big Mac* meal," consisting of a *McDonald's Big Mac,* a chocolate shake, and fries. As the profiles show, that meal is decidedly top-heavy with calories, protein, and fat.

Overall, fast-food entrées do not pack enough vitamins and minerals to justify all the calories. Profiles for other foods of the same type would show more similarities than differences. The fast-food chains' hamburger dishes are long on protein and fat, with skimpy amounts of vitamins and minerals for such high-calorie sandwiches.

By contrast, a roast-beef sandwich packs just as much iron as a *Mac* but without so much excess baggage. A plain roast-beef sandwich from Arby's, Hardee's, and Roy Rogers, with no sauce, carries fewer calories than the big hamburgers—sometimes 250 fewer—with almost as much protein, just as much iron, but only a fraction of the fat. Even with a little barbecue sauce, a roast-beef sandwich still puts the big burgers to shame.

Chicken and fish are perceived as lighter fare than red meat. But deep-frying adds enough fat and calories to dampen any advantage over hamburgers. The profile of *Kentucky Fried Chicken* pretty much sums up what you can expect from fast-food chicken. (Chicken nuggets offer fewer calories, but the calories still carry a heavy load of fat along with their protein.)

The profile of one chain's burger or french fries is much the same as another's, so the items generally show what you can expect from any such item. The Roy Rogers roast-beef sandwich shows a rather good balance; other roast-beef sandwiches aren't quite as lean.

The McDonald's profile shows that the classic fast-food order of burger, shake, and fries adds up to a very lopsided meal. The McDonald's meal provides only about half of a woman's daily need for calories, but most of the day's protein and 96 percent of its saturated fat, with little of its vitamins and minerals. Two other meals during the day might provide the needed vitamins and minerals, but they would almost certainly add up to an excess of calories and an excess of saturated fat.

The really bad news is that french fries are loaded with fat, which provides almost half their calories. Some good news is that most fast-food french fries provide their calories' share of vitamin C, but they're not plentiful sources compared with, say, an orange. French fries typically contain less than one-sixth the daily need. A medium-size orange provides more than a day's worth, with far fewer calories.

Chocolate shakes supply their calories' share of protein and calcium, though the vitamin A they contain is disappointingly scant. By contrast, 10 ounces of 2 percent lowfat milk contains about half the calories, with about as much protein and more calcium.

Only a few fast-food items seem unduly high in sodium for the calories they contribute to the diet. That calculation is based on a quota of 3,300 milligrams of sodium a day, what the National Research Council considers the upper limit of safe and sufficient intake for healthy adults. (Many people in fact eat far more than that.) But for someone on a sodium-restricted diet, 3,300 milligrams a day is still too much. Only some fast-food chains' french fries might be allowed in a restricted diet.

McDonald's Big Mac

% of daily intake		0	25	50	75	100
Calories	572					
Protein	25 g.					
Calcium	202 mg.					
Iron	3 mg.					
Vitamin A	251 I.U.					
Vitamin C	4 mg.					
Total fat	34 g.					
Saturated fat	15 g.					
Sodium	794 mg.					

Profiles are based on an average woman's daily dietary needs. The quotas of an average man are 35 percent greater for calories, fat, and saturated fat and 27 percent greater for protein. Children's needs are proportionately lower. An asterisk indicates less than 2 percent of an adult's need.

As published in a **June 1988** report.

McDonald's Fries

% of daily intake		0	25	50	75	100
Calories	222					
Protein	3 g.					
Calcium	8 mg.					
Iron	1 mg.					
Vitamin A	* I.U.					
Vitamin C	6 mg.					
Total fat	12 g.					
Saturated fat	5 g.					
Sodium	121 mg.					

McDonald's Chocolate Shake

% of daily intake		0	25	50	75	100
Calories	356					
Protein	11 g.					
Calcium	291 mg.					
Iron	2 mg.					
Vitamin A	324 I.U.					
Vitamin C	* mg.					
Total fat	10 g.					
Saturated fat	6 g.					
Sodium	278 mg.					

McDonald's Big Mac Meal

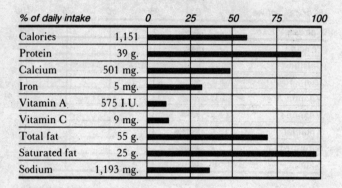

% of daily intake		0	25	50	75	100
Calories	1,151					
Protein	39 g.					
Calcium	501 mg.					
Iron	5 mg.					
Vitamin A	575 I.U.					
Vitamin C	9 mg.					
Total fat	55 g.					
Saturated fat	25 g.					
Sodium	1,193 mg.					

Burger King Whaler

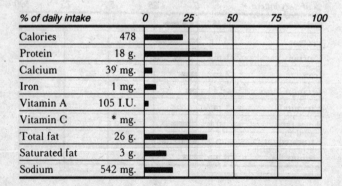

% of daily intake		0	25	50	75	100
Calories	478					
Protein	18 g.					
Calcium	39 mg.					
Iron	1 mg.					
Vitamin A	105 I.U.					
Vitamin C	* mg.					
Total fat	26 g.					
Saturated fat	3 g.					
Sodium	542 mg.					

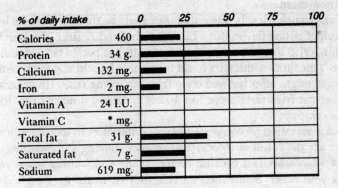

Kentucky Fried Chicken
(two pieces)

% of daily intake		0	25	50	75	100
Calories	460					
Protein	34 g.					
Calcium	132 mg.					
Iron	2 mg.					
Vitamin A	24 I.U.					
Vitamin C	* mg.					
Total fat	31 g.					
Saturated fat	7 g.					
Sodium	619 mg.					

Roy Rogers Roast Beef

% of daily intake		0	25	50	75	100
Calories	335					
Protein	25 g.					
Calcium	107 mg.					
Iron	3 mg.					
Vitamin A	59 I.U.					
Vitamin C	* mg.					
Total fat	11 g.					
Saturated fat	3 g.					
Sodium	743 mg.					

Flavor

It is common to find taste differences in an item from store to store within a chain.

Take french fries. In one outlet they could be thick, with skins left on, full of potato flavor, but a bit soggy. In another store, they might be thin, crisp outside, soft within, but with less potato taste. A third outlet's medium-width fries could turn out to be cold and soggy. And a fourth might offer hot and crisp fries of varying sizes. (In general, thicker-cut fries taste more like baked potatoes; thinner ones, like potato chips.)

Some variation no doubt stems from differences in food suppliers. Some are the result of inconsistent or poor cooking and handling.

Fast foods are fast because they're ready and waiting when you place your order. Sometimes, though, they've waited too long. Fried foods have an especially short shelf life. If held too long, crispy items like chicken nuggets and fried chicken can become rubbery or go soggy on the underside. Perhaps that's why McDonald's reportedly throws out batches of unsold french fries every so often.

In one Consumers Union test series, there were differences in the quality of ingredients and the cooking among chains. *Wendy's Big Classic* contained the juiciest, thickest patty; the other brand-name burgers were drier and more gristly. Of the roast-beef sandwiches, Roy Rogers' was juiciest and most flavorful. Of the chicken nuggets, only Burger King's *Chicken Tenders* were made solely of breast meat. Kentucky Fried's *Kentucky Nuggets* and McDonald's *Chicken McNuggets* are both blends of white and dark meat (McDonald's also throws in ground chicken skin).

Shakes were variously concocted from chain to chain and from store to store, depending on the type of shake mix and syrup, how much chocolate syrup was siphoned, and how the drink was mixed. The best shake came from a Hardee's outlet that had an ice-cream parlor. It made an old-fashioned milkshake with ice cream and milk; the three other Hardee's in the test series poured the more usual

froth-filled shake. The texture of *Wendy's Frosty* was more reminiscent of ice cream than shake—thick enough to be eaten with a
spoon. But to some people its taste might resemble chocolate milk of
magnesia.

Recommendations

A steady diet of typical fast-food items will overload you with protein, fat, and calories while shortchanging you on vitamins, minerals, and fiber. To balance one meal of burger, shake, and fries, you'd
have to search out lowfat, vitamin-and-mineral-rich fare the rest of
the day.

But by choosing from the fast-food menus with an eye toward
damage control, you can put together a fairly well balanced meal.
Here are some tactics for dining defensively:

- Choose roast beef over burgers if you can. Roast beef is often
  leaner than a hamburger. Roy Rogers' roast-beef sandwich may
  be the leanest and best balanced of all the entrées—and it's tasty,
  too. By adding tomatoes and lettuce from Roy Rogers' "Fixin's
  Bar," you can add other nutrients.
- Choose small plain burgers instead of the giant mouth-filling
  burgers with all the works. Skip the mayonnaise and cheese. You
  can save nearly 150 calories on a Burger King Whopper, for
  example, just by having them hold the mayo. Cheese, while a
  source of protein and calcium, also carries some fat.
- Choose regular fried chicken, not the "extra crispy" recipe. Extra
  fat adds the crispiness—up to 100 extra calories per piece for
  Kentucky Fried Chicken's extra crispy recipe.
- Order milk instead of a shake. Lowfat milk provides much more
  protein and calcium per calories than the fast-food concoctions.
  Or order a diet soda.

- If you're looking to cut calories, go easy on the french fries. Split an order with someone else. When you're at Wendy's or Roy Rogers, consider a plain baked potato instead.
- Choose a boxed fast-food salad or one from the salad bar. If you try a boxed salad, one with chicken or shrimp will supply some protein along with the fiber, complex carbohydrates, vitamins, and minerals from the vegetables. At a salad bar, choose carrots, tomatoes, and dark-green vegetables. And go easy on dressings, fatty croutons, taco chips, and mayonnaise-laden pasta and potato salads. The packet of Thousand Island dressing that comes with a McDonald's salad can give it more calories than a Big Mac.

Ratings of Fast Food

Listed by food types; within types, listed alphabetically.
As published in a **June 1988** report. Information has been updated to December 1989.

Food	Price	Weight, oz.	Calories	Protein, g.	Total fat, g.	Saturated fat, g.	Sodium, mg.	Calcium, mg.	Iron, mg.	Vitamin A, i.u.	Vitamin C, mg.	Sensory comments
Hamburgers												
Burger King Whopper	$2.39	9	584	28	33	13	769	61	4	103	11	Soft bun with thin, slightly gristly, juicy meat. Crisp lettuce. Tomato, pickle. Mayonnaise, ketchup add moistness.
McDonald's Big Mac	2.39	7	572	25	34	15	794	202	3	251	4	Cottony bun soggy from sauce, with thin, dry, gristly meat, cheese, and limp lettuce.
Wendy's Big Classic	2.39	8	500	26	28	11	739	106	3	139	12	Hard seeded roll toasted, not soggy. Meat thick and juicy, slightly gristly, with rich beef flavor. Crisp romaine lettuce.

Nutrient levels

Ratings of Fast Food (cont'd)

Food	Price	Weight, oz.	Calories	Protein, g.	Total fat, g.	Saturated fat, g.	Sodium, mg.	Calcium, mg.	Iron, mg.	Vitamin A, I.U.	Vitamin C, mg.	Sensory comments
Roast beef												
Arby's Roast Beef (regular)	$2.09	5	365	23	19	7	771	31	4	30	1	Soft, thinly sliced meat seemed fabricated, salty, with taste like ham.
Hardee's Roast Beef (regular)	1.55	5	338	22	17	6	754	39	3	76	*	Soft, soggy seeded bun with juicy, salty, flavorless beef.
Roy Rogers Roast Beef	2.44	6	335	25	11	3	743	107	3	59	*	Soft, soggy bun with thinly sliced, juicy, salty roast beef. Nice color.
Fish												
Burger King Whaler	1.99	6	478	18	26	3	542	39	1	105	*	Soft bun with bland fish, sweet tartar sauce. Breading slightly crisp.
McDonald's Filet-O-Fish	1.79	5	415	14	23	5	568	126	2	169	*	Cottony bun with bland fish, cheese, and gummy, slightly bitter tartar sauce. Breading soggy.

Nutrient levels

Chicken

	Price										Comments
Arby's Chicken Breast Sandwich	2.59	7	567	26	32	7	965	61	2	109	*	Varied among stores. Bun burned or soggy. Patty with spicy coating tender and juicy to tough and dry.
Burger King Chicken Tenders	2.19	3	223	18	12	3	519	13	1	26	*	Varied among stores from crisp and tender to tough and chewy, with slight chicken flavor. Spicy coating.
Hardee's Chicken Fillet Sandwich	1.79	7	431	24	20	6	937	58	2	125	*	Soft sesame-seed bun, with spicy coated chicken, usually crisp, tender, and juicy. Sometimes patty was tough.
Kentucky Fried Chicken, 2 pc.	1.99	6	460	34	31	7	619	132	2	24	*	Crisp, well-seasoned coating with greasy meat. Sometimes tough, chewy, or steamed-tasting.
Kentucky Fried Chicken Nuggets	1.79	4	281	18	17	4	634	11	1	17	*	Generally hot, crisp, well-seasoned coating on tender, juicy chicken.
McDonald's Chicken McNuggets	1.99	4	286	19	18	5	443	11	1	21	2	Varied among stores from crisp, tender, and juicy to tough, dry, soggy, bland, and salty. Little chicken flavor.
Roy Rogers Chicken, 2 pc.	2.55	6	519	33	35	8	728	44	4	31	*	Crisp, well-seasoned coating on juicy meat. If held too long before serving, tough and chewy.

Ratings of Fast Food *(cont'd)*

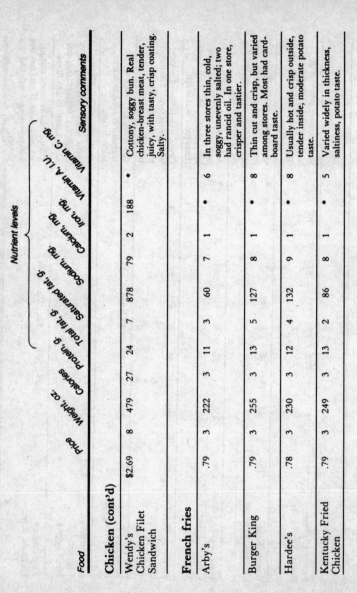

Food	Price	Weight, oz.	Calories	Protein, g	Total fat, g	Saturated fat, g	Sodium, mg	Calcium, mg	Iron, mg	Vitamin A, I.U.	Vitamin C, mg	Sensory comments
Chicken (cont'd)												
Wendy's Chicken Filet Sandwich	$2.69	8	479	27	24	7	878	79	2	188	*	Cottony, soggy bun. Real chicken-breast meat, tender, juicy, with tasty, crisp coating. Salty.
French fries												
Arby's	.79	3	222	3	11	3	60	7	1	*	6	In three stores thin, cold, soggy, unevenly salted; two had rancid oil. In one store, crisper and tastier.
Burger King	.79	3	255	3	13	5	127	8	1	*	8	Thin cut and crisp, but varied among stores. Most had cardboard taste.
Hardee's	.78	3	230	3	12	4	132	9	1	*	8	Usually hot and crisp outside, tender inside, moderate potato taste.
Kentucky Fried Chicken	.79	3	249	3	13	2	86	8	1	*	5	Varied widely in thickness, saltiness, potato taste.

McDonald's	.89	3	222	3	12	5	121	8	1	*	6	Thin, crisp, and tender outside, soft inside, slight potato taste.
Roy Rogers	.89	3	237	3	13	4	120	8	1	*	7	Thin, variable in texture. Soggy, cardboardy, little potato taste.
Wendy's	.85	3	287	3	14	4	108	7	1	*	9	Medium thickness, crisp outside, tender inside, some potato taste.

Chocolate shakes

Arby's	.99	11	426	10	14	7	294	281	2	307	5	Usually thick and a bit icy. Chocolate flavor varied.
Burger King	.99	11	351	8	10	5	514	371	2	342	*	Moderately thick and a bit icy, with little chocolate flavor.
Hardee's	1.03	11	349	9	11	6	247	239	2	261	*	Different ingredients and preparation methods used from store to store.
McDonald's	1.09	11	356	11	10	6	278	291	2	324	*	A bit icy, varying in thickness and flavor from real milk chocolate to slight fruitiness of artificial chocolate.
Roy Rogers	1.09	12	430	13	11	6	435	363	2	380	*	Moderately thick and chocolatey, a bit icy.
Wendy's Frosty	.99	9	351	8	13	6	257	207	1	233	*	Very thick, little chocolate flavor. Left chalky, gritty residue in mouth.

* Contains less than 2 percent of daily quota.

19

Chain Restaurants

Roadside restaurants such as Denny's, Ponderosa, Friendly, Red Lobster, and Shoney's offer less speed but more variety and ambience than the fast-feeders and pizza chains. They not only are competing with one another but are also engaged in a tug-of-war with the likes of McDonald's and Pizza Hut for your dining-out dollar.

That's good news if you eat frequently, or even occasionally, at chain restaurants. In their attempt to win customers, the chains must offer more—more value, more variety, more convenience, more atmosphere.

To foster distinctiveness, the chain restaurants have been going "high concept," packaging ambience so that eating out becomes rather like stepping into a movie set.

Menus offer more choices, including salads, international dishes, regional cooking, and plenty of desserts. Salad bars have expanded, sometimes into all-you-can-eat buffets and smorgasbords. Special audiences—the young, the old, the diet-conscious—are wooed with special menus. More and more chains offer a take-out menu as well.

The chains differ considerably in the types of food available and how it is served. You can find meat loaf or elegantly presented Cajun cuisine, plastic plates and plastic-wrapped cutlery or table settings of crockery and cloth, cafeteria-style trays and lines or individual dining rooms.

Most of these moderately priced chains fall into three basic types, as defined by the restaurant trade. The "family" restaurant, also known as the coffee shop, is big on breakfast and is fairly inexpensive. The "steak house" aims for lunch and dinner trade but is also fairly low-priced, often with a cafeteria-like line. The fanciest type of chain is the "dinner house," a class that includes many styles, often with a bar, almost always with "atmosphere."

Speed and Service

Even the harshest critic of fast food has to admit it's convenient. You don't have to go far or wait long to get it.

Chain restaurants have more or less conceded that they can't match the fast-food chains for sheer numbers of outlets. But many are trying to serve food faster, so they can appeal to eaters who are used to the speed of fast-food service.

One way to speed up service is the do-it-yourself approach, and many chains offer salad bars, breakfast bars, pasta bars, or full-fledged buffets. One steak-house chain, Ponderosa, offers "Express Lunch," which allows salad-bar customers not only to get food faster but to pay faster than customers ordering entrées.

Friendly, a chain famous for its ice cream, has promised to whip up certain lunch entrées within five minutes of your order or you get a free dessert. Chains such as Bennigan's, Po Folks, and Red Lobster have said they would deliver your lunch within 15 minutes of the order or it's free. (The loophole, of course, is that your order may not be taken right away.)

Take-out food, once the exclusive domain of fast fooderies, is one of the fastest-growing segments of the entire restaurant business. Chains are using various strategies to jump on the bandwagon. The Bob Evans chain, for instance, promotes a limited take-out menu of quickly prepared items. Other chains are less inhibited. Po Folks offers everything on its menu for take-out, while pointing out some selections it does "extra good." Nor is Po Folks shy about catering, a service also offered on its menu.

Chain restaurants will probably never be able to beat fast-food chains on *speedy* service, but they certainly can beat them on service. Unlike fast-food outlets, where your only contact with a human is brief and monosyllabic, the chains can use personal contact to make an impression.

The service at many chain restaurants begins at the door rather than at the table. Chains are discovering that a well-dressed host or hostess adds a pleasant touch to the dining experience. The employee greets you, consults a seating chart—even if the place is empty—and leads you to a table. Once you are seated, the service is likely to be good.

Atmosphere

Dinner houses have known all along the value of creating a "dining experience." With their relatively high prices, they have to convince patrons that the meals are worth extra.

Atmosphere in a restaurant is a combination of psychology and design. The elements may be as obvious as the architecture of the building or as subtle as the restaurant layout, interior colors, lighting, even the background music. The sum of those elements can be as important as the food in getting you to come back.

Nearly all dinner houses score highly in atmosphere. Stuart Anderson's has its message fine-tuned. Its stark, windowless buildings with barnboard siding set the stage for its cowboy theme and steak specialties. Inside, customers are led to private corrals constructed of rough-hewn wood and smoked glass. The effect is so understated and unique that you might not suspect you're in one unit of a large chain.

Other dinner houses also use thematic ambience. Bennigan's,

T.G.I. Friday, and Chili's resemble fancy saloons. El Torito and Chi-Chi's are unmistakably Mexican. Steak and Ale, usually found in Tudor-style houses, takes an aristocratic approach to serving steak.

Brown Derby, a chain based in Ohio, takes myriad shapes. From unit to unit, the only constants are the name borrowed from the now defunct Hollywood nightspot, the trademark hat, and the basic menu.

Until not very long ago, atmosphere was about the last thing you'd ascribe to chains in the coffee-shop class. The likes of Shoney's, Big Boy, and International House of Pancakes projected no coherent image. Recently, the image of good value was being actively promoted.

Other chains in the coffee-shop class—Village Inn and Perkins, for instance—cultivate a more elegant look, using polished brass, Americana, and greenhouse seating. The most successful restaurant of this type at establishing an atmosphere is Marie Callender's.

This western chain combines sentimentality, nostalgia, and Americana. Standing out like a storybook illustration amid the gray of roadside and mall architecture, it's grandma's house, complete with fragrant flowers lining the walk and lace curtains at the windows. Freshly baked pies greet you inside the door. Antiquey furniture and flowery prints complete the picture.

Another family restaurant that has a theatrical flair is Bob Evans. The incandescent red ranch house of Bob Evans restaurants is hard to miss through Texas, Florida, and the Midwest. Inside, the country decor is subdued but unmistakable. The restaurant may be laid out to display the part of the kitchen where the biscuits are baked.

Many steak houses retain the predictable motifs of ranch-house architecture—exposed beams, high ceilings, and wagon wheels. Often, the layout is confusing, so a customer isn't sure which way to walk after entering. In some cases, glimpses of the kitchen and work areas behind the serving line seem unplanned and not appetizing.

Some steak-house chains, however, have started to come out of the dark. The biggest—Bonanza, Ponderosa, and Sizzler—have added windows and brass and glass detailing.

Background music can help or hinder atmosphere. Music can be used deliberately, to soothe diners—or to make them eat more quickly. According to an industry study, the time diners took to complete their meal and leave, called "table turn," was speeded up nearly 20 percent with fast-tempo music.

A casual atmosphere makes a restaurant more attractive to families with small children. Dinner houses, with their bars, pricier entrées, and rather formal dining areas, are not as good as the other types when children are along. (Ground Round, which offers special children's promotions, is an exception.)

Restaurants that appeal to children and parents are less expensive. They also have plenty of room, possibly booths, and often a "fun" theme. Po Folks is a favorite restaurant for families. Like Marie Callender's and Country Kitchen, Po Folks takes a homey approach to serving food.

Food Quality

Respondents to CU's survey liked Bob Evans's and Marie Callender's rather traditional family-restaurant fare, although Marie Callender's also includes such items as tostada salad and chicken lasagna. The dinner houses that specialize in steak—Stuart Anderson's and Steak and Ale—also got high marks for their food, as did Red Lobster (seafood and steak) and T.G.I. Friday and Chili's (broad, international menus).

Part of the appeal of any chain is the familiarity of the food. Some chains try to cash in on a well-known, predictable specialty: Friendly's ice cream, Howard Johnson's fried clams, or Chi-Chi's fajitas, for instance.

But, unlike fast-food outlets, these restaurants can offer a wide variety of food, including regional specialties. Choices abound. In general, you'll find that the variety includes more salads, chicken, and seafood and less beef than in the past.

Food offerings are growing lighter and presumably more nutritious. But at the same time, restaurants are tempting customers to top off those meals with rich desserts. This "dietary schizophrenia," as it's called in the restaurant industry, is fueling the growth of "house" bakeries that turn out breads and biscuits as well as desserts. Marie Callender's is perhaps the best known, specializing in pies.

Even though chains usually have a core menu that's the same wherever you go, they often encourage their restaurants to develop their own regional dishes. So it's possible to encounter anything from Cajun cooking to catfish to fried ice cream.

While the quality of the food is clearly the most important aspect of any restaurant, it has taken on even more importance of late. Fast-food competition is part of the reason. But at the chain restaurants with bars, it's also because of "lighter" life-styles and a resultant drop in alcohol sales, which have traditionally been a big profit-maker for them. Those chains are now especially motivated to showcase their food. Chili's, Bennigan's, and T.G.I Friday are known for having big menus loaded with fashionable food.

Consumers Union's survey respondents judged T.G.I. Friday as having the best selection of food. Friday's menu is a thick notebook, with several pages devoted to beverages and two each to appetizers, soups and salads, and sandwiches. Entrées range from the Southwestern to the Oriental.

The selection at steak houses was once only average, but chains have been expanding their menus. Bonanza was one of the first, adding salad, chicken, and seafood; more recently, steak accounted for only one-third of Bonanza's sales. Bonanza and other steak houses have found the salad bar particularly useful in making up for business lost as people eat less red meat. At Quincy, Western Steer, and Ponderosa, for example, the salad bar is a full-fledged buffet, with meats, hot vegetables, and desserts.

Prices

Breakfast is still the cheapest meal to eat out. An examination of some of the menus from the restaurants that serve breakfast shows prices ranging from $3 or so for plain but hearty meals, up to $6 or more at Perkins for fancy omelets.

A typical lunch—hamburger and fries, say, or a club sandwich—would cost around $5 at most chains. That's also about what a salad bar costs during the lunch hour.

The dinner prices at family restaurants and steak houses aren't much higher than lunch prices. If you choose the salad bar for dinner, it will usually run you $1 or $2 more than the lunchtime price.

Dinner houses are more expensive. The Po Folks chain got the highest marks for value. The prices at Po Folks aren't unusually low, but the chain's portions are unusually large. Shoney's received nearly as high marks in value—probably because of its all-you-can-eat breakfast bar and because of its salad bar, which is included with any lunch or dinner entrée you order.

All-you-can-eat salad bars and buffets are good values for those with hearty appetites. A buffet's variety may also satisfy a picky or fussy child. Light eaters might do better at one of the chains that serve smaller (and cheaper) portions. Several chains have special menus or selections for children or senior citizens—small portions for kids, small and light entrées for seniors.

Guide to the Ratings

1. Restaurant. Listed by type; within type, listed in order of overall score based on a Consumers Union survey. Within a type, differences of three points or more in score are meaningful. As published in a July 1988 report, with information on number of units updated November 1989.

2. Overall score. Respondents to the survey rated overall quality on a five-point scale ranging from excellent to poor. These judgments are summarized as the overall score. Had everyone judged a chain excellent, its score would have been 100; had everyone judged it poor, its score would have been 0. Regular patrons gave higher scores than onetime visitors, but both types of patron rated the chains in the same order. Most respondents were repeat customers.

3. Food. These ratings are comparative, showing how a chain differed from the median for all 31 chains. In general, *taste* and *selection* tracked with the overall score. Ratings were higher at the more expensive dinner houses than at the other types.

4. Service. Only a couple of standouts here—at least at the time of the survey.

5. Atmosphere. It's set by such things as the color and style of decor, music, lighting, noise level, and privacy. Not surprisingly, dinner houses got the highest marks.

6. Cleanliness. Only a few chains stood out as really superior.

7. Value. An estimation of what you get for your money.

8. Kids. Whether it's a matter of children's menus, availability of high chairs, informal settings, roomy dining rooms, or low prices, the answer is clear—dinner houses aren't as good as other places to take children.

Ratings of Restaurant Chains

As published in a **July 1988** report.

Legend: ◉ ◐ ○ ◑ ● Better ←——→ Worse

1 Restaurant	Overall score 2	Taste	Selection	Service 4	Atmosphere 5	Cleanliness 6	Value 7	Kids 8
Family restaurants								
Bob Evans	71	◐	○	◐	○	◐	○	◉
Marie Callender's	70	◐	○	○	◉	◐	○	○
Shoney's	68	○	○	○	○	○	◐	◐
Po Folks	67	○	○	○	○	○	◉	◉
Perkins	65	○	○	○	○	○	○	◐
Country Kitchen	64	○	○	○	○	○	○	○
Village Inn	64	○	○	○	○	○	○	○
Big Boy	60	◐	○	◐	◐	○	○	○
Denny's	60	◐	○	◐	◐	○	○	○
Waffle House	59	○	●	○	●	●	○	◐
Friendly	59	◐	◐	◐	◐	◐	○	◐
International House of Pancakes	58	○	○	◐	●	●	○	○
Howard Johnson's	55	●	◐	◐	◐	○	◐	○
Steak houses								
Western Steer	67	○	○	○	○	○	○	○
Quincy	66	○	○	○	○	○	○	○
Mr. Steak	66	○	○	○	○	○	○	○

1 Restaurant	Overall score 2	3 Food		Service 4	Atmosphere 5	Cleanliness 6	Value 7	Kids 8
		Taste	Selection					
Steak houses (cont'd)								
Golden Corral	66	○	○	○	○	○	○	○
Sizzler	62	○	○	○	○	○	○	○
Bonanza	62	○	○	○	◐	◐	○	○
Western Sizzlin'	62	○	○	○	◐	◐	○	○
Ponderosa	59	◐	○	◐	◐	●	○	○
Dinner houses								
Stuart Anderson's	71	◐	○	○	◉	◐	○	●
Steak and Ale	71	◐	○	◐	◉	◐	◐	●
Brown Derby	71	○	◐	○	◉	○	○	◐
T.G.I. Friday	69	◐	◉	○	◉	○	◐	●
Red Lobster	68	◐	◐	○	◐	○	◐	◐
Chi-Chi's	67	○	○	○	◉	○	○	◐
Bennigan's	66	○	◐	○	◉	○	◐	●
El Torito	66	○	○	○	◉	○	○	◐
Chili's	66	◐	○	○	◉	○	○	◐
Ground Round	61	○	○	◐	○	◐	◐	○

A Guide to the Chains

Restaurant	Type [1]	No. of units	Location	Menu	Character
Bennigan's	D	222	Atlantic & Central	Wide-ranging with emphasis on S/SW regional dishes. Kids' menu. Take-out. Bar.	Sophisticated saloon—lots of polished wood and brass, ceiling fans, stained glass.
Big Boy	F	912	National	Famous for double-decker burgers but offers a variety of entrées. Salad bar. "Heart Smart," seniors' [2], kids' menus. Take-out.	The pudgy boy in red-checkered overalls has become a roadside icon. Functional decor. Counter service [3].
Bob Evans	F	223	East Central, Tex., & Fla.	Emphasis on breakfast entrées but also beef, chicken, and regional dishes. Seniors', kids' menus. Take-out.	Red farmhouse outside; country theme inside, complete with fresh-made biscuits. Counter service.
Bonanza	S	612	Central, Atlantic, & New England	Posted menu. Equal emphasis on beef, chicken, seafood. Salad bar. Kids' menu. Seniors' discounts.	Steak-house decor. New and renovated units more contemporary, according to company. Cafeteria-style serving line.
Brown Derby	D	70	Ohio & Fla.	Mostly steak, some seafood. Salad bar. Kids' menu. Seniors' discounts. Take-out. Bar.	Upscale dinner spot. Menu the same but decor varies from unit to unit.
Chi-Chi's	D	192	Central & Atlantic	Mexican, featuring fajitas (meat strips). Kids' menu. Bar.	Mexican pottery, Aztec statues, stuffed parrots, and wall hangings reinforce unmistakable theme.
Chili's	D	183	Central, Atlantic, & Calif.	Mexican specialties, burgers, salads. Kids' menu. Bar.	Bright, eclectic decor with SW flair. Entrées typically served in baskets.
Country Kitchen	F	252	Central & Mountain	Breakfasts and sandwiches plus some poultry, beef, seafood entrées. Salad bar. Beer, wine [3]. Take-out [3].	Breakfast house in the midst of upgrading image; country theme shows mainly on waitresses' aprons and knickknacks. Counter service [3].

Name					
Denny's	F	1299	National	Known for breakfast menu, but also offers chicken, seafood, and some beef. Mother Butler pies [3]. Seniors', kids' menus. Take-out.	Standard roadside coffee shop. Counter service.
El Torito	D	179	National	Distinctly Mexican. Known for fajitas (meat strips). Kids' menu. Take-out. Bar.	Festive, colorful establishment that plays Mexican theme to hilt.
Friendly	F	848	Atlantic, New England, Ohio, & Fla.	Ice cream is mainstay but also popular for breakfast and offers entrées for lunch and dinner. Kids' menu. Seniors' discounts. Take-out.	Unpretentious, no-nonsense approach to casual dining. Counter service.
Golden Corral	S	502	National, except New England	Posted menu. Salad/sundae/potato bar. Seniors', kids' menus.	Standard budget steak house. Cafeteria-style serving line.
Ground Round	D	285	Atlantic & Central	Mostly beef and seafood entrées. Seniors' [3], kids' menus. Take-out. Bar.	More akin to steak house than dinner house.
International House of Pancakes	F	437	National	Extensive breakfast menu, including lots of pancakes; a limited number of meat and seafood entrées. Salad bar [3]. Seniors', kids' menus. Take-out.	Updated slogan "man does not live by pancakes alone" attempts to de-emphasize pancakes.
Marie Callender's	F	152	Mountain & Pacific	Fresh-baked pies. Wide-ranging selection—pot pies to pasta to chicken. Salad bar. Kids' menu. Seniors' discounts. Take-out. Bar.	The country theme executed to perfection in Laura Ashley style. Homey outside and in. Counter service [3].
Mr. Steak	S	125	National	Mostly steak, but few chicken and seafood items. Seniors' discounts. Salad bar [4]. Take-out. Bar.	Contemporary look.
Perkins	F	341	North Central, Middle Atlantic, Colo., Wash., Fla.	Breakfast plus sandwiches and burgers. "House" bakery. Salad bar [3]. Seniors', kids' menus. Take-out.	A roadside standby with a new look.

Restaurant	Type [1]	No. of units	Location	Menu	Character
Po Folks	F	149	National	Homestyle "Kuntry cookin," plain and simple, in generous portions. "Young-uns" menu. Seniors' discounts. Take-out.	The country theme again, hillbilly-style.
Ponderosa	S	718	Atlantic & New England	Posted menu of steak but also some chicken and seafood. Salad/pasta/sundae bar. Kids' menu. Seniors' discounts. Take-out. Beer [3].	No-frills steak house. Cafeteria-style serving line.
Quincy	S	211	South Atlantic & South Central	Posted menu, mainly steaks. "Country Sideboard" buffet includes salads, meats, hot vegetables, soups, desserts. Kids' menu. Seniors' discounts.	Typical steak house decor—ceiling fans, darkly stained beams, wooden booths.
Red Lobster	D	512	National	Seafood but also chicken and steak. Kids' menu. Take-out. Bar.	Contemporary, nautical decor.
Shoney's	F	636	Atlantic & Central	Standard American roadside fare. Salad bar. Breakfast bar. Seniors', kids' menus. Take-out.	Simple, functional decor.
Sizzler	S	625	National, except for New England	Posted menu of steak, but also chicken and seafood. Salad/soup/taco/pasta bar. Seniors', kids' menus. Take-out. Beer, wine.	Upgraded, well-polished eatery that's changed its steak-house image.
Steak and Ale	D	159	Atlantic & Central	Mostly beef and seafood. Salad bar. Kids' menu. Take-out. Bar.	Posh restaurant in Old English style. Dining areas in small private rooms.

Stuart Anderson's	D	84	Mountain & Pacific	Steak and more steak. A few chicken, seafood entrées. Seniors', kids' menus. Bar [3]. Take-out.	Sumptuous steak-house decor. Tables are nestled in minicorrals of barn wood and smoked glass.
T.G.I. Friday	D	136	National	Varied menu with international entrées. Kids' menu. Take-out. Bar.	Upscale, eclectic eatery with saloon decor. Known as the granddaddy of singles bars.
Village Inn	F	272	National	Breakfast still the emphasis but recently expanded menu for lunch and dinner. Seniors', kids' menus. "House" bakery. Take-out.	Light and airy decor gives this chain a classy, modern feeling. Baked pies and breads displayed at entrance.
Waffle House	F	667	Central & South Atlantic	Breakfast entrées plus limited selection of sandwiches and dinner plates. Take-out.	The traveler's beacon for no-frills food, fast. Counter service.
Western Sizzlin'	S	550	Central, Atlantic, & Mountain	Posted menu, still mostly steak. Salad/potato bar. Kids' menu. Take-out.	Budget steak-house decor. Cafeteria-style serving line.
Western Steer	S	221	South Atlantic	Posted menu, mostly steak. Features "All American Food Bar," an extensive buffet with meat, vegetables, desserts. Take-out.	Typical ranch decor. Cafeteria-style serving line.

[1] D—Dinner house; F—Family restaurant; S—Steak house.
[2] Seniors' discounts in some locations.
[3] In some locations.
[4] In a few locations.

33

2

*E*ating In

Breakfast Foods

Butters and Margarines

Americans eat more than twice as much margarine as butter—10.5 pounds of margarine a year to every 4.6 pounds of butter.

Margarine is a relatively cheap, national-brand product with an advertising budget far bigger than butter's. (Most butter is sold under supermarket or regional labels; only *Land O Lakes* is a national brand.)

More persuasively, margarine makers have enlisted health as a powerful selling tool. One brand's box virtually orders consumers to "Get Heart Smart," an idea it reinforces with a photo of a heart-shaped pat of margarine—and a recap of the federal government's dietary guidance on the "clear association between elevated blood cholesterol and increased risk of coronary heart disease." Another brand's commercials use heart-attack victims—real people, says the company—to tell margarine's no-cholesterol story.

Federal regulations require margarine, like butter, to be at least 80 percent fat. But butterfat (the real, the natural) is a highly saturated fat. Margarines, made from vegetable oil, are usually much less saturated. Consumption of saturated fat, of course, has been heavily implicated in heart disease.

Then there are the margarine substitutes. Products containing less than 80 percent fat—typically, 45 to 75 percent fat overall—are called "spreads." (Food manufacturers reduce the percentage of overall fat by adding water.) "Diet" margarines generally have even less fat.

Flavor

Butter tastes better than margarine. An excellent butter should have a dairy, fresh-cream flavor. It should be slightly to moderately salty (unless it's sweet butter), with no sour or bitter notes and no hint of rancidity or other off-flavors. It should melt fairly quickly and may leave a bit of a coating in the mouth.

By contrast, an excellent margarine has less dairy flavor and a somewhat softer texture than butter; it also has some oil flavor and perhaps a slight sour note. It may melt in the mouth more quickly. Like butter, it may leave a bit of a coating in the mouth. Margarine may have a bit of imitation-butter flavor, like that common to movie-house popcorn.

Lower-quality margarine has even less dairy flavor, a reluctance to melt in the mouth, unwanted "fruity" notes, or an unyielding mouthcoating reminiscent of solid shortening. In reduced-fat margarines, loss of flavor seems to go along with the reduction in fat content.

Nutrition

Nearly all the calories in butter or margarine come from fat. One tablespoon (about three pats) of most butters or margarines supplies about 100 calories and 11 grams of fat. Some reduced-fat vegetable-oil spreads have less fat, perhaps 50 percent fat by weight—not the 80 percent found in regular margarine—and supply just 60 calories a tablespoon. A tablespoon of whipped butter or margarine has about 35 fewer calories than nonwhipped—because air replaces food. Ounce for ounce, of course, the whipped version is just as fattening.

In 1988, the Surgeon General urged Americans to cut down on cholesterol and fat, especially saturated fat. A year later, a committee of the National Research Council echoed the theme and gave specific advice: Consume less than 300 milligrams of cholesterol daily and cut fat intake to no more than 30 percent of all calories. (Most Americans get closer to 37 percent of their calories from fat.) No more than one-third of the fat eaten should be saturated fat, the NRC committee added.

Margarine, derived from vegetable sources, has no cholesterol. Only animal products—meat, dairy, eggs, seafood—contain cholesterol. A tablespoon of butter contains 25 to 30 milligrams of cholesterol—about one-tenth of the daily quota.

Saturated fats tend to raise the body's blood-cholesterol level more than cholesterol-rich foods do. Here, the picture is more troubling for butter lovers. About 65 percent of the fat in butter is saturated. By contrast, the saturated-fat level in margarine ranges from about 9 percent of total fat to 27 percent.

A margarine's saturated-fat level depends on the oil used. Safflower oil, for instance, has less saturated fat than corn or soybean oil, which in turn are far less saturated than cottonseed oil. The saturated-fat level also depends on how hydrogenated, or hardened, the oil is. More thorough hydrogenation saturates an oil's polyunsaturated fat, converting some of it to monounsaturates and some monounsaturates into fully saturated fat. Assuming the same oil is used, soft margarines (in tubs) or semiliquid margarines (in squeeze bottles) tend to be less hydrogenated—and thus less saturated—than regular margarines.

Following the NRC committee's recommendations, a woman who consumes 2,000 calories daily should have no more saturated fat over an entire day—and from all sources—than the amount in about three tablespoons of butter. A man who consumes 2,700 calories a day would nearly reach his daily saturated-fat quota with about four tablespoons of butter.

Note that merely eating a product low in saturated fat doesn't guarantee you'll eat less than the quota. If you eat enough of a regular margarine that's high in unsaturates, you could wind up consuming more saturated fat than from a lower-fat, more highly saturated product.

Recommendations

Unlike butter, margarine has no cholesterol. Its calories are the same as butter's, but it typically has less than one-third the saturated fat of butter. High-quality margarine tastes quite good, with some dairy flavor and an appropriate hint of oil flavor. Its texture is a bit softer than butter's. And margarine typically costs less than half as much as butter.

Margarine isn't less fattening than butter. Both products contain 100 calories per tablespoon, virtually all from fat. But the fat in each is quite different. Butterfat is highly saturated, the kind of fat that health experts have been warning Americans to avoid.

Guide to the Ratings

1. Package. Products generally come in sticks (S) or tub containers (T); two margarines come in squeeze bottles (B).

2. Variety. Regular margarines (M), like butter, are 80 percent total fat by weight. Vegetable-oil spreads (Sp) are roughly 45 to 75 percent fat. Diet margarines (D) generally have even less total fat. The products may be unsalted (U) and/or whipped (W).

3. Calories. Calories track the fat content. Most products supply about 100 calories per tablespoon (11 grams of fat). Some reduced-calorie margarine products have as little as 50 calories (about 6 grams of fat). Whipped products supply less than 100 calories per tablespoon because of their air; ounce for ounce, though, the calorie count is the same as unwhipped.

4. Sodium. Salted products typically provide 90 to 120 milligrams of sodium per tablespoon.

5. Saturated fat. The percentage of a product's total fat content that is saturated. (The remainder consists of monounsaturated and poly-unsaturated fat.) In addition, butter carries 25 to 30 milligrams of cholesterol per tablespoon; margarine has none.

6. Sensory comments. Most products meet most of their criteria of excellence; this column lists noteworthy exceptions and unique char-acteristics. An excellent *butter* should: have a distinct dairy flavor; coat the mouth only a bit; melt quickly in the mouth; have no hint of sourness, bitterness, rancidity, or other off-notes. An excellent *margarine* should: have some oil flavor and some dairy flavor; have a softer texture and may melt in the mouth faster than butter. In all products, a range of saltiness is acceptable.

Ratings of Butters and Margarines

Listed by types; within types, listed in order of sensory index.
Except as noted, products are salted.
As published in a **September 1989** report.

Product	Sensory index	Variety / Package	Price per pound	Calories	Sodium, mg.	Saturated fat	Sensory comments
Butters							
Land O Lakes	Very good	S —	$2.46	100	115	64%	Distinct dairy, with fresh-cream flavor.
Land O Lakes Whipped	Very good	T W	2.28	63	75	65	Distinct dairy, with fresh-cream flavor.
Breakstone's	Good	S —	2.56	103	88	64	Distinct dairy. A bit more mouth-coating.
Breakstone's Sweet Unsalted	Good	S U	2.60	103	0	64	Distinct dairy flavor.
A&P	Good	S —	2.27	99	110	64	Less dairy flavor. A bit more mouthcoating.

Sensory index columns: Poor, Fair, Good, Very good, Excellent

Per tbsp.: Calories, Sodium, mg., Saturated fat

Product								Comments
A&P Unsalted		S	U	2.19	99	0	64	Distinct dairy flavor, with cheesy/sour note.
Land O Lakes Unsalted		S	U'	2.49	100	2	64	Distinct dairy flavor, with cheesy/sour note.
Challenge		S	—	2.58	96	115	66	Less dairy flavor. A bit slow-melting and a bit more mouthcoating.
Challenge Whipped Unsalted		T	U,W	2.88	62	1	66	Moderate dairy flavor, with cheesy/sour note. A bit more mouthcoating.

Margarine products

Product								Comments
I Can't Believe It's Not Butter! 75% Vegetable Oil Spread		S	Sp	1.48	90	95	20	Some dairy flavor.
Parkay		S	M	.84	100	115	18	Some dairy flavor.
Blue Bonnet		S	M	.84	100	95	18	Some dairy flavor.
I Can't Believe It's Not Butter! 75% Vegetable Oil Spread		T	Sp	1.53	90	90	20	Some dairy flavor.
Parkay Whipped		T	M,W	1.42	60	75	14	Saltier than most.
Land O Lakes Soft		T	M	1.23	100	115	9	Very slight "nutty" flavor.
Mazola Premium		S	M	1.19	100	100	18	—
Parkay Soft		T	M	1.34	100	115	18	Saltier than most.
Shedd's Spread Country Crock Classic Quarters 64% Vegetable Oil		S	Sp	.88	80	110	22	—

Ratings of Butters and Margarines (cont'd)

Product	Sensory index	Package 1	Variety 2	Price per pound 3	Calories 4	Sodium, mg 5	Saturated fat 6	Sensory comments
Margarine products (cont'd)								
A&P Soft		T	M	$ .69	100	100	18%	Saltier than most.
Lucerne Vegetable Oil (Safeway)		S	M	.69	100	95	27	—
Fleischmann's		S	M	1.27	100	95	18	—
Promise 72% Vegetable Oil Spread		S	Sp	1.29	90	90	20	—
Shoprite 100% Corn Oil		S	M	.69	100	100	19	A bit slow-melting.
Land O Lakes		S	M	.84	100	115	9	Slight "nutty" flavor.
Lucerne 100% Corn Oil (Safeway)		S	M	.89	100	95	18	—
Mazola Sweet Unsalted		S	M,U	1.19	100	0	18	Less dairy flavor.
Promise 72% Vegetable Oil Spread		T	Sp	1.50	90	90	10	—
Saffola		S	M	1.04	100	95	18	—
Blue Bonnet Soft		T	M	1.41	100	95	18	—

Per tbsp.

Sensory index: Poor, Fair, Good, Very good, Excellent

44

Product									Notes
Fleischmann's Sweet Unsalted				T	M,U	1.61	100	0	18	Less dairy flavor.
Blue Bonnet Spread 52% Vegetable Oil				T	Sp	.86	60	100	14	Some dairy flavor, with "fruity" note.
Chiffon Soft				T	M	1.09	90	105	20	Saltier than most.
Fleischmann's Sweet Unsalted				S	M,U	1.22	100	0	18	Less dairy flavor.
Imperial Light 45% Vegetable Oil Spread				T	Sp	.71	60	110	19	Less salty than most, with "fruity" note. A bit slow-melting.
Parkay Squeeze				B	M	1.52	100	100	18	Less dairy flavor, with strongest imitation-butter note; saltier than most.
Parkay Spread 50% Vegetable Oil				T	Sp	.80	60	110	14	"Fruity" note; less salty than most.
Albertsons Corn Oil				S	M	.84	100	120	18	Less dairy flavor. More mouthcoating and a bit slow-melting.
Weight Watchers Reduced Calorie				S	D	.97	60	110	14	"Fruity" note; less salty than most. More mouthcoating and a bit slow-melting.
Fleischmann's Light Corn Oil Spread 60% Oil				S	Sp	1.29	80	70	25	"Fruity" note; less salty than most. A bit slow-melting.
Lady Lee Vegetable Oil (Lucky)				S	M	.61	100	95	18	More mouthcoating, with *Crisco*-like mouthfeel; a bit slow-melting.
Fleischmann's Squeeze				B	M	1.56	100	95	18	Less dairy flavor, distinct oily taste; less salty than most.

Ratings of Butters and Margarines (cont'd)

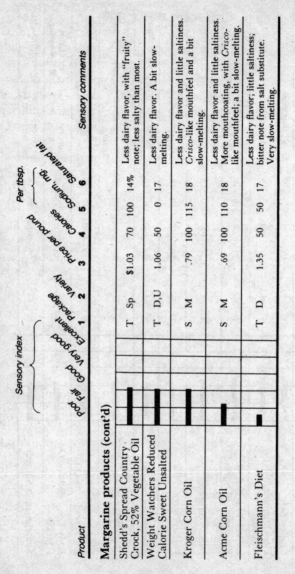

Product	Sensory index (Poor, Fair, Good, Very good, Excellent)	1 Excellent Package	2 Variety	3 Price per pound	4 Calories	5 Sodium, mg.	6 Saturated fat	Sensory comments
Margarine products (cont'd)								
Shedd's Spread Country Crock, 52% Vegetable Oil	Fair		T	Sp	$1.03	70	100	14%	Less dairy flavor, with "fruity" note; less salty than most.
Weight Watchers Reduced Calorie Sweet Unsalted	Fair		T	D,U	1.06	50	0	17	Less dairy flavor. A bit slow-melting.
Kroger Corn Oil	Fair		S	M	.79	100	115	18	Less dairy flavor and little saltiness. *Crisco*-like mouthfeel and a bit slow-melting.
Acme Corn Oil	Poor		S	M	.69	100	110	18	Less dairy flavor and little saltiness. More mouthcoating, with *Crisco*-like mouthfeel; a bit slow-melting.
Fleischmann's Diet	Poor		T	D	1.35	50	50	17	Less dairy flavor; little saltiness; bitter note from salt substitute. Very slow-melting.

Bacon and Eggs

The traditional and tasty meal based on bacon and eggs has come on hard times, together and separately. Fat is responsible for a large percentage of bacon's calories (but two slices of bacon contain only as much fat as one egg), and salt has a lot to do with the way it tastes. Not only that: Bacon is high in chemical nitrosamines, a suspected carcinogen. Nevertheless, Americans still eat a lot of bacon because of its appealing taste and smell.

As for eggs, the case isn't quite as bad. Eggs *are* nutritious, but they contain a lot of cholesterol, and they have been implicated in food poisoning. The truth, however, is that properly handled eggs won't make you sick. Nor will an occasional meal based on eggs send your cholesterol count soaring (any more than an occasional rasher or two of bacon). If health concerns have induced you to abandon eggs, you owe yourself a second look.

Eggs and Health

Eggs are a good source of high-quality protein, riboflavin, phosphorus, and vitamins A, D, and B12. And those nutrients come at a low cost in calories—about 75 per egg, on average. Eggs are also a good choice for dieters and the elderly—two groups who can have trouble obtaining the nutrients they need.

The average large egg contains about 213 milligrams of cholesterol, however. Does that outweigh its nutritional value when considering heart-attack risk? For most people, probably not. Part of the worry about eggs stems more from confusion than from scientific fact.

An elevated level of cholesterol in the blood does increase the risk of heart attack. All foods of animal origin contain cholesterol. But, contrary to a common misconception, cholesterol on the hoof or in the shell doesn't automatically translate into cholesterol in the arteries. People differ in the way dietary cholesterol affects their blood-cholesterol level.

The body, in fact, produces cholesterol on its own, about 800 to 1,500 milligrams daily, which serves a variety of important functions. Generally, the more cholesterol you eat, the less your body produces. That "feedback" process helps to regulate blood-cholesterol levels.

Unfortunately, in many individuals—about one-fourth to one-third of the population—that process doesn't work efficiently. Those people may experience a sharp rise in blood cholesterol after a cholesterol-laden meal. Since most people have no way of knowing whether they belong to that group, public-health officials caution everyone to go easy on cholesterol. The American Heart Association accordingly advises limiting dietary cholesterol to less than 300 milligrams a day, including no more than four egg yolks a week (cholesterol is in the yolk; you can eat all the egg whites you want).

If your blood-cholesterol level is too high, your physician will recommend that you lower it through diet and, in some cases, medication. While reducing dietary cholesterol may help somewhat, the most effective measure is to eat less saturated fat, which has a much greater impact on your cholesterol count. Typically, that means eating more fruit, vegetables, and grain products, and less food from animal sources—especially fatty meats and dairy products, and rich baked goods.

Unlike many foods of animal origin, eggs are relatively low in saturated fat, only about 1.5 grams each. That's roughly the amount in an eight-ounce glass of buttermilk or lowfat (1 percent) milk—and less than the amount in a tablespoon of margarine.

"It's not true to say that cholesterol has no effect," says Dr. John LaRosa, former head of the American Heart Association's nutrition committee. "But critics have misused cholesterol by focusing on that instead of saturated fat." Food marketers, of course, often promote "cholesterol-free" products without mentioning saturated-fat content.

Whether you can adopt a low-fat diet but eat eggs liberally remains a controversial issue. Blanket advice is difficult because individuals respond differently to excess dietary cholesterol. The prudent course is to follow the recommendation of major health organizations: Moderate your intake of eggs, particularly if your blood-cholesterol level is elevated. But don't feel that you have to banish them from the breakfast table.

Salmonella from Eggs Like any animal product, eggs can harbor bacteria that cause food poisoning. In 1988, a study published in *JAMA*, the *Journal of the American Medical Association*, showed that the link between eggs and salmonella food poisoning had been dramatically underestimated.

Researchers from the U.S. Centers for Disease Control reviewed salmonella outbreaks that occurred in eight eastern states between January 1985 and May 1987. Of those cases where the offending food could be identified, some 77 percent were linked to eggs or to foods containing them. In more than half of those incidents, eggs were eaten raw or undercooked.

Prior to the CDC study, food-safety specialists assumed that the bacteria responsible for egg contamination, like other salmonella strains, resided in animal feces. Efforts to prevent contamination were based on keeping the shell clean after the eggs were laid. Researchers theorized that the new outbreaks originated from salmonella transmitted from the hen's ovaries to the egg before the shell was fully formed. If that theory is correct, the only sure way to destroy the bacteria is to cook the egg thoroughly.

Only a small fraction of the commercial egg supply is thought to be contaminated; so the risk of contracting salmonella from eggs remains extremely slight, especially if you live outside the Northeast. Most of the reported incidents occurred in the New England states, New York, and Pennsylvania.

For most people, the symptoms of salmonella infection—nausea, vomiting, diarrhea, and fever—are unpleasant but not dangerous. However, the infection can prove fatal to some vulnerable groups, including infants, the elderly, and those with weakened immune systems, such as AIDS patients, people undergoing cancer treatments, and organ-transplant recipients. The fetus is also at higher risk.

The federal government responded to the CDC report by instituting a voluntary testing program to identify salmonella at its source—infected hens. Producers can divert eggs from affected flocks to processing plants for pasteurization, which kills salmonella. Those eggs can then be used safely in commercial food products.

You can virtually eliminate the risk of food poisoning by taking appropriate steps. The USDA and the U.S. Food and Drug Administration offer the following tips:

Don't eat raw eggs or foods made with raw eggs, such as Caesar salad and homemade mayonnaise, hollandaise sauce, eggnog, or ice cream (unless it's made from a cooked custard base). Commercial forms of these products are safe because they are made with pasteurized eggs.

Cook eggs until both the white and yolk are firm, not runny. Researchers found, for example, that contaminated eggs fried "sunny-side up" still harbored viable salmonella bacteria. Egg-rich foods that are only lightly cooked—soft custards, meringues, French toast—may also be risky, particularly for elderly people and other vulnerable groups.

Buy only clean, uncracked eggs that have been stored under refrigeration, then refrigerate them at home promptly in their original carton. The egg shelf on the refrigerator door is the worst place to store eggs. Constant jostling and temperature changes cause eggs to deteriorate more quickly.

Don't keep eggs out of the refrigerator for more than two hours, including preparation and serving time. (Hard-boiled eggs such as Easter eggs should also be stored in the refrigerator within two hours.)

Use fresh eggs within five weeks and hard-cooked ones within a week. Leftover whites and yolks should be refrigerated immediately and discarded after four days.

Wash food-preparation surfaces that come in contact with eggs with hot, soapy water, and always serve eggs and egg-rich foods soon after cooking.

Reducing Cholesterol in Eggs   Any attempt to produce a low-cholesterol egg runs smack into Mother Nature. Cholesterol is vital to the growing embryo. If a hen's blood cholesterol is reduced, the hen simply stops producing eggs.

A dozen or so egg producers, most concentrated in Pennsylvania, have marketed "low cholesterol" eggs, which were labeled as having only 185 to 210 milligrams of cholesterol. John H. Albright, president of Environmental Systems, which had sold such eggs under the brand name *Full Spectrum Farms,* claimed his company's secret was special feed and a less-stressful environment for the hens.

Albright may have happier hens, but they're producing much the same eggs as less indulged birds. Claims from Albright's company and others led the government to reexamine the federal norm for cholesterol in a Grade A large egg, which had stood at 274 milligrams for more than a decade. New and more accurate measuring techniques showed that the average egg actually contains 213 milligrams of cholesterol—about the same amount subsequently measured in those Pennsylvania eggs.

You can buy cholesterol-free substitutes for beaten eggs, however. Products such as *Egg Beaters, Scramblers,* and *Second Nature* combine egg whites with vegetable oil, emulsifiers, and various vitamins and minerals to compensate for the lack of a yolk. Besides having no cholesterol, such products also have less fat and fewer calories than whole eggs. A serving of an egg substitute contains most of the known nutrients found in a real egg, thanks to a heavy dose of fortification.

When Consumers Union tested egg substitutes several years ago, the tasters judged French toast, brownies, and sponge cakes made with *Egg Beaters* to be practially identical to those made with fresh eggs. Omelets, scrambled eggs, and soufflés, however, were somewhat disappointing.

Less cholesterol costs more money. Egg substitutes sell for roughly twice the price of their real counterparts.

Eggs' Grading and Price

If you took a freshly laid egg and cracked it into a skillet, you'd see no distinct orange yolk. It would barely show through the center of a thick, opaque white. When you cooked it, the egg would have a mild aroma and a delicate flavor.

Eggs you buy in the supermarket, even the freshest AA grade, probably won't look—or taste—quite like that.

Whereas an egg may retain its nutritional value for several months, it starts to lose sensory quality from the moment it's laid. The white gradually becomes runnier, the yolk more likely to break. With each passing day the mild flavor gives way to a stronger, "eggier" taste.

The quality of an egg, as determined just before packing, is reflected in a letter grade. Top-quality eggs, Grade AA and A, are sold in supermarkets. Grade B eggs go to manufacturers to be used in other food products.

Skilled workers assess egg quality in a process called "candling." Eggs pass over a strong beam of light that illuminates defects both inside and outside the egg. The grader looks for eggs with clean, intact shells of proper shape and texture. Cracked eggs and those with blood spots are discarded. The grader also notes the visibility of the yolk. The fresher the egg, the less delineation between the yolk and the white.

Eggs that have been graded by a government inspector usually have a USDA shield on the carton. Government grading is a voluntary process, paid for by the egg producer. For the consumer, the USDA seal may offer some assurance of freshness. The government stipulates that eggs it grades be refrigerated before and after packing and that cartons bear a packing date. Eggs not graded by federal inspectors are subject to grading laws of the state in which they are sold. Most states follow guidelines similar to those of the USDA.

Despite such grading procedures, there's no guarantee that a top-quality egg will still be Grade AA at the point of sale. After eggs leave the plant, the quality of care they receive depends on the shipper and the store that sells them. A change in temperature or humidity will adversely affect freshness.

Will you notice if a Grade AA egg has slipped a bit? Unless your palate is accustomed to the freshly laid variety, probably not. Chances are, you won't even taste much difference between different grades of supermarket eggs, particularly if you scramble them or use them in recipes. White eggs and brown eggs also taste pretty much the same. Although brown eggs are often priced higher, the only real difference between the two is shell color.

Accordingly, unless you know that a store takes pains to ensure freshness, you're likely to get the most for your money if you simply shop for price. Eggs come in six sizes—jumbo, extra large, large, medium, small, and pee wee—with each size about 10 percent smaller than the one before. So if large eggs are selling for $1.00, extra-large eggs should be priced at about $1.10. If the larger ones are selling for less than that 10 percent difference, you've found a bargain.

Some Facts About Bacon

Three-quarters of bacon's calories come from fat. Much of its good taste is the taste of salt. And bacon is also among the main dietary sources of nitrosamines, a suspected carcinogen.

There's really no reason to eat bacon—except for the way it smells and tastes. That's reason enough, apparently, for Americans to spend almost $3 billion a year on it. If you're among the millions who do eat bacon at least occasionally, here are some facts that may make you feel less guilty.

Bacon does contain lots of fat. But it's no more fatty than many other foods, just more visibly so. One egg, for instance, contains about as much fat as two slices of bacon. While 74 percent of bacon's calories come from fat, that's the same as the percentage of calories from fat in cheddar cheese. Surprisingly, only about one-third of bacon's fat calories comes from saturated fat. Bacon contains twice as much unsaturated fat as saturated fat.

Bacon is clearly a salty food. Besides the salt that's used in curing, it contains some sodium from other curing ingredients, as well as the sodium that's naturally in the meat. At 303 milligrams per three-slice serving, bacon is not as bad as a hot dog or a few slices of American cheese, but it's something to avoid if you're on a sodium-restricted diet.

The nitrite present in bacon from the curing process is also a worry. But the connection between nitrite and cancer is far from clear, as noted below.

Flavor   It's difficult to find taste differences from one brand of bacon to another. The variation from package to package of the same brand is sometimes as great as the difference between brands.

On the plate, an excellent-tasting pork bacon is crisp, reddish brown, and moist. The flavor artfully blends the smoky, sweet, and salty components of the curing and of the meat. The fat adds its own distinctive note and contributes to a pleasant oily coating in the mouth. Alternating bands of fat and lean give the slices a pleasing mixture of tenderness and chewiness.

Yield   It's often said that bacon shrinks less when baked in the oven or the microwave than when pan-fried. That isn't true. Bacon's yield is roughly the same, no matter how you cook it. But bacon in an oven or microwave makes less mess than in a pan, and an oven or even a microwave should be able to hold more slices at a time.

Yield among brands varies considerably, though, with yields ranging from about 25 to 45 percent.

Nitrite and Bacon   It's known that the nitrite used in bacon may combine during cooking with natural components of foods called amines to form nitrosamines. It's known that nitrosamines cause cancer in laboratory animals, and probably in humans. It's known that cooked bacon contains traces of several nitrosamines.

But it's not known whether the risk bacon poses is worth worrying about. Government regulations don't eliminate nitrite or nitrosamines from bacon; they simply put ceilings on permissible amounts. Manufacturers rely on nitrite to prevent botulism and to impart desirable color and flavor characteristics to cured meats, including frankfurters, most cold cuts, and corned beef as well as bacon. Manufacturers claim there's no viable alternative that serves all those functions adequately.

Even if nitrite were banned from cured meats, you couldn't avoid it. It's a natural constituent of some vegetables. And the human body makes nitrite from nitrate, another widespread natural compound. Nitrite is present in human saliva, too. In fact, some studies show that saliva is an even larger source of nitrite than foods.

In theory, nitrite and amines, both naturally present in foods, could combine inside the stomach to form nitrosamines. If that occurs, eliminating exposure to nitrosamines would be a practical impossibility. But researchers can't yet say how much the body itself contributes to the total amount of nitrosamines you are exposed to. Nor can they say how important, by comparison, are bacon and other sources of preformed nitrosamines.

To reduce the formation of nitrosamines, bacon manufacturers have for several years been adding substances related to vitamin E, called tocopherols, as well as substances related to vitamin C. Both vitamins C and E inhibit the formation of nitrosamines. (Taking a vitamin supplement may help a bit, too, but the vitamins would have to be eaten with the food for maximum effect.)

If you don't want to live without bacon, you can reduce its nitrosamine content by cooking it in a microwave oven. Some studies have found that the lower cooking temperatures in the microwave result in *no* detectable nitrosamines in the bacon.

If you fry your bacon, don't reuse the grease; nitrosamine levels in leftover bacon fat are at least double the levels in the bacon strips. And ventilate your cooking area; nitrosamines are volatile and may be present in the air as well as in the cooked bacon.

To sum up: Don't eat bacon every day. It isn't especially good for you, and it costs too much. Save it to celebrate Sunday morning.

Listings of Bacon

Listed by types; within types, listed in
order of increasing cost per cooked
pound.

As published in an **October 1989**
report.

Product	Cost per pound	Yield after draining fat
Regular Pork Bacon		
Bar-S Lower Salt	$1.55	38%
Janet Lee Thick Sliced (Albertsons)	1.50	34
Lady Lee (Lucky)	1.40	31
Smok-A-Roma Lower Salt	1.45	31
Corn King	1.55	32
Kwick Krisp Brand (Kroger)	2.00	41
Hormel Range Brand Thick Sliced	2.25	43
Wilson	1.90	36
Safeway	2.10	39
Swift Premium	1.90	35
Farmland Foods	1.95	33
A&P	2.00	34
Farmer John Brand	2.00	32
Dak	1.60	25
Dubuque Premium	2.20	33
Farmstead	1.90	29
John Morrell	1.70	25
Smithfield Smokehouse No Sugar Added	2.00	30
Armour	2.15	29

Product	Cost per pound	Yield after draining fat
Regular Pork Bacon (cont'd)		
Oscar Mayer	$2.70	36%
Gwaltney/Williamsburg Brand No Nitrite Added	2.80	37
Thorn Apple Valley Brand Lower Salt No Sugar Added	2.10	27
Hormel Black Label	2.70	35
West Virginia Brand Thick Sliced	2.65	32
Kahn's American Beauty No Sugar Added	2.55	32
Oscar Mayer Thick Sliced	2.80	34
Armour Lower Salt	2.40	29
Jones	2.85	34
Jones Thick Sliced	2.80	33
Thorn Apple Valley Brand Thick Sliced	2.35	27
Plumrose Premium	2.50	30
West Virginia Brand	2.35	27
Rath Black Hawk	2.60	25
Oscar Mayer Center Cut	4.05	30
Breakfast strips		
Sizzlean Pork	2.20	37
Sizzlean Beef	2.55	32
The Real McCoy Beef Bacon	3.20	36
Oscar Mayer Lean 'n Tasty Beef	3.20	30
Best's Kosher Breakfast Beef	6.50	42
Bacon analogue		
Morningstar Farms Cholesterol Free Breakfast Strips	6.20	58

Cereals

Breakfast-cereal manufacturers have always promoted their products as nutritional miracles. The latest pitches focus on the supposed cholesterol-lowering capabilities of oats and oat bran, the finely ground, fiber-rich outer coating of oats after they're hulled.

Cereal makers have built slender experimental evidence of oat bran's benefit into a marketing bonanza. For a time during 1988, Quaker Oats couldn't produce enough oats to satisfy the demand for oatmeal and oat bran. The company had to ration its products and posted apologetic "Dear Customer" letters in supermarket cereal aisles. Sales of hot cereal, long a minor and sleepy part of the business, soared 25 percent in 1988, thanks largely to the sudden demand for oat bran.

Oat bran has found its way into muffins, bagels, pasta, potato chips, tortillas, pretzels—and more breakfast cereals.

Established cereals are playing up the oats they've always had. The *Cheerios* box sports a bright blue banner: "For Nearly 50 Years, Excellent Source of OAT BRAN." And after more than a century on the *Quaker Oats* cardboard canister, the smiling Quaker shares his cameo space with a headline: "Can Help Reduce Cholesterol . . ."

The oat-bran action is happening on the upper cereal shelves, those at an adult's eye level. Meanwhile, down where kids can see (and grab), cereal makers are still packaging grain as candy. There's even an oat-based product with four-and-a-half teaspoons of sugar per serving. The cereal's gimmick: a squeeze-packet of a jam-like substance ("made with real fruit") for kids to use as a food decoration.

Nutrition

Until the processors get hold of them, cereal grains pack lots of desirable nutrients for their calories: complex carbohydrates (starches and fiber), B vitamins, some protein, and iron. Cereal grains are also naturally low in fat. But ready-to-eat cereals are among the most highly processed of foods. Such processing—grains are milled, steamed, toasted, puffed, mashed, gnashed, and extruded—can upset the balance of nutrients or even destroy some almost entirely.

To turn grain into a product with a selling point, manufacturers usually add some form of fat, sugar, or salt. All cereals are enriched to restore B vitamins, iron, and other nutrients depleted during manufacture. And some are transformed into food supplements—fortified with extra vitamins and minerals—to satisfy a marketing goal irrelevant to the needs of a typical consumer's diet.

Manufacturers usually do less to the grain in making a hot cereal. Oatmeal, for example, is typically cut-up oat groats, steamed and flattened between heavy rollers. The size of pieces largely determines cooking time—from instant or quick-cooking varieties to regular oatmeal.

Some hot cereals are more highly processed. In farina, for example, the grain's bran is removed, leaving just the "cream of wheat," the starchy center that's known as the endosperm.

The nutrition of cereal products focuses on four key ingredients: fiber, protein, sugar, and fat. There are also micronutrients to consider ("micro," because the body needs minute quantitites of vitamins and minerals).

Here are some details:

Fiber The National Cancer Institute recommends that Americans consume 20 to 30 grams of fiber a day, but most get only about 11 grams. To get about that much fiber from fresh fruit or vegetables you'd have to eat almost five apples or three cups of spinach. (According to the spokesperson for a fig industry trade association, three dried figs of average size have the fiber content of seven grapefruit, five cups of grapes, five prunes, one-and-a-half cantaloupes, five peaches, or two-and-one-fourth apples.)

There are two types of fiber. Insoluble fiber, in wheat bran, can shorten the time food lingers in the intestines, which not only eases constipation but, according to some experts, may also play some role in the prevention of colorectal cancer.

Soluble fiber, in oat bran, may help lower cholesterol by binding with the cholesterol that the liver has released into the intestine, the theory goes. Studies show that such fiber has some effect, but only when part of a diet low in saturated fats.

Although the National Cancer Institute doesn't recommend any set dietary amount for either type, CU's medical consultants recommend that intake of fiber be divided equally between the two types.

Many ready-to-eat cereals contain between two and five grams of fiber per serving. But a few ultra-high-fiber products pack at least 10 grams. Many hot oatmeals and oat brans provide three or more grams of fiber, though instant oatmeals often provide less.

Protein   Cereal isn't a high-protein food. Most products supply only two or three grams of protein without milk. A half-cup of milk adds another four grams and improves the quality of the cereal protein as well.

Sugars   This is mainly a measure of sucrose and fructose. Grain naturally contains a little of those sugars. Manufacturers add plain sugar, sugary substances such as corn syrup, and sweet ingredients such as raisins.

The more sugar in a serving of cereal, the less room for other nutrients. Sugars make up as much as half the calories in some of the highly sweetened products aimed at children. They often contain three or four teaspoons of sugars per ounce of cereal. Dried fruit can boost the percentage of calories that come from sugars substantially, especially if the cereal part of the product is high in fiber (and thus low in calories). A few high-fiber cereals are sweetened with aspartame, an artificial sweetener.

Fat   Only a few brands contain more than a gram or two of fat (many have less). Oils are often added to soften texture, carry flavorings, or keep a cereal crisp longer in milk. Most companies have removed coconut oil, a highly saturated fat, from cereals.

Micronutrients People with vitamin deficiencies should speak to a doctor about multivitamin supplements and buy them in the drug section of the supermarket, not on the cereal shelves. While you're unlikely to be harmed by the excess of vitamins and minerals you'd ingest by adding a highly fortified cereal to a normal diet, you're unlikely to be helped, either.

Products that are merely "enriched" generally provide 25 percent of the U.S. RDAs (Recommended Daily Allowances) for various vitamins and minerals in every serving. "Fortified" cereals provide 100 percent, as their ads loudly proclaim. You can quickly tell the level of fortification by looking at the cereal's nutritional labeling.

Sodium Most people needn't be concerned about how much sodium they ingest. For those who *are* concerned, sodium levels as noted on labels may range from near zero to around 300 milligrams per serving.

Information on the Box

The label on a cereal box tells you a great deal about the product inside:

Serving Size Usually described as a one-ounce portion. A cereal with fruit or fruit and nuts can be quite dense, with a surprisingly small serving weighing in at an ounce. A puffed cereal is much less dense; a serving of such a cereal can look quite substantial. It's also useful if a label notes a serving's volume, in cups. An ounce of *Grape-Nuts,* one of the densest cereals, fills up only a quarter cup. An ounce of *Cheerios* occupies five times that volume. If you're serious about counting calories, you may want to measure out a serving and note the level on your favorite bowl.

Calories A high-fiber brand typically has about 90 calories per ounce. But 110 calories an ounce is more typical for a food that is largely carbohydrates and not high in fiber. Fattier cereals may pack more calories; high-fiber brands, fewer (since, as previously mentioned, fiber isn't digested and hence has no calories).

Nutrients   The list of nutrients must give calories, protein, carbohydrates, and fat. Cholesterol is generally zero. Since cereals are grain-based products, fat should be low.

Nutrients with Milk   Many cereal brands specify skim milk, which keeps fat figures as low as possible. One-half cup of skim milk adds about 40 calories and considerable protein and calcium. Whole milk adds the same amount of protein and calcium, along with four grams of fat and about 35 extra calories.

U.S. RDAs   Package labels give percentages of the daily quota for protein, vitamins, and minerals for people over age four. Processors are required to list only protein, vitamin A, vitamin C, thiamin, riboflavin, niacin, calcium, and iron. Additional items are optional, unless there is a nutritional claim involving their use.

Ingredients   These are listed in descending order, by weight. Sweeteners (sugar, brown sugar, corn syrup, maltodextrin, honey, etc.) are listed separately, which can give the impression that there's less sweetener than is actually the case. If only one sweetener is used, it might well be at the top of some of the ingredient lists.

Carbohydrate   Cereal should be high in complex carbohydrates and low in sucrose and other sugars. Some labels list the sugar content of added fruit separately, which makes the numbers look even lower. Fiber information is also found in the same place on the label as the figures for carbohydrates. If there isn't any fiber data, there's probably little fiber in the product. Some brands give a breakdown of soluble and insoluble fiber.

Flavor

A good cereal should taste of its constituent grains—generally, wheat, oats, corn, or rice—with cooked and toasted variations. There may also be flavorings such as vanilla, brown sugar, spices, honey, cocoa, dried fruits, and nuts.

Most cereals, especially the ones not too heavily sugared, have a moderate toasted-grain taste. Not surprisingly, some kids' cereals taste excessively sweet—more like candy or cookies than cereal—with the heavy sweetness masking the grain flavor.

A good ready-to-eat cereal should be firm and crispy in texture but not too hard, even in milk. Most stay fairly crisp, though some turn soggy. Some, like various shredded-wheat biscuits, are tough but chewy. Other cereals linger unpleasantly in the mouth, either as loose particles or masses packed into teeth.

Economy

Compared with other breakfasts, cereal and milk are an inexpensive way to start the day. Ready-to-eat cereals average about 19 cents a serving; hot cereals are a nickel cheaper. Add milk and some fresh fruit and the breakfast is still cheap. Here are more ways to economize:

- *Forgo fortification.* High-vitamin cereals usually cost considerably more than their less fortified counterparts.
- *Think big.* Larger packages are generally cheaper. So are bulk canisters of hot cereals, compared with single-serving packets.
- *Add your own toppings.* Generally, the more fruit and nuts the company adds, the more it charges—and the more the markup. The same goes for added sugar.
- *Try generics.* Generic and supermarket-label cereals are nutritionally equivalent to the big-name products, save for possible minor differences in fortification. The generics may even come from the same factory. Yet such cornflakes, bran flakes, shredded wheat, puffed wheat, and crisped rice cost much less than national brands.

Recommendations

Cereal with milk and fruit is an easy-to-fix breakfast and a healthful, inexpensive way to start the day. If you're like most people, your taste buds will likely determine which brand you buy, but you'll probably want to choose good nutrition, too.

Of course, you needn't wed yourself to one cereal or even one type of cereal. American families typically have four different brands on hand and breakfast on one or another as the spirit moves them. Maintaining a well-balanced diet is a long-term effort; if you choose a less-than-exemplary cereal for breakfast, you can make up for it with what you eat the rest of the day.

Hot cereals generally cost a bit less than ready-to-eat brands and can be almost as convenient to prepare. Virtually all can be microwaved in a minute or two right in the bowl.

If you're concerned about fiber but your favorite cereal doesn't supply much, try adding a teaspoon or two of millers bran. But go easy at first and gradually increase the amount, or you may become gassy and develop diarrhea. You should also go easy if you switch to an ultra-high-fiber cereal.

Guide to the Ratings

1. Product. Products are grouped according to their overall nutritional profile. An ideal cereal that would provide, say, 5 percent of your daily caloric need would also supply 5 percent of your quota for all nutrients. But no food is perfectly balanced. What matters is how all the foods you eat in a day or in a week add up. Ideally, what you eat over time provides 100 percent of your needs for both calories and nutrients, without excesses or deficiencies.

The profiles are based on an average woman's daily dietary needs: 2,000 calories, 20 grams of dietary fiber, 45 grams of protein, 50 grams of sugar, and 67 grams of fat. The quotas for the average man would be 35 percent higher for calories and fat. Micronutrients are a composite score of the U.S. RDA percentages for calcium, folic acid, iron, magnesium, potassium, vitamin B6, and zinc.

2. Manufacturer. Stores often group cereals by companies. Major ones include: General Mills (G), Kellogg (K), Nabisco (N), General Foods' Post (P), Quaker Oats (Q), and Ralston Purina (R). Others include: American Home Food (A), Nutrition Industries (H), Malt-O-Meal Co. (M), and United Mills (U).

3. Nutrients. An indication of the amounts of fiber, protein, sugar, fat, and vitamins and minerals the cereal provides for the calories it contains. If a nutrient is about in proportion to the cereal's calories, it scores O. If it supplies more fiber or protein than its calories' share, or less sugar and fat than its calories' share, it scores ◐ or ●. The micronutrient score includes the vitamins and minerals listed above.

4. Calories. Per one-ounce serving.

5. Sodium. Per one-ounce serving.

Ratings of Cereals

Listed by types; within types, listed in order of nutritional quality. Except where separated by bold rules, differences between closely ranked products were slight. Prices generally are for a 10- to 16-ounce package.

As published in an **October 1989** report.

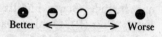

Better ● ◐ ○ ◑ ● Worse

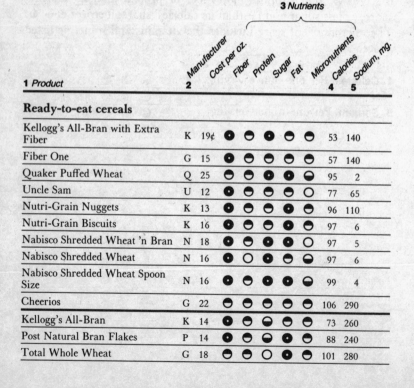

1 Product	Manufacturer 2	Cost per oz.	Fiber	Protein	Sugar	Fat	Micronutrients	Calories 4	Sodium, mg. 5
Ready-to-eat cereals									
Kellogg's All-Bran with Extra Fiber	K	19¢	●	●	◐	●	◐	53	140
Fiber One	G	15	●	◐	●	◐	◐	57	140
Quaker Puffed Wheat	Q	25	◐	◐	●	●	◑	95	2
Uncle Sam	U	12	●	●	◐	◐	○	77	65
Nutri-Grain Nuggets	K	13	●	◐	◐	●	◐	96	110
Nutri-Grain Biscuits	K	16	●	◐	◐	●	●	97	6
Nabisco Shredded Wheat 'n Bran	N	18	●	◐	◐	●	○	97	5
Nabisco Shredded Wheat	N	16	●	○	◐	◐	◐	97	6
Nabisco Shredded Wheat Spoon Size	N	16	●	◐	◐	●	◐	99	4
Cheerios	G	22	◐	◐	◐	◐	◐	106	290
Kellogg's All-Bran	K	14	●	◐	◑	◐	◐	73	260
Post Natural Bran Flakes	P	14	●	◐	◑	●	◐	88	240
Total Whole Wheat	G	18	◐	◐	○	●	◐	101	280

3 Nutrients

Ready-to-eat cereals (cont'd)

1 Product	2 Manufacturer	Cost per oz.	Fiber	Protein	Sugar	Fat	Micronutrients	4 Calories	5 Sodium, mg.
Grape-Nuts	P	14¢	◐	◐	◑	◉	◐	96	170
Kellogg's Bran Flakes	K	13	◉	◐	◑	◐	◐	95	220
Fruit & Fibre Cinnamon Apple Crisp	P	20	◉	◐	●	◐	◐	86	190
Post Natural Raisin Bran	P	14	◉	○	●	◉	◐	84	180
Common Sense Oat Bran	K	20	◉	◐	◑	◉	◐	97	260
Mueslix Bran	K	25	◉	◐	●	◉	◐	89	72
Nabisco 100% Bran	N	12	◉	◐	●	○	◐	74	190
Total Raisin Bran	G	19	◉	○	●	◉	◐	89	127
Post Oat Flakes	P	22	◐	◐	◑	◉	◐	103	140
Wheaties	G	15	◐	◐	○	◉	◐	105	270
Just Right	K	20	◐	◐	◑	◉	◐	105	190
Kellogg's Raisin Bran	K	15	◉	○	●	◉	◐	89	164
Mueslix Five Grain	K	24	◐	◐	●	◉	◐	94	38
Strawberry Squares	K	18	◉	○	◑	◉	◐	96	5
Blueberry Fruit Wheats	N	17	◉	○	◑	◉	◐	95	15
Frosted Wheat Squares	N	17	◐	◐	◑	◉	◐	104	2
Strawberry Fruit Wheats	N	16	◉	○	◑	◉	◐	96	15
Nutrific Oatmeal Flakes	K	21	◉	◐	●	◐	◐	89	160
Quaker Oat Squares	Q	15	◐	◐	◑	◐	◐	110	160
Frosted Mini-Wheats	K	15	◉	○	◑	◉	◐	99	7
Fruitful Bran	K	20	◉	○	●	◐	◐	96	177
Life	Q	15	◐	◐	◑	◐	◐	104	180
Honey Nut Cheerios	G	19	◐	◐	●	◉	◐	102	250
Oat Bran Options	R	17	◐	◐	●	◉	○	97	131

Ratings of Cereals (cont'd)

1 Product	2 Manufacturer	Cost per oz.	Fiber	Protein	Sugar	Fat	Micronutrients	4 Calories	5 Sodium, mg.
Ready-to-eat cereals (cont'd)									
Raisin Squares	K	18¢	◒	○	◒	◓	◓	103	10
Clusters	G	21	◒	◒	◒	○	◒	103	160
Cracklin' Oat Bran	K	21	◉	○	◒	○	◓	112	140
Raisin Nut Bran	G	19	◒	◒	◒	○	◒	107	140
Ralston Muesli Raisins, Dates & Almonds	R	22	◒	○	◒	◓	◓	107	79
Ralston Muesli Raisins, Peaches & Pecans	R	22	◒	○	◒	◓	◓	107	79
Oatmeal Raisin Crisp	G	17	◒	○	●	◒	◒	102	140
Apple Cinnamon Cheerios	G	20	◒	○	●	◒	◓	105	170
Quaker 100% Natural	Q	15	◒	○	◒	○	◐	121	15
Quaker Puffed Rice	Q	22	◐	○	◉	◉	◐	111	2
Special K	K	22	◒	◒	○	◉	◓	107	230
Crispy Critters	P	17	○	○	○	◉	◓	103	230
Kellogg's Corn Flakes	K	15	○	○	◒	◉	○	101	290
Product 19	K	20	○	○	○	◉	◓	112	320
Total Corn Flakes	G	25	◐	○	◒	◉	◐	110	280
Kix	G	22	○	○	◒	◉	◓	109	290
Double Chex	R	17	○	○	◒	◉	◓	108	280
Corn Chex	R	17	◐	○	○	◉	◐	109	310
Crispix	K	18	◐	○	○	◉	○	112	220
Rice Chex	R	17	◐	◐	○	◉	○	107	280
Rice Krispies	K	21	●	○	○	◉	○	110	290
Lucky Charms	G	22	◒	○	●	◉	◒	106	180

			3 Nutrients						
1 Product	Manufacturer **2**	Cost per oz.	Fiber	Protein	Sugar	Fat	Micronutrients	Calories **4**	Sodium, mg. **5**

Ready-to-eat cereals (cont'd)

Product	Mfr	Cost	Fiber	Protein	Sugar	Fat	Micro	Cal	Sodium
Honey-Comb	P	22¢	◐	◐	●	⊙	○	108	130
Almond Delight	R	17	○	◐	◐	◑	●	114	200
Froot Loops	K	21	○	◐	●	⊙	○	113	125
Apple Jacks	K	21	○	◐	●	⊙	○	116	125
Super Golden Crisp	P	19	◐	◐	●	⊙	○	112	45
Dinersaurs	R	21	◑	◐	●	⊙	○	105	70
Nut & Honey Crunch	K	18	◐	○	●	⊙	◑	110	200
Honey Smacks	K	17	○	◐	●	⊙	○	113	70
Golden Grahams	G	20	○	◐	●	⊙	○	105	280
Cap'n Crunch	Q	15	◐	◐	●	◑	○	119	250
Frosted Flakes	K	18	◐	◐	●	⊙	◑	109	200
Oh's Crunchy Nut	Q	18	◐	◐	◐	○	◑	125	170
Cap'n Crunch's Crunch Berries	Q	17	○	◐	●	◑	◑	113	260
Cocoa Puffs	G	22	◐	◐	●	⊙	○	110	200
Ice Cream Cones Vanilla	G	21	◑	◐	●	◑	○	112	170
Ice Cream Cones Chocolate Chip	G	22	○	◐	●	◑	○	113	160
Cinnamon Toast Crunch	G	20	○	◐	●	◑	○	115	220
Corn Pops	K	18	◐	◐	●	⊙	◑	112	90
Trix	G	22	◐	◐	●	⊙	○	110	150
Fruity Pebbles	P	21	◐	◐	●	⊙	○	111	160

Hot cereals

Product	Mfr	Cost	Fiber	Protein	Sugar	Fat	Micro	Cal	Sodium
H-O Quick Oats 'n Fiber	H	11	⊙	◑	⊙	◑	○	81	3
Quaker Extra Oatmeal, regular [1]	Q	20	●	◑	⊙	◑	◑	90	220

Ratings of Cereals (cont'd)

			3 Nutrients						
1 Product	Manufacturer **2**	Cost per oz.	Fiber	Protein	Sugar	Fat	Micronutrients **4**	Calories **5**	Sodium, mg.
Hot cereals (cont'd)									
Wheatena	A	07¢	◓	◒	◓	◒	◒	90	3
Wholesome 'n Hearty Oat Bran	N	12	◓	◒	◓	◒	◒	94	3
Quaker Instant Oatmeal, regular 🔟	Q	18	◒	◒	◓	◒	◒	94	270
Total Instant Oatmeal, regular ②	G	22	◓	◒	◒	◒	◒	94	220
Quaker Oat Bran	Q	11	◓	◒	◓	◒	○	93	1
Quaker Quick Oats	Q	08	◒	◒	◓	◒	○	97	6
Quaker Old Fashioned Oats	Q	08	◒	◒	◓	◒	○	97	1
Maypo 30 Second Oatmeal, Maple	A	10	◒	◒	◓	◒	◒	91	2
Total Instant Oatmeal, Apple Cinnamon ③	G	22	◒	◒	●	◒	◒	107	112
Quaker Instant Oatmeal, Apples & Cinnamon ②	Q	17	◒	○	●	◒	◒	99	102
Quaker Instant Oatmeal, Maple & Brown Sugar ②	Q	15	◒	◒	●	◒	◒	97	213
Quaker Instant Oatmeal, Peaches & Cream ②	Q	18	◒	○	●	◒	◒	101	143
Quaker Instant Oatmeal, Strawberries & Cream ②	Q	18	◒	○	●	◒	◒	105	163
Oatmeal Swirlers Instant, Strawberry ③	G	18	◒	○	●	◒	◒	94	78
Nabisco Quick Cream of Wheat	N	10	○	◒	◓	◓	○	101	80
Nabisco Instant Cream of Wheat	N	11	○	◒	◓	◓	◒	101	4
Nabisco Regular Cream of Wheat	N	10	○	◒	◓	◓	◒	102	2

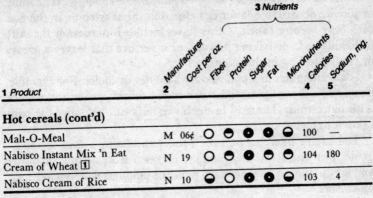

				3 Nutrients				
1 Product	Manufacturer	Cost per oz.	Fiber	Protein	Sugar	Fat	Micronutrients	Calories	Sodium, mg.
	2						**4**	**5**

Hot cereals (cont'd)

Product	Manufacturer	Cost per oz.	Fiber	Protein	Sugar	Fat	Micronutrients	Calories	Sodium, mg.
Malt-O-Meal	M	06¢	○	◑	●	●	◑	100	—
Nabisco Instant Mix 'n Eat Cream of Wheat ①	N	19	○	◑	●	◑	◑	104	180
Nabisco Cream of Rice	N	10	◑	○	•	●	◑	103	4

① Box contains 12 single-serving packets.
② Box contains 10 single-serving packets.
③ Box contains eight single-serving packets.

Pancake Mixes

Pancake mixes are made for people who love pancakes but not the labor. Some mixes don't spare you much effort, though, for you have to add milk, eggs, and oil. Other types are more complete—all you add is water or milk. If you don't want to do any mixing at all, you can buy frozen batter or even frozen, fully formed flapjacks that need only be heated in the oven or microwave.

Flavor

Pancakes are a simple dish. They should have the grain taste of wheat, with egg and dairy flavors plus a slight sweetness. A pancake should be tender when you bite into it, and it should be neither leaden and soggy nor too fluffy and airy.

Some flavors are out of place in a pancake. It shouldn't taste tinny or like cardboard; the latter is a clue that the shortening in the mix may have become rancid. Other flaws include bitterness or the taste of baking soda or baking powder, or a texture that leaves a greasy or chalky feeling in the mouth.

Some attributes in a pancake are a matter of choice. For example, people who favor light, tender pancakes probably prefer those made with buttermilk. The acid in the buttermilk can help give the pancakes a lighter texture.

You aren't likely to find the ideal pancake in a mix or ready-made. But just about any pancake makes a suitable foil for butter and syrup; indeed, the standard pancake toppings would mask most off-flavors.

Nutrition

Pancakes make a fairly nutritious breakfast, but not one you want to have often if you're counting calories or watching your sodium intake.

Most products contain 60 to 100 calories per four-inch pancake. Reduced-calorie brands deliver about 30 to 40 calories. Lather on a pat of butter and a few tablespoons of syrup and you add another 300 calories or so.

For most products, sodium content ranges from 167 to 350 milligrams per pancake. Reduced-calorie brands have less than 50 milligrams per pancake. Butter and syrup add about another 140 milligrams. For many of these products, then, three pancakes topped with butter and syrup provide about half of the recommended daily allotment of sodium for most people.

Pancakes offer varying amounts of nutrients, according to the nutritional labels: one to three grams of protein per pancake, zero to four grams of fat, and seven to 17 grams of carbohydrates.

Check labels for FD&C Yellow #5, an artificial color that can cause allergic reactions, especially in aspirin-sensitive individuals.

Recommendations

The tastiest pancakes, unfortunately, are not the quickest to make. The best versions come from the recipe on page 80 or from mixes that require the addition of fresh eggs, oil, and milk. You can save a little time in the kitchen by choosing one of the complete mixes, which require only water or milk to make a batter.

Convenience has its price. The dry mixes are by far the cheapest to use—usually less than a nickel per pancake. Pancakes made with frozen batter cost about a dime apiece, whereas the frozen ready-made products cost quite a bit more. The frozen batters also require some advance planning because they take at least a day to thaw. (You can't defrost them quickly in a microwave oven; that will cook the batter.)

Guide to the Ratings

1. Type. Most of the products are mixes. Some are regular mixes (RM), which require you to add eggs, milk, and, usually, oil. The others are nearly complete (CM) and need only be mixed with water or milk. A few come as frozen, premixed batter (FB); the rest are frozen, precooked pancakes (FP) that need only be reheated.

2. Sensory index. An excellent pancake should have the flavor and aroma of baked grain, especially wheat, with a balanced mix of egg and milk aromas. It should be somewhat sweet, moist, and tender, not gummy or chewy. The comments highlight significant flavors, aromas, and textures. Except as noted, the pancakes were judged suitably dense.

3. Calories. Per pancake, based on the manufacturer's nutrition labeling (except for our own recipe). Syrup and butter add to the freight, of course. The average syrup contains about 250 calories per five-tablespoon serving; a teaspoon of butter contains 36 calories.

4. Sodium. Per pancake, based on the manufacturer's data (except for the recipe on page 80). Figure that five tablespoons of syrup and a pat of butter will add about 140 milligrams of sodium.

5. Thickness. This is the height of a cooked pancake. The *thick* ones, made according to package instructions, cook up to at least five-eighths-inch high; the *medium* ones are about three-eighths-inch high, and the *thin* ones are no more than one-quarter-inch high. You can add more liquid to any batter if you like thinner pancakes; you can let the batter stand for a while if you want thick pancakes.

Ratings of Pancake Mixes

Listed in order of sensory quality, as depicted by the sensory index.

As published in a **January 1988** report.

Product	Type	Sensory index	Cost per pancake	Calories	Sodium, mg	Thickness	Sensory comments
Hungry Jack Buttermilk	RM	Good	4¢	80	190	Medium	Suitably subtle egg and dairy flavors.
Aunt Jemima Buttermilk	RM	Good	5	100	330	Medium	Suitably subtle egg and dairy flavors.
Lady Lee Old Fashioned	RM	Good	6	100	283	Medium	Suitably subtle egg and dairy flavors.
CU's recipe	—	Good	4	89	156	Medium	Suitably subtle egg and dairy flavors.
Betty Crocker Buttermilk	RM	Good	4	93	270	Medium	Suitably subtle egg and dairy flavors.
Hungry Jack Extra Lights	RM	Good	3	70	163	Thin	Suitably subtle egg and dairy flavors.

Ratings of Pancake Mixes (cont'd)

Product	Type [1]	2 Sensory index Poor / Fair / Good / Very good / Excellent	Cost per pancake [3]	Calories [4]	Sodium, mg [5]	Thickness	Sensory comments
Bisquick Buttermilk Baking Mix	RM [1]		6¢	80	233	Thick	Suitably subtle egg and dairy flavors.
Aunt Jemima Original	RM		3	67	183	Medium	Suitably subtle egg flavor.
Betty Crocker Buttermilk	CM		3	70	167	Medium	Suitably subtle dairy flavor. Slightly chewy.
A&P [6]	RM		4	67	227	Medium	Suitably subtle egg flavor.
Aunt Jemima Buttermilk	CM		4	87	320	Thick	Suitably subtle dairy flavor. Slightly chewy.
Pillsbury Microwave Buttermilk	FP		16	87	197	Medium	Suitably subtle dairy flavor. Sweet aromatics. Slightly chewy.
Jiffy Baking Mix	CM		2	[2]	[2]	Thick	Suitably subtle egg and dairy flavors. Slightly chewy.
Aunt Jemima	FB		10	67	333	Medium	Sweet aromatics. Too chewy. Slightly dense. Slight greasy mouthfeel.

Mrs. Wright's Buttermilk Baking Mix	CM	6	2	2	Medium	Suitably subtle dairy flavor.
Krusteaz Buttermilk	CM	3	2	2	4	Slightly chewy.
Aunt Jemima Buttermilk	FP	16	80	330	3	Sweet aromatics. Slightly chewy.
Aunt Jemima Buttermilk	FB	10	67	287	3	Sweet aromatics. Slightly dense. Too chewy.
Pillsbury Microwave Original	FP	16	80	183	3	Sweet aromatics. Too chewy.
Aunt Jemima Original	FP	16	80	350	3	Suitably subtle dairy flavor. Sweet aromatics. Too chewy.
Aunt Jemima	CM	3	93	320	Medium	Too much leavening flavor. Slightly bitter.
Skaggs Alpha Beta Buttermilk	CM	2	87	320	Thick	Too much leavening flavor. Slightly bitter.
Hungry Jack Pan-shakes [6]	CM	7	67	280	Medium	Too much leavening flavor. Slightly chewy.
Downyflake Original [6]	FP	18	80	250	Medium	Sweet aromatics. Slightly salty. Slight greasy mouthfeel.
Downyflake Buttermilk [6]	FP	18	80	250	4	Suitably subtle egg and dairy flavors. Slightly chewy. Sweet aromatics. Slightly salty. Slight greasy mouthfeel.
A&P	CM	2	93	320	Medium	Too much leavening flavor. Slightly bitter.

Ratings of Pancake Mixes (cont'd)

Product	Type (1)	Sensory index (2) Poor · Fair · Good · Very good · Excellent	Cost per pancake (3)	Calories (4)	Sodium, mg (5)	Thickness	Sensory comments
Kroger	CM	▮ (Fair)	2¢	60	210	Medium	Too much leavening flavor. Slightly bitter. Slightly chewy.
Martha White Flapstax Buttermilk	CM	▮ (Fair)	5	[2]	[2]	[5] Medium	Too much leavening flavor. Too chewy.
Hungry Jack Extra Lights	CM	▮ (Fair)	3	60	235	Medium	Too much leavening flavor. Slightly chewy.
Kroger Buttermilk	CM	▮ (Fair)	3	60	210	Thick	Too much leavening flavor. Slightly bitter. Too chewy.
Lady Lee Buttermilk	CM	▮ (Fair)	3	90	290	Thick	Too much leavening flavor. Slightly bitter. Too chewy.
Hungry Jack Buttermilk	CM	▮ (Fair)	3	60	237	Thick	Too much leavening flavor. Slightly bitter. Slightly chewy. Cardboard off-flavor.
Dia-Mel	CM	▮ (Poor)	5	33	45	Medium	Slightly bitter. Too chewy. Cardboard off-flavor. Slightly dense. Slight corn flavor.

Sweet 'N Low	CM	6	35	10	Thin	Too much leavening flavor. Slightly bitter. Cardboard off-flavor.
Featherweight	CM	8	43	23	Thin	Too much leavening flavor. Bitter. Slightly chewy. Cardboard off-flavor. Slight metallic off-flavor.

[1] Unlike other regular mixes, no oil required.
[2] Manufacturer does not provide nutritional information.
[3] Thickness varies from medium to thick.
[4] Thickness varies from thin to medium.
[5] Medium when made with milk, thick when made with water.
[6] Contains artificial color with FD&C Yellow #5.

Pancakes from Scratch

Pancakes made from this recipe should be right up there with the best of the bunch. They should make an almost-perfect match for butter and syrup.

These pancakes take about the same time to make as one of the add-everything mixes. Here's what you'll need:

2 cups white all-purpose flour
2 tbsp. baking powder*
¼ cup sugar
2 large eggs
2 tbsp. oil
2 cups whole milk

Let the griddle preheat while you prepare the batter. (If the griddle has a thermostat, set it for 400° F; otherwise, set the control for medium-high.) Grease the griddle very lightly with vegetable oil, margarine, or butter.

Sift the dry ingredients together in a large bowl. In a separate bowl, beat the eggs, oil, and milk until well blended. Add the liquids to the dry ingredients, stirring lightly with a wire whisk or a fork until the batter is creamy with some small lumps.

Spoon or ladle the batter onto the hot griddle. Turn the pancakes when their edges look dry and bubbles cover the top. Flip them only once; more will give them a tough texture. This recipe yields 19 four-inch pancakes.

Hint: For less-dense pancakes, separate the eggs when you mix the batter. Add the yolks with the other liquids; whip the whites until soft peaks form and add them after you've combined the other ingredients.

For thinner pancakes, add more milk or water to the batter.

---

*The 156 milligrams of sodium in this recipe come from the baking powder. Try adding a little more sugar and salt if the recipe seems too bland. For palates that

Pancake Syrups

To most people, real maple syrup is the ideal topping for a stack of flapjacks. Yet maple syrup is basically just sugar-water, and in that respect no different from the maple-flavored corn syrups sold in supermarkets as pancake syrup. Maple sugar is no more "natural" than any other sugar and a serving offers little more than calories.

True, there are differences between maple and nonmaple "maple" syrups. Real maple syrup is scarce and expensive because nature is fickle, the sugaring season short, and the process of collection painstaking. As a result, maple syrup is relatively expensive.

Maple syrup can be clear and thin or dark and thick. It all depends on when the farmer collects the sap from the sugar-maple tree.

Food processors can be more creative when they concoct a pancake syrup. They usually start with corn syrup. Some add a dollop of butter or butter flavoring. Some use other sugars. Some even add a soupçon of real maple syrup or a concoction derived from maple syrup.

By mixing and matching corn syrup and other sugars, food processors can create a contradiction in terms—light (or "lite") sugar-water. Here's how it's done: Sucrose (table sugar) is sweeter than regular corn syrup, though equal in calories. By removing some of the corn syrup and replacing it with a smaller amount of sucrose, it's possible to create a product that tastes just as sweet but contains fewer calories. In the world of syrups, though, "light" is a relative term. Even a light syrup can pack 140 calories or more in a five-tablespoon serving. Real maple syrup has about twice as many calories per serving.

Food processors also add a stiff dose of sodium to the low-calorie products, in the form of salt as a flavor enhancer. Salt may actually make syrup seem sweeter. A light syrup may contain as much as

---

find the recipe too sweet and the pancakes too fluffy, cut the sugar by half and the baking powder by one-third.

244 milligrams of sodium in a five-tablespoon serving. Real maple syrup has about 20 to 40 milligrams per serving.

Flavor

Beyond sweetness, pancake syrup should have, at most, only the merest hint of the flavor of corn syrup. It should be thick enough to stick to pancakes but not so thick that it doesn't pour easily. And it shouldn't taste of artificial butter or maple flavors. Real maple syrup has a woody, smoky taste; it may also have a note of caramelized sugar. And, like other syrups, maple syrup leaves a coating in your mouth.

Sweetness levels vary. Sweetest of all is pure maple syrup, followed by most of the regular syrups that contain 2 percent real maple syrup.

Some products are cagily named to imply that butter has been mixed in. But that's not always the case; they may contain artificial flavoring. Some products actually do contain a dab of butter, which is not always a flavor asset. If you want butter on your pancakes, add a pat yourself.

Recommendations

In at least one respect, all syrups are alike: They're a nutritional luxury, offering precious little besides calories. Real maple syrup could be considered an economic luxury as well.

Maple syrup is by far the best choice if you're watching your intake of sodium, however. And you'll probably also use a real maple syrup more sparingly than an unmaple syrup. Maple syrup is extremely sweet, with a stronger and more complex flavor than regular syrup.

Maple syrups are subject to a grading system that defines color and flavor. Grade AA, the first of the season, is almost clear and lacks a strong maple flavor. More common is Grade A, dark amber in color with a pronounced maple flavor. You probably won't find the much stronger Grades B and C outside the sugaring states.

Ratings of Pancake Syrups

Listed in order of overall sensory quality as depicted by the sensory index. Products lost points for being too thick or too thin; for having an artificial-maple or artificial-butter flavor; or for having a notable corn-syrup flavor.

As published in a **January 1988** report.

Product	Sensory index	Cost	Calories	Sodium, mg	Sensory comments
Camp Pure Maple (Dark Amber)	Good	90¢	277	37	Very sweet; strong maple flavor; woody, smoky flavor; moderate carmelized-sugar flavor.
Reese Pure Maple (Dark Amber)	Good	$1.24	269	29	Very sweet; strong maple flavor; woody, smoky flavor; moderate carmelized-sugar flavor.
Vermont Maple Orchards Pure Maple (Dark Amber)	Good	90¢	271	21	Very sweet; strong maple flavor; woody, smoky flavor.
Vermont Maid (2% Maple Syrup)	Good	25	273	34	Sweet; moderate maple flavor; slight artificial-maple flavor.

Ratings of Pancake Syrups (cont'd)

Product	Sensory index					Per serving			Sensory comments
	Poor	Fair	Good	Very good	Excellent	Cost	Calories	Sodium, mg.	
Golden Griddle (2% Maple Syrup)			■			25¢	278	47	Sweet; corn-syrup flavor; slight artificial-maple flavor.
Kroger (2% Maple Syrup)			■			25	276	52	Thick and sweet; corn-syrup flavor; slight artificial-maple flavor.
Log Cabin (2% Maple Syrup)			■			25	270	99	Thick; corn-syrup flavor; slight artificial-maple flavor.
Log Cabin Country Kitchen			■			20	280	63	Corn-syrup flavor; slight artificial-maple flavor.
Aunt Jemima Lite			■			25	143	185	Not as sweet; corn-syrup flavor; slight artificial-maple flavor.
Mrs. Butterworth's Lite (Thick 'N Rich)			■			25	157	160	Corn-syrup flavor; slight artificial-maple flavor.
Aunt Jemima (Extra Thick)			■			25	280	134	Thick; corn-syrup flavor; slight artificial-maple flavor.
Cost Cutter (Kroger)			■			15	281	58	Thick; corn-syrup flavor; slight artificial-maple flavor.
Mrs. Butterworth's (Thick 'N Rich)			■			25	280	91	Thick and sweet; corn-syrup flavor; slight artificial-maple flavor.

Product				Comments
Aunt Jemima Butter Lite		25	142	185	Not as sweet; corn-syrup flavor; moderate artificial-butter flavor; slight artificial-maple flavor.
Kroger Buttered Syrup		25	277	84	Thick; corn-syrup flavor; strong artificial-butter flavor; slight artificial-maple flavor.
Kroger Lite		25	174	244	Thick; moderate corn-syrup flavor; slight artificial-maple flavor.
Log Cabin Lite		25	168	200	Not as sweet; thick; moderate corn-syrup flavor; slight artificial-maple flavor.
Karo		20	319	123	Very thick; very little maple flavor; strong corn-syrup flavor.
Log Cabin Buttered Syrup		25	284	195	Thick; very little maple flavor; strong artificial-butter flavor; moderate corn-syrup flavor; slight artificial-maple flavor.

Strawberry Jams and Preserves

Strawberry is the most popular flavor in jams and preserves. (The distinction between "jams" and "preserves" has been blurred. Historically, preserves usually contained larger pieces of fruit and were made with more sugar than jams. Now, the terms seem to be used interchangeably.)

Flavor

It goes without saying that strawberry jam should taste and smell like strawberries. But some of the flavor of the fresh berry is lost even when you "put up preserves" the old-fashioned way, by cooking the fresh fruit with sugar and pouring it into jars.

When you start with frozen fruit, as the commercial makers usually do, a lot of the fresh berry flavor is lost. A commercial strawberry jam, then, can't be expected to match a good homemade jam. Still, it should capture as much of the aroma and flavor of the berries as possible.

Jam may or may not contain large pieces of strawberry. Jam lovers express strong feelings about the size of the fruit pieces. The fruit pieces in jams should be relatively firm, and the gel around the fruit should be soft yet cohesive. The jam should also be easy to spread. And it shouldn't have the caramel flavor of overcooked strawberries; the flavor of any berry or fruit other than strawberry; or any bitter, artificial, or off-flavor taste.

Sugar Content

A quality jam should be sweet, but not *overwhelmingly* sweet. Jam is sweet by nature and, preferably, naturally sweet. Sugars show up on the ingredients lists in several guises—sucrose, corn syrup, cane sugar, and even honey. Jams are usually composed of 60 to 65 percent sugars, the level that retards spoilage. That much sugar translates into many calories. Most regular jams contain about 65 calories per one-tablespoon serving.

Low-calorie jam uses less sugar or sometimes substitutes saccharin. Instead of using a lot of sugar to prevent spoilage, the low-calorie jams use harmless preservatives such as ascorbic acid, sorbates, and propionates.

Recommendations

Forget the fancy labels and prices. In Consumers Union's last tests of jams (August 1985), the most expensive "gourmet" jams—*Crabtree & Evelyn* and *Fortnum & Mason*—did not distinguish themselves from the average jam. Neither did most of the other gourmet jams.

The *Knott's Berry Farm* preserves tasted best by a slight margin. Close to it in quality were brands such as Kraft, Smucker's, Polaner, Bama, and supermarket brands from Kroger and Safeway.

For the calorie conscious or for those cutting down on sugar, light jams may contain only half the calories of the regular jams and still taste good.

Orange Juice

Processed orange juice can't match the taste and character of freshly squeezed juice. What's missing is primarily the zesty, eye-opening, sweet taste of a fresh orange, a stimulation of tongue and nose easy to discern but hard to describe.

Of all the processing methods, frozen concentrated orange juice comes closest to saving some of that elusive fresh-orange flavor.

By contrast, the high heat used in canning orange juice leaves behind little of the fruit but its color. Canned juice's best attribute is that it doesn't require refrigeration. It has increasingly been crowded off the supermarket shelf by boxed juice, another product that needs no refrigeration.

The most popular type of orange juice is chilled juice, the ready-to-drink beverage found in the supermarket's dairy case. It accounts for slightly more than half of all the orange juice sold. Although chilled juice may look like fresh-squeezed juice, most of it is made from frozen concentrate that's shipped in bulk to a regional plant, where it's reconstituted and packed in bottles or cartons. The extra processing and handling takes its toll: The average chilled juice doesn't taste as good as the average juice you make from concentrate. Chilled juice is usually more expensive, too.

Freshly squeezed orange juice is even more expensive, and it adds time and effort to making breakfast.

Flavor

Much of the delicate flavor in an orange comes from dozens of volatile esters and aldehydes. During processing, heat vaporizes most of the compounds, but some are captured and condensed into an "orange essence," which is later added back to the frozen concentrate. Cold-pressed peel oil can also restore some zest to frozen concentrate. Or the processor may overconcentrate the juice in the evaporator, then dilute it a little with freshly squeezed juice called "cutback."

But even the best of those processes saves only a fraction of a fresh orange's delicacy. Processors do better with what specialists call "orange complex," that characteristic aroma and flavor we sense as "orange."

In addition to the zesty fresh-orange flavor and the basic orangey taste, an excellent orange juice should be sweet, yet refreshingly tart. It should contain a little of the tang that comes from the peel oil but little or no bitterness.

Processed juice can have off-flavors. Chief among them: the cooked-orange taste characteristic of overprocessed orange juice, especially canned juice. Other defects suggest poor treatment after processing. Over time, exposure to air can start orange juice fermenting in the container or give rise to oxidation, which leaves a taste like multivitamins. Another symptom that the orange oils are deteriorating is a cardboard taste.

Some processed juice contains pulp. The presence or absence of pulp is a matter of taste, not of quality.

You probably will find the best frozen concentrates entirely satisfactory as a morning eye-opener, especially if you were raised on that type of orange juice.

Chilled juice is processed more than frozen concentrate, making chilled orange juice more vulnerable to taste defects. Most chilled juice starts out as extraconcentrated frozen concentrate that is shipped in bulk from a juice plant to a regional center where it is mixed with water and packed in bottles or cartons. At that time, chilled juice is generally pasteurized—a heat treatment that juice sold as frozen concentrate escapes.

Chilled juice has a tendency to show off-flavors caused by improper handling; it's more susceptible to such problems than frozen concentrate, which can last months in the freezer. Chilled juice has a shelf life of four to five weeks if it's kept properly chilled at 35° F. But if chilled juice is stored at 45°, it lasts only half that long.

Boxed orange juice is heated, quickly cooled, then packed in multilayer laminated cartons without any air space. The "aseptic" in this "aseptic packaging" refers to the closed, germ-free environment in which the packing takes place. Like cans, aseptic cartons can be stored at room temperature and packed in a lunchbox or bought from a vending machine without fear of spoilage.

Unfortunately, boxed orange juice doesn't taste any better than canned juice. Cartoned juice also seems prone to the same sort of metallic off-flavors that affect the taste of canned orange juice. Boxed juices contained virtually no trace of fresh-orange flavor.

Aseptically packed orange juice is just a small part of the boxed-juice market, a market that's aimed mainly at kids. The individual-portion cartons typical of this product help explain the boxed juices' relatively high cost per serving. Most cost more than the most expensive chilled juices.

Nutrition

Orange juice is the major natural source of vitamin C in the American diet. A six-ounce serving of juice made from frozen concentrate provides an adult's Recommended Daily Allowance of 60 milligrams of vitamin C. Chilled and boxed juices average a little less than 60 milligrams per serving, probably because of processing or storage vagaries. But it isn't enough less to be significant nutritionally.

Orange juice is also a good source of potassium, as are many other common foods, such as meat, potatoes, bananas, and peanut butter. Since potassium is so abundant, healthy people rarely develop a potassium deficiency. There is no formal RDA for potassium. A six-ounce serving of orange juice, of any type, contains about 350 milligrams.

Although orange juice is a nutritious drink, it's not a diet drink. Ounce for ounce, orange juice has about as many calories as a cola or beer: roughly 80 calories per six-ounce serving. More than 10 percent of orange juice is fruit sugar. That's why people on a diet are advised to eat an orange rather than drink a glassful of juice, which is the caloric equivalent of three or four oranges.

Recommendations

Not only is juice sold as frozen concentrate apt to taste better than chilled juice, it often costs less, too.

People who think they are buying a higher-quality product when they buy chilled juice might switch to frozen concentrate and stop carrying home the extra water.

If frozen and chilled juice aren't stored properly, their flavor—and their vitamin C content—can deteriorate. If you make up more juice than you'll drink within a day or two, store what's left in an airtight jar. Both the orange flavor and vitamin C degrade rapidly in the presence of air.

Consider boxed juice only for situations in which the package's convenience and portability demand that you put up with the poor flavor.

Ratings of Orange Juice

Listed by types; within types, listed in order of overall sensory quality, as depicted by the sensory index.
As published in a **February 1987** report.

Product	Sensory index (Poor, Fair, Good, Very good, Excellent)	Cost per 6 oz. serving	Sensory comments
Fresh-squeezed		30¢	Very pulpy.
Frozen concentrate			
Florida Gold 100% Valencia		15	Moderately pulpy.
Minute Maid Country Style		20	Very pulpy.
Citrus Hill Select		15	Moderately pulpy.
Skaggs Alpha Beta		10	Very pulpy.
No Frills (Pathmark)		10	Some vitamin flavor; moderately pulpy.
Minute Maid Reduced Acid		25	Some vitamin flavor; moderately pulpy.
Minute Maid		20	Moderately pulpy.
Janet Lee (Albertson)		15	Some metallic flavor; very pulpy.

Ratings of Orange Juice (cont'd)

Sensory index

Product	Poor	Fair	Good	Very good	Excellent	Cost per 6 oz. serving	Sensory comments

Frozen concentrate (cont'd)

Product	Sensory index	Cost per 6 oz. serving	Sensory comments
Tropicana Home Style		20¢	Some fermented, metallic, and vitamin flavors; very pulpy.
Bel-Air (Safeway)		10	Moderately pulpy.
Donald Duck Higher Pulp		10	Some vitamin flavor; moderately pulpy.
Kroger		15	Some vitamin flavor; moderately pulpy.
Tree Sweet		15	—
Lady Lee (Lucky)		10	Some vitamin flavor; moderately pulpy.
Pathmark		10	Cardboard flavor; moderately pulpy.
Sunkist		20	Some vitamin flavor.
Donald Duck		15	Some vitamin flavor.
A&P		15	Some vitamin and cardboard flavor.
Tropicana		20	Some metallic and vitamin flavors; moderately pulpy.
Cost Cutter (Kroger)		10	Some vitamin flavor.
Vita Gold		15	Some metallic and vitamin flavors.
Avondale (Kroger)		10	Fermented taste; strong vitamin flavor.
Scotch Buy (Safeway)		10	Some vitamin flavor; strong metallic flavor.

Chilled

Brand		Rating	Comments
Tropicana Pure Premium		25	—
Minute Maid		20	Some vitamin and metallic flavors.
Knudsen		25	—
Minute Maid Country Style		15	Some metallic flavor; moderately pulpy.
Citrus Hill Select		15	—
Tropicana Home Style		20	Some vitamin flavor; very pulpy.
Lucerne (Safeway)		15	—
Tropicana (from concentrate—jar)		25	Some vitamin flavor.
Janet Lee (Albertson)		15	Some vitamin flavor.
Tropicana (carton)		15	Fermented taste; some vitamin and metallic flavors.
Sunkist		20	Fermented taste; strong vitamin flavor.
Pathmark		15	—
A&P		10	Fermented taste; some metallic flavor.
Skaggs Alpha Beta		15	Some metallic and vitamin flavors.
Donald Duck		15	Fermented taste; some vitamin and strong metallic flavors.
Safeway (jar)		25	Fermented taste; some metallic flavor.
Tropicana (not from concentrate—jar)		15	Fermented taste.
Kroger		15	Some metallic and vitamin flavors.

Ratings of Orange Juice (cont'd)

Chilled (cont'd)

The sensory index is shown as a horizontal bar graph with the scale: Poor — Fair — Good — Very good — Excellent.

Product	Sensory index (bar reaches)	Cost per 6 oz. serving	Sensory comments
Tropicana Home Style	Very good	20¢	Some fermented, metallic, and vitamin flavors; very pulpy.
Bel-Air (Safeway)	Very good	10	Moderately pulpy.
Donald Duck Higher Pulp	Very good	10	Some vitamin flavor; moderately pulpy.
Kroger	Good–Very good	15	Some vitamin flavor; moderately pulpy.
Tree Sweet	Good	15	—
Lady Lee (Lucky)	Good	10	Some vitamin flavor; moderately pulpy.
Pathmark	Good	10	Cardboard flavor; moderately pulpy.
Sunkist	Good	20	Some vitamin flavor.
Donald Duck	Good	15	Some vitamin flavor.
A&P	Good	15	Some vitamin and cardboard flavor.
Tropicana	Fair–Good	20	Some metallic and vitamin flavors; moderately pulpy.
Cost Cutter (Kroger)	Good	10	Some vitamin flavor.
Vita Gold	Fair	15	Some metallic and vitamin flavors.
Avondale (Kroger)	Fair	10	Fermented taste; strong vitamin flavor.
Scotch Buy (Safeway)	Poor	10	Some vitamin flavor; strong metallic flavor.

Some Facts About Oranges

Most juice oranges grown in the United States come from Florida, where the growing conditions are nearly ideal. Juice oranges need warm, moist days, cool nights, and plenty of rain—weather found in Florida for nine months of the year. While some juice oranges, notably the *Sunkist* brand, come from California, the orange-growing counties in that state are hot and dry, a climate that produces a drier fruit with a thicker skin, more suitable to eat than to squeeze.

As the Florida orange season progresses from October to July, different varieties mature on the trees. First comes the Hamlins variety, a tart, thin-skinned orange high in acid and vitamin C. It's followed by Pineapples and, finally, the late-maturing Valencias, which are the biggest crop, and prized for their deep orange color, sweetness, and juiciness.

To produce a uniform-tasting juice year round, processors blend frozen concentrate from different harvests. Thus, concentrate from Valencias—highly colored, sweet, but relatively low in acidity and vitamin C—may be held frozen after the spring harvest and blended the following fall with some high-acid, tart, light-colored Hamlins concentrate.

One factor the orange packers can't control is the weather. Serious freezes are disastrous.

But Brazil has filled in where Florida left off. Brazil is now the world's largest producer of concentrate. In one recent year, roughly half the orange juice consumed in the United States came from Brazilian concentrate, which was blended with homegrown.

Brazil grows its own orange varieties, including vast acreages of the Pera, an orange quite similar to the Florida Valencia.

To keep Florida as the orange-juice capital of the world, the Florida juice lobby has erected a series of barricades. A protective tariff levied on imported juice keeps Brazil from swamping the U.S. market. And the state of Florida sets legal standards for orange juice that are a bit more stringent than the federal government's standards. While those standards ostensibly ensure that Florida orange juice is a high-quality product, they also tend to tilt the definition of quality toward the type of oranges that Florida produces in abundance.

The Florida Department of Citrus has come up with a couple of label logos to distinguish products of the Florida industry from out-of-state competition, launching big advertising campaigns to make the point. The first logo was the "Sunshine Tree," a stylized orange tree. When that symbol shows up on a container, it means that the juice inside is from oranges all grown in Florida.

But since so much juice is now Brazilian, the Sunshine Tree needed a graft. Enter "Florida's Seal of Approval." That seal means that the contents meet Florida's quality standards. It doesn't mean that the juice necessarily comes from Florida. All it really signifies is that the juice was marketed by a Florida shipper. Perfectly good juice from California or Texas won't have the seal. It's worth noting that compliance with the seal program is not total, even in Florida. One of the biggest brands, *Minute Maid,* a Florida-based division of Coca Cola, doesn't carry the seal.

Apple Juice

The delicate taste of freshly pressed apple cider is hard to find in a commercial product. If you see a jug of cider in the supermarket, chances are that it really contains pasteurized apple juice.

Fresh juice could be available for a few weeks each year—around harvest time. But fresh juice lasts only a couple of weeks even under refrigeration. That's why some juice is bottled and pasteurized, and much of the harvest winds up concentrated to one-seventh of its original bulk and frozen. Most bottlers of the apple juice found on supermarket shelves rely mainly on concentrated juice stock to keep their plants running year round.

Freezing slows the activity of microorganisms that ferment apple juice, but when water is added and the temperature rises, the fermentation begins again. If you buy frozen apple-juice concentrate and add water at home, you must refrigerate the juice and use it within a couple of weeks.

The juice in the bottles, cans, and boxes that sit on open shelves in the market, whether straight from the apple or made up from concentrate, has been pasteurized—heated to something like 170° to 190°F. Heat kills the microorganisms that cause fermentation, and the result is a juice that has a stable, unrefrigerated shelf life of up to a year.

Most American concentrate comes from the same few types of eating and cooking apples that are likely to be available in the produce department just an aisle or two away from the juice. When apple juice started to soar in popularity in the 1970s, American orchards couldn't keep pace. Consequently, roughly half the concentrate that bottlers use is imported, mostly from central Europe. (In some European countries, the chemical *Alar* is used on apples. It's up to the processor to find out whether the concentrate contains this controversial chemical [see pages 98–99].)

The ample supply of various concentrates gives bottlers the luxury of making their blends from a bigger variety of supply stocks. Apple juices and ciders are normally blends of several apple types, each chosen for its own distinct contribution of flavor notes and for what it adds to the sugar and acid levels.

And what the bottlers blend tastes bland. A consistent failure in commercial apple juice is a virtual absence of *appleness*. In addition to killing microorganisms, pasteurization cooks off some of the volatile flavor notes that make fresh apple juice taste fresh. The cooking also produces other permanent flavor changes, so that the juice tastes more like applesauce than fresh apples.

When apple juice is pasteurized, the higher the heat used, the quicker the process. So there's an inclination to crank up the heat to move more product through the plant. But the higher the heat, the more the fruit sugars will caramelize, creating a distinctive flavor that is easy for a trained palate to pick up.

The tartness of apple juice hinges on the balance between the fruit's natural malic acid and its natural fruit sugars—fructose, sucrose, and glucose. Children drink a big share of all apple juice, and sweetness would be attractive to them. Still, very few products are excessively sweet. Many makers do find a way to cater to children's point of view, though. Many of them blend their products to be conspicuously low in malic acid. That unmasks more of the juice's natural sweetness by reducing the counterbalancing sourness.

A touch of fermented flavor might be excused—even welcomed—in the juice of freshly squeezed apples. A properly handled pasteurized product should have none of it, though.

Children seem to prefer "regular" apple juice, which in juice jargon means a product filtered to crystal clarity. Many adults go for the cloudier, darker, so-called natural juice, which is likely to be the same pasteurized, reconstituted juice, but merely screened and not filtered. Natural-style juice feels slightly thicker in the mouth.

Although natural-style juice may look and feel as if it has useful fiber, that's a delusion. There's no difference in nutritional content between regular and natural types.

Apart from small amounts of minerals—iron, boron, and such—apple juice offers little nutritionally. A glass contributes practically nothing except about 100 calories, mostly from fruit sugars. Some brands may be fortified with vitamin C to about half the level naturally found in orange juice. Otherwise, orange juice, grapefruit juice, tomato juice, even pineapple juice contribute more nutrients for their calories than apple juice.

What about *Alar?*

Uniroyal Chemical Company announced early in June 1989 that it was halting sales of *Alar,* the controversial chemical used as a growth regulator on apples. (Earlier, the federal government proposed a ban on *Alar* because the chemical posed a cancer risk.) Uniroyal said it was offering refunds to U.S. apple growers who had purchased *Alar*.

Before the Uniroyal announcement, the International Apple Institute urged its membership to stop using *Alar* in orchards. At the same time, the trade group representing apple processors urged the Environmental Protection Agency to go forward with its ban and asked Uniroyal to stop selling *Alar*.

Uniroyal, maintaining that *Alar* was safe, said it had halted domestic sales because the chemical became the center of "a needless controversy that is hurting the industry and the American public." An attorney for the Natural Resources Defense Council, the group that helped spark the concern about *Alar*, said Uniroyal was trying to make "a virtue out of necessity." According to one industry estimate, the publicity about *Alar* cost apple growers about $100 million and severely depressed sales of apple juice and other apple products.

Milk for People Who Can't Drink Milk

Some 30 to 50 million Americans risk bloating, gas, cramps, and diarrhea when they drink milk or eat ice cream. These symptoms result from a deficiency of lactase, an intestinal enzyme needed to digest the milk sugar, or lactose, in dairy products. It's the undigested sugar that causes the intestinal problems. Adults of all races may suffer from lactose intolerance; the problem affects a far greater percentage of nonwhites than whites.

If you like milk and other dairy foods but have trouble tolerating them, several products sold nationwide under the *Lactaid* name can help.

Lactaid milk is a lowfat milk treated with lactase. The *Lactaid* milk has lactose levels 80 to 85 percent below those of regular milk. But you pay a premium for *Lactaid*'s benefit; it costs a bit more than regular lowfat milk.

Lactaid tastes slightly sweeter than ordinary lowfat milk and has a slightly caramelized flavor. The sweetness comes from the sweeter simple sugars into which the enzyme breaks milk sugar. The caramelized flavor comes from ultrapasteurization; the milk is briefly heated to a much higher temperature than regular pasteurized milk to give it a longer shelf life—at least six weeks in the dairy case.

Lactaid Inc. also sells *Calcimilk,* a lowfat, lactose-reduced milk with about two-thirds more calcium than *Lactaid* and other lowfat milks. And early in 1989 the company started producing *Lactaid* skim milk, fat-free and with 20 percent fewer calories than *Lactaid* lowfat.

Lactaid lactase drops, sold in drug and health-food stores, let you treat your own milk to cut lactose. Typically, you use five drops per quart, shake, and refrigerate the milk. You must wait a day for results. At usual refrigerator temperatures, the drops reduce milk sugar by about 70 percent after 24 hours. More time or more drops do an even more thorough job.

The product works well. Treated milk tastes more like regular milk than *Lactaid* does, and adding drops is a little cheaper.

Lactaid enzyme tablets, sold over the counter, can help when you dine out or indulge in ice cream or some other dairy product for which there is no lactose-reduced equivalent. You take the pills right before eating. The dosage varies from one-half to three tablets, depending on the meal and your system—you'll have to experiment.

Coffees

The United States, which claims scarcely one-twentieth of the world's population, drinks one-third of the planet's coffee—about 360 million cups a day.

And U.S. coffee drinkers are becoming fussy about what brew they drink. The consumption of instant coffee has dipped appreciably. By contrast, the number of coffee drinkers choosing decaffeinated—many for health reasons—has increased markedly.

Flavor

Cultivating premium coffee requires the most exacting conditions—rich soil, mild climate, painstaking care—and a labor-intensive harvest that comes down to handpicking.

Coffee beans are actually the seeds of the blood-red cherries that grow on coffee trees, two beans per cherry. Since each tree yields perhaps only a pound of finished coffee, billions of trees must be harvested to quench the world's thirst. The trees—evergreens with waxy leaves and jasmine-like flowers—thrive on windblown tropical hills at heights up to 6,000 feet, the higher the better.

Various processes are used to separate the green (unroasted) beans from the cherries. The beans are then shipped and finally roasted. Roasting alters the complex chemistry of the beans' carbohydrates, oils, and other constituents to bring out desirable flavors and coffee aroma. Too much roasting, though, can be as bad as too little, charring the delicate beans and sending much of their good coffee essence up the chimney.

Botanists have named the two main coffee species *Coffea robusta* and *Coffea arabica*. The robusta strain, as its name implies, is the hardier, more impervious to bad weather and plant disease. But experts describe its taste as harsh, rubbery, even a bit like cereal. So processors often shunt the cheaper robusta beans into instant or institutional-grade coffees or use them in bargain blends. Arabica beans—the name pays homage to coffee's Middle Eastern beginnings—are reserved for the world's premium coffees. Such coffees are often identified by the ports of call from which their beans hail. Here's a sensory sampler:

Arabian Rich and heavy-bodied, with smooth flavor, notable acidity.

Brazilian   Lighter, thinner in flavor and aroma, often slightly harsher than Colombian; often blended. The best: Bourbon Santos—smooth, sweet, and medium-bodied.

Colombian   Sometimes sold unblended as "100 percent Colombian" coffee; sometimes blended with other beans. Full-bodied taste, moderate acidity, fine aroma.

Haitian   Mellow yet rich, with a touch of smoothness and medium body.

Hawaiian Kona   Often grown on soil rich in volcanic deposits, said to lend Kona its full, smooth body. Limited production makes it expensive, but it's nonetheless in demand.

Indonesian   Home to Java, a full-bodied, very rich coffee; often mixed with Yemeni beans—themselves described as "gamy" tasting with heavy acidity—to make Mocha-Java. Sumatra Mandheling or Lintany Indonesian coffees are known for their body.

Kenyan   From slopes around Mount Kilimanjaro. Mild, aromatic, with good body. Slightly superior to Colombian.

Great coffee starts with fine beans and a good coffee maker. But a delicious cup can't be taken for granted. Coffee is a finely tuned admixture of more than 100 different chemicals—aromatic molecules, proteins, starches, oils, bitter phenols—each contributing its scent or taste.

There are numerous pitfalls between good coffee beans and good coffee. Probably the worst are time and temperature. Ground coffee ages rapidly, even if packed in a hermetically sealed can. Once the can is open, exposure to air can also turn coffee stale, its oils rancid. It's best to start with whole coffee beans, if you can. Grind only as much as you need, and freeze unused coffee—beans or ground—in a dry, airtight container to preserve taste.

When you're set to brew coffee, always use cold, fresh water—bottled, if necessary—and scrupulously clean utensils. Oils that accumulate in the coffee pot can and will spoil flavor. Use the grind correct for your coffee maker. And don't stint on coffee by trying to squeeze too many cups from too little coffee. If you prefer weak coffee, it's best to make a full-strength cup and then dilute it with hot water. Using too little coffee results in overextraction and a bitter taste.

Coffee is best prepared with water just below the boil—about 190° F. Serve it promptly, though you can keep coffee hot in a thermally insulated bottle or carafe for a few hours with little loss in quality. You can also warm it in the microwave oven with little loss in taste. But keeping coffee on a low burner too long—or worse, reheating or boiling it—can turn the taste flat, harsh, sour, or bitter as volatile molecules are driven off and delicate chemical bonds are broken.

Pricing and Packaging

Like many commodity prices, the price of coffee is volatile—buffeted by international politics and inclement weather.

Supermarkets don't make much profit selling coffee. "It's a break-even item like sugar, salt, eggs, flour, and butter," one executive has said. But manufacturers do have an incentive to hold down prices, lest they alienate the less dedicated drinkers. Packaging and processing tricks help.

Stretching the Coffee The soaring prices of more than a decade ago inspired manufacturers to introduce "high yield" coffees—13 ounces (and sometimes less) of fluffed-up coffee to a can. Originally, the cheaper 13-ounce packages were supposed to make the same number of cups as a regular can. Nowadays, though, some don't make any such claim.

One way a manufacturer can stretch a brew is by "flaking" the beans instead of grinding them. Another technique uses a heat process to increase the beans' overall surface area, somewhat like popped corn. Both methods expose relatively more surface area and supposedly make brewing more efficient.

Sometimes these flaked and puffed coffees make as much coffee as you get with a one-pound can. Sometimes they don't.

Bricks Brick packs landed in Europe a generation ago and have virtually replaced coffee cans there. In this country, bricks have been widely sold for only a few years. The brick is nothing more than a fancy bag—a multilayered laminate of plastic, foil, and nylon that is vacuum-sealed for freshness. Supermarkets like bricks because they're lighter and take up less shelf space than coffee cans. More important for consumers, bricks cost far less to make than cans, a saving that can be passed on.

Brick packaging does have drawbacks. Punctures and pinholes make messes and rob coffee of freshness. And the bricks can't be resealed very well. So you'll have to transfer the coffee to an airtight container—perhaps an old coffee can with a tightly fitting plastic lid.

Freshness Dates and "Locks" Some brands stamp a freshness date on packages, but the date may be so optimistic as to be unreliable. Besides, even in sealed cans, roast coffee loses much of its freshness in the first hours and days after it's ground and packaged.

Recommendations

Millions of Americans drink coffee to help them wake up in the morning. For many of them, any cup of coffee that's hot, wet, and caffeinated will do. But many others relish coffee's unique taste as well as its caffeine jolt.

These people might enjoy coffee roasted from a blend containing Colombian or other premium beans like Konas.

Buying beans to grind just before brewing makes for an undeniably better-tasting brew, compared with using coffee ground days or even months beforehand. Intact beans practically guarantee intact freshness. If you invest in a coffee grinder, you'll likely taste the difference. Don't forget, though, to freeze all unused coffee—whether whole beans or ground—in a dry, airtight container. Otherwise, you risk losing the delicate coffee scents and flavors. Finally, milk, cream, or sugar will blunt any coffee's taste. If you pour either with a heavy hand, you may be able to settle for one of the less flavorsome but cheaper coffees. You won't know what you're missing.

Coffee and Your Health

The majority of Americans drink coffee—an average of three and one-third cups a day. But many of the drinkers worry that coffee or its caffeine will harm them.

Caffeine is one of the most commonly consumed substances, found naturally in coffee and tea, added to soft drinks, and compounded into more than 1,000 over-the-counter drugs. It is a mild stimulant and somewhat addictive. It's the coffee ingredient responsible for the quick energy and "lift" that many coffee drinkers count on.

Caffeine stimulates the brain's cortex to improve attention and concentration, and it makes muscles work more powerfully and with less fatigue. It also speeds up the heart, stimulates the stomach to secrete more acid, and acts on the kidneys to step up urine production.

Too much caffeine leads to distressing symptoms popularly called "coffee nerves." These can include nervousness, heart palpitations, disturbed sleep, stomach problems, and diarrhea. Some people can drink several cups of coffee a day—with from 50 to 200 milligrams of caffeine or more per cup—and never suffer from coffee nerves; others experience symptoms after only a cup or two.

Coffee or caffeine—some studies haven't distinguished which—has also been suspected of contributing to far more serious problems: heart disease, pancreatic cancer, benign breast cysts, and birth defects. But the research on each of those topics is far from conclusive. Given the variety of foods people eat, it is difficult to disentangle the effects of any one food—or one ingredient—in order to track its influence on health years later.

Heart Disease Scientists have taken a two-pronged approach, studying coffee's impact on cholesterol—and thus its indirect influence in heart disease—and studying the incidence of heart disease in coffee drinkers.

A 1985 study of tens of thousands of men and women by the Kaiser-Permanente Health Organization in California found a relationship between coffee drinking and elevated blood cholesterol. Since no similar link was found for tea-drinking, something in coffee other than caffeine presumably was involved.

Research the same year at Stanford University confirmed the finding in a smaller sample of men, even after relevant factors like age, diet, body weight, and smoking were accounted for. A more recent Norwegian study has revealed that people who drink a lot of coffee and who have high cholesterol levels can lower their cholesterol an average of 13 percent by giving up coffee. But other research has failed to confirm a clear-cut relationship between coffee and cholesterol.

Late in 1986, researchers at Johns Hopkins University published a long-term study of the link between coffee and heart disease. The study had followed more than 1,100 physicians for 20 years or longer and noted a significant association between coffee drinking and coronary heart disease—heart attacks, angina pectoris, and milder chest pains. The doctors who drank three or four cups a day were about twice as likely to suffer such problems as those who drank no coffee. Those who drank five or more cups a day were nearly three times as likely to report such problems.

But the number of heart "events" was small—less than 5 percent of the doctors reported one. And some of the cases may have been indigestion, not heart disease. Further, although the study controlled for its participants' smoking, it failed to consider variables like diet, lack of exercise, and stress, all of which can contribute to coronary disease. The study has also been faulted for focusing solely on white males.

Birth Defects Since 1980, the U.S. Food and Drug Administration has advised pregnant women to limit their caffeine intake. The warning followed an FDA study in which pregnant rats that were fed large amounts of caffeine bore offspring with missing toes. That study has been criticized for its massive caffeine dosages—the human equivalent of up to 24 cups a day of strong coffee—and the fact that the rats were force-fed.

A subsequent FDA study, publicized early in 1986, also used high dosages of caffeine but let the rats sip it at a more natural rate in caffeine-laced drinking water. This time, the rats' offspring showed delayed skeletal development, but there were no missing toes. More important, the pups' delayed bone development reversed itself almost entirely within a week of birth.

No well-controlled studies have linked caffeine consumption to human birth defects. Still, it's prudent for pregnant women to put coffee on the list of pleasures to forgo for a while.

Decaffeinated Coffee

If you want to cut down on caffeine, you can drink fewer cups, brew weaker coffee, or try one of the lower-caffeine regular coffees. You can also switch to decaffeinated coffee.

A few years back, a packet of instant *Sanka* alongside a cup of boiled water was the best that restaurant diners could hope for when ordering decaffeinated coffee. Now, most restaurants keep a pot of freshly brewed decaffeinated on hand. Likewise, a host of ground decaffeinated brands compete against regular coffees for precious supermarket shelf space.

Decaffeinated coffee need not be a weak-flavored imitation. Some taste just as good as the real thing, some even better.

A cup of any decaffeinated coffee contains negligible caffeine—a few milligrams at most.

Ratings of Ground Coffee

Listed by types; within types, listed in order of overall sensory quality, as shown on the sensory index. Manufacturers' "suggested servings" (level tablespoons of coffee per six-ounce cup) were used to brew coffee for tastings and chemical analyses.

As published in a **September 1987** report.

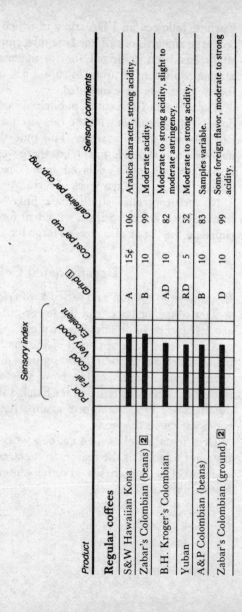

Product	Sensory index (Poor / Fair / Good / Very good / Excellent)	Grind T	Cost per cup	Caffeine per cup, mg	Sensory comments
Regular coffees					
S&W Hawaiian Kona	Excellent	A	15¢	106	Arabica character, strong acidity.
Zabar's Colombian (beans) [2]	Very good	B	10	99	Moderate acidity.
B.H. Kroger's Colombian	Very good	AD	10	82	Moderate to strong acidity, slight to moderate astringency.
Yuban	Very good	RD	5	52	Moderate to strong acidity.
A&P Colombian (beans)	Very good	B	10	83	Samples variable.
Zabar's Colombian (ground) [2]	Very good	D	10	99	Some foreign flavor, moderate to strong acidity.

Brown Gold Colombian	A	10	109	Moderate to strong acidity.
Zabar's Special Blend (beans) [2]	B	10	102	Moderate to strong acidity.
A&P Colombian (ground)	AD	10	83	Strong acidity.
Brown & Jenkins Colombia Supremo (beans) [3]	B	20	115	Burned (overroasted) flavor.
MJB Premium Colombian	A	5	62	Slight to moderate acidity.
Brown & Jenkins Special Blend (beans) [3]	B	20	110	Moderate to strong burned (over-roasted) character.
S&W Colombian	D	10	93	Moderate to strong acidity.
Zabar's Special Blend (ground) [2]	D	10	102	Acidic.
Pathmark Premium (brick)	AD	5	71	Slight off-aroma/flavor; caramel flavor.
Brown & Jenkins Colombia Supremo (ground) [3]	D	20	115	Strong burned (overroasted) character.
Hills Bros. Gold	A	5	48	Moderate acidity.
Brown & Jenkins Special Blend (ground) [3]	D	20	110	Moderate to strong burned (over-roasted) character.
Martinson Mr. Automatic	AD	5	123	Moderate to strong robusta character.
Edwards (Safeway)	D	10	103	Strong acidity.
MJB Premium	AD	5	62	Moderate to strong robusta character.
Melitta Gourmet Filter	EF	5	80	Slight robusta flavor.
Maryland Club Filter Blend	F	5	63	Robusta flavor variable across samples.
A&P Eight O'Clock (ground)	AD	5	79	Variable samples.

Ratings of Ground Coffee (cont'd)

Product	Sensory index (Poor / Fair / Good / Very good / Excellent)	Grind [1]	Cost per cup	Caffeine per cup, mg	Sensory comments
Regular coffees (cont'd)					
Folgers		AD	5¢	63	Robusta flavor variable across samples.
A&P Eight O'Clock (beans)		B	5	79	Moderate robusta flavor.
Yuban		D	5	51	Strong acidity, lacks flavor.
Folgers Special Roast Flaked		AD	5	54	Strong robusta character.
Maxwell House Master Blend (brick)		AD	5	65	Strong robusta character.
Chock Full O' Nuts		A	5	111	Strong robusta character.
Chock Full O' Nuts (brick)		A	5	110	Robusta flavor variable across samples.
Maxwell House ADC (brick)		AD	5	74	Strong robusta aroma and flavor.
Kroger		AD	5	89	Moldy foreign flavor, slight acidity.
Maxwell House ADC		AD	5	76	Strong robusta character.
Ann Page (A&P)		AD	5	62	Strong robusta character.
Folgers (brick)		AD	5	61	Strong robusta character.
Cost Cutter (Kroger)		A	10	195	Strong robusta character; stale taste in two samples.

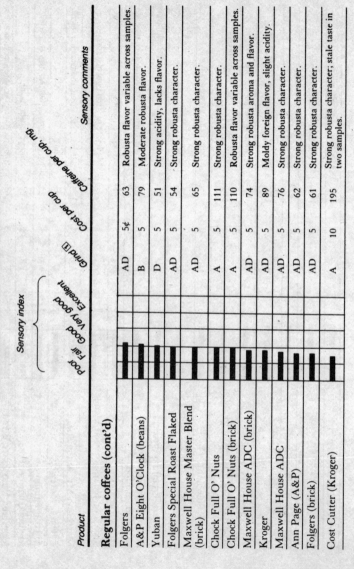

			Flavor notes
Scotch Buy (Safeway)	A	5	74	Moderate robusta character, foreign aroma and flavor.
Maxwell House Master Blend	AD	5	51	Moderate to strong robusta flavor.
Savarin	AD	5	55	Moldy flavor, moderate to strong robusta character.
Chase & Sanborn	A	5	54	Strong robusta flavor.

Decaffeinated coffees

S&W Colombian	D	15	—	Moderate acidity.
Hills Bros. Gold	A	5	—	Moderate acidity.
Brown Gold Colombian	A	15	—	Strong acidity.
Martinson Premium	A	10	—	Moderate to strong acidity.
A&P Eight O'Clock (beans)	B	10	—	Slight to moderate acidity; samples variable.
Hills Bros.	AD	5	—	Slight to moderate acidity.
Yuban	AD	5	—	Caramel flavor, moderate to strong acidic flavor, lacks flavor.
A&P Colombian (beans)	B	10	—	Moderate to strong acidity; moderate caramel flavor.
Chock Full O' Nuts 98 Caf Free	A	10	—	Caramel flavor, slight to moderate acidity.
Edwards (Safeway)	A	5	—	Foreign flavor.
Sanka	AD	5	—	Slight to moderate acidity.
Brim Regular Roast	AD	5	—	Moderate to strong acidity.
Maryland Club Premium	F	5	—	Foreign flavor, strong acidity.
A&P Eight O'Clock (ground)	AD	10	—	Slight to moderate acidity.

Ratings of Ground Coffee (cont'd)

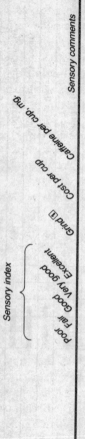

Product	Sensory index (Poor / Fair / Good / Very good / Excellent)	Grind [1]	Cost per cup	Caffeine per cup, mg.	Sensory comments
Decaffeinated coffees (cont'd)					
A&P Colombian (ground)		AD	10¢	—	Moderate acidity, odd flavor.
Folgers		AD	5	—	Lacks flavor.
Pathmark (brick)		A	5	—	Very variable samples.
Chase & Sanborn		A	5	—	Slight to moderate acidity.
Savarin		A	10	—	Caramel flavor, variable samples.
MJB Premium		A	5	—	Strong robusta flavor.
Brim Dark Roast		AD	5	—	Moderate acidic flavor, lacks aroma and flavor.
Maxwell House		AD	5	—	Weak flavor, moderate acidity.
Melitta Filter		EF	5	—	Weak flavor, foreign flavor in two samples.
Kroger		AD	5	—	Samples variable.
Ann Page 97 Caf Free (A&P)		AD	5	—	Low flavor, foreign flavors.

[1] A—All-purpose; B—Whole beans (ground just before brewing); AD—Autodrip; D—Drip; EF—Extra fine; F—Filter; RD—Regular/drip. [2] Available from Zabar's, 2245 Broadway, New York, N.Y. 10024. [3] Available from Brown & Jenkins, Box 1570, Burlington, Vt. 05402. [4] At most, decaffeinated coffees had six milligrams caffeine per six-ounce cup.

Teas

Increasingly, Americans are drinking more and more tea, as a look at the supermarket shelf reveals. You'll find there a wide variety of teas beyond the basic-black blends.

The traditional tea—the brew drunk ritually with finger sandwiches or pastry at "afternoon tea," the one drunk anytime by those who eschew coffee—is black tea. It's a lively brew with a hearty flavor, made from the leaves of the evergreen shrub *Camellia sinensis*.

For people who like the flavor of black tea but don't want its caffeine, there are decaffeinated products. And for those who like something a bit more exotic than plain black tea, there are flavored fruity or floral black teas, with and without caffeine.

Also available are dozens of herbal teas—mixes of chamomile, rose hip, peppermint, orange, almond, cinnamon, lemon, apple, and more. Herbal teas, which used to be found only in health-food stores, can be made from any part of just about any plant—stems, leaves, seeds, or roots.

Black Teas

All teas sold in America are blends. The blended black teas that grace the tea table can also be found at the kitchen table in bags. Common domestic brands tend to be blends of black Indian or Ceylon teas. (The "orange pekoe" or "pekoe" on their label indicates the size of the leaf, not the name of the tea.) English brands offer a variety of black-tea blends with names like English Breakfast and Irish Breakfast (which mean nothing in themselves) and Darjeeling (which refers to one variety of black Indian tea used in the blend). Some imports are marketed at double, triple, even quadruple the price of U.S. brands.

Flavor

An excellent black tea is full-bodied, not thin. It does not taste flat but has the character specialists call "brisk" or "lively"—it tingles on the tongue. It should have some pungency and bitterness. Often it may contain floral or malty notes—and sometimes both. (Maltiness in a tea refers to the actual aroma and flavor of malt—which can be described as cooked, sweetish, slightly reminiscent of caramel.) An excellent tea has no off-flavors, such as hints of wood, weeds, hay, or fermented fruit. Unless it's a smoky tea, it does not have a smoky flavor.

Caffeine

Tea contains caffeine. The amount can vary widely, depending on the type of tea leaves used and the strength of the brew. The longer you steep tea, the more caffeine it will have.

Black tea contains an average of 60 milligrams of caffeine per tea bag—about half what you get in a cup of coffe. (And a cup of *weak* tea might provide only one-fourth the caffeine of coffee.) Loose tea contains much less caffeine than a brand-name equivalent in bags.

If you're sensitive to caffeine, you might want to try decaffeinated black tea. But be aware that some decaffeinated tea may contain enough caffeine to bother someone sensitive to the stimulant.

Flavored and Herbal Teas

Early herbal-tea elixirs, made of herbs collected from the woods and fields, were used as medicines. By the time herbal teas came into the health-food store, they had become a soothing drink, a mild and caffeine-free alternative to coffee or black tea.

The popularity of the flavored herbals inspired a new flowering among black teas, too—tea with flavor added: black currant, strawberry, blackberry, and other fruity/nutty tastes. The best herbal or flavored tea is the one that tastes best to you.

Flavored Black Teas These combine the malty character of their black tea leaves with various flavors and aromas including orange, cinnamon, mint, cherry, almond, black currant, blackberry, strawberry, and apple. There's also a specialty tea called Earl Grey, which has a floral quality. Earl Grey is a blend of black teas flavored with oil of bergamot, a citrus-rind oil often used in perfumery. The bergamot lends a floral quality to the tea, which should also have a subtly sweet aroma.

Flavored black teas are mild, light brews. Some develop a more distinct flavor or aroma if allowed to steep an extra minute or two.

Herbal Teas These are mildly flavored and relatively lively, but watery. And, except for the smooth herbal citrus and spice teas, most are somewhat harsh in the mouth.

Anyone switching from regular tea or even coffee would probably prefer the heartiest of the herbals.

Orange seems to be a favorite among all kinds of tea drinkers. But having it in the name doesn't mean it shows up strongly in the flavor.

Light Lunches

Breads

The daily bread of most Americans is still packaged white bread, despite the best advice of mothers, grandmothers, and recently, a fair number of physicians. But, as anyone who has bought fresh bread at a bakery knows, plastic-wrapped supermarket white bread doesn't match the flavor, texture, and aroma of an excellent white bread. By contrast, some packaged and sliced whole-wheat and multigrain breads can be very good.

Most white bread also falls short nutritionally. For instance, the typical packaged white provides only about 40 percent of the fiber of the typical wheat or multigrain.

White bread is low in fiber because it's made from refined wheat flour. The refining process removes the wheat's outer coating, the bran, and the kernel that is the seed for a new plant, the germ. Lost with the bran and the germ is more than 90 percent of the fiber natural to grain.

That loss is keenly felt in the American diet. Although bread is a good source of nutrients other than fiber (see following section), there's generally no shortage in the average American diet of most of the other nutrients bread has to offer. Fiber, however, is found mainly in grains, fruits, and vegetables. So bread is, or should be, a principal fiber source.

Grains provide mostly insoluble fiber. This type of fiber speeds the elimination of waste, preventing constipation and possibly lowering the risk of serious problems such as diverticulitis and colon cancer. Fruits, vegetables, and oats provide soluble fiber. Increasing one's intake of that type of fiber is believed to be beneficial in other ways as well.

Adults should have a daily intake of about 20 grams of fiber, divided about equally between the insoluble fiber found in breads and cereals and the soluble fiber in fruits, vegetables, and oats.

Some bakers of white bread add soy or cellulose fiber to the flour, to replace what milling has removed. That accounts for the high fiber content of some packaged white breads. But it may also account for some off-flavor.

Whole-wheat and multigrain breads are far more successful products than white bread, both in sensory characteristics and in the amount of fiber they contribute.

More on Nutrition

Bread is a good source of the B vitamins—thiamin, niacin, and riboflavin. These nutrients, natural to grain, must by law be returned to their premilling levels, and they vary little from one bread to another.

Bread, especially whole-grain bread, provides more than its calories' share of several other vitamins and minerals, such as folic acid, phosphorus, zinc, magnesium, copper, manganese, and potassium. Some bakers add milk to the dough, which gives you a little extra calcium. In general, though, the nutrients in bread are also available in plenty of other foods.

Bread is very low in fat. It's also quite densely packed with protein for its calories. The protein in grain is of lower quality than protein from meat or dairy products, but those foods also have a fair amount of fat. Many Americans would do well to get more of their daily protein requirement from bread and less from meat.

Breads vary in their sodium content. The National Research Council of the National Academy of Sciences recommends a maximum intake of 3,300 milligrams of sodium per day. Most packaged breads have sodium levels roughly in balance with their calorie content. But some breads, especially ryes, carry too high a sodium load for their contribution to daily caloric needs.

As for oil, the amount used in bread is too small to have a significant impact on total fat in the diet.

The profiles that follow illustrate the average nutrient densities of wheat and white bread (excluding the fiber-enriched products). Ideally, the bars for the positive nutrients—the ones you want to get more of—should be at least as long as the calorie benchmark. The shorter the bars for the negative nutrients—sodium and fat—the better.

Two differences stand out in these profiles. The most dramatic difference between the two profiles is in the fiber bars. Wheat bread offers two and a half times as much fiber per calorie as white bread. Two slices of wheat typically give you about 15 percent of your daily 20-gram need. Another disparity is in protein—it's higher in the wheat bread.

Note that the calcium density for both the wheat and the white bread is low. Bread is not normally a primary source of this mineral.

Average Wheat Bread, Two Slices
(excludes fiber-supplemented brands)

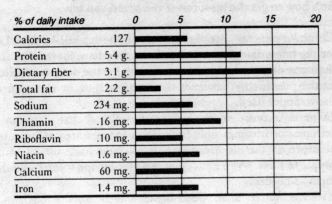

% of daily intake		0	5	10	15	20
Calories	127					
Protein	5.4 g.					
Dietary fiber	3.1 g.					
Total fat	2.2 g.					
Sodium	234 mg.					
Thiamin	.16 mg.					
Riboflavin	.10 mg.					
Niacin	1.6 mg.					
Calcium	60 mg.					
Iron	1.4 mg.					

Average White Bread, Two Slices
(excludes fiber-supplemented brands)

% of daily intake		0	5	10	15	20
Calories	127					
Protein	4.1 g.					
Dietary fiber	1.2 g.					
Total fat	2.4 g.					
Sodium	208 mg.					
Thiamin	.19 mg.					
Riboflavin	.13 mg.					
Niacin	1.6 mg.					
Calcium	58 mg.					
Iron	1.1 mg.					

Profiles are based on an average woman's daily dietary needs. Quotas for an average man are greater for calories, protein, and fat; for children, lower. Data from USDA.

As published in an **October 1988** report.

Recommendations

Here's how to get the most out of the bread you buy.

- *Check the date tag*. Bread comes labeled with a sell-by date. Look for the latest date. Store shelves frequently have loaves with more than one date. You may have to search for the date. Look closely on the plastic clip that holds the wrapper shut, or in a corner of the wrapper itself.
- *Don't store bread in the refrigerator*. Bread that's kept in the refrigerator becomes stale faster than bread stored at room temperature, in the old bread-box. If you won't use up a loaf in a couple of days, wrap individual servings for the freezer and thaw them as needed.
- *Kick the butter habit*. Good bread may be good enough to eat without butter or anything else. It's worth a try.
- *Use bread as a diet food*. Filling up on a few slices of relatively low-calorie bread can keep you from eating fattening things.

Ratings of Breads

Listed by types; within types, listed in order of sensory quality, as depicted by the sensory index.
As published in an **October 1988** report.

Product	Sensory index	Cost per lb.	Calories	Dietary fiber, g.	Sodium, mg.	Sensory comments
White breads						
Earth Grains Sandwich Very Thin	Good	$1.30	51	0.3	101	A,B,C
Arnold Extra Fiber Brick Oven	Good	1.10	64	1.1	101	B,D,U
Home Pride Butter Top	Good	.85	68	0.5	116	C,D,F
Wonder	Good	1.05	63	0.7	124	A,C,F
Pepperidge Farm	Good	1.15	71	0.5	114	B,D,H,I,J,K,L
Mrs. Wright's Super Soft	Good	.65	60	0.5	79	A,F,M
Northridge Premium Old Fashion	Good	1.40	67	0.7	92	B,C,D,I,J,L,N
Arnold Brick Oven Premium	Good	1.10	66	0.4	103	B,D,O,U
Taystee	Fair	.95	64	0.6	104	C,F,M

Sensory index scale: Poor, Fair, Good, Very good, Excellent.
Per slice: Calories, Dietary fiber, Sodium.

121

Ratings of Breads (cont'd)

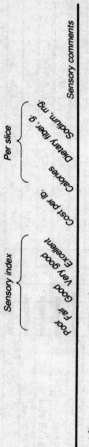

Product	Sensory index	Cost per lb.	Calories	Dietary fiber, g	Sodium, mg	Sensory comments
White breads (cont'd)						
Less Reduced Calories	Fair	$1.05	45	2.4	118	F,P,Q,M
Roman Light	Fair	1.05	43	2.3	66	Q,R,S,T
Wonder Light Reduced Calorie	Poor	1.20	44	2.0	84	A,Q,R,S,T
Whole-wheat breads						
Oroweat Bran'nola Natural w/Bran	Very good	1.00	89	2.5	161	U
Earth Grains Whole Wheat Full Slice	Very good	1.35	73	0.8	160	N,S
Millbrook Buttercrown	Very good	1.05	71	1.0	144	F,V,W
Northridge Premium 100% Whole Wheat	Very good	1.35	53	2.4	94	A,M,S
Arnold Brick Oven 100% Whole Wheat	Very good	1.10	61	1.2	93	U,X
Pepperidge Farm	Good	1.25	61	1.5	95	A,S,CC
Mrs. Wright's 100% Whole Wheat	Good	.80	54	1.5	98	A,F,S,V,W,Y,CC
Home Pride Butter Top	Fair	.80	63	1.1	137	A,F,M,S,V,Y,Z
Taystee	Fair	1.15	53	1.7	86	A,Q,R,S,V,Y,AA
Wonder Soft 100% Whole Wheat	Fair	1.10	57	1.7	101	F,G,Q,S,V,Y,BB,CC

Per slice: Calories, Dietary fiber (g), Sodium (mg)

Sensory index scale: Poor, Fair, Good, Very good, Excellent

Less Reduced Calorie		1.10	46	2.6	113	A,F,G,P,Q,S,V,W,Y,CC
Wonder Light Reduced Calorie		1.20	43	2.0	94	A,F,G,Q,S,V,W,Y,CC

Multigrain breads

Pepperidge Farm Honey Bran		1.10	89	1.2	120	B
Pepperidge Farm Multi-Grain Very Thin		1.30	43	1.1	68	Y
Oroweat Bran'nola Country Oat with Bran		.95	103	1.9	169	EE
Pepperidge Farm Honey Wheat Berry		1.40	63	1.9	105	B,FF
Arnold Honey Wheat Berry		1.05	76	2.0	136	B,FF,GG,HH
Home Pride 7 Grain Butter Top		.65	69	1.3	110	F,EE
Mrs. Wright's Multi-Meal		.60	51	1.4	114	F,EE,II

Rye breads

Pepperidge Farm Seeded		1.00	76	1.7	183	B
Mrs. Wright's with Seeds		1.00	55	0.9	135	F
Taystee NY Soft Rye		1.25	76	0.4	119	B,N
Arnold Jewish Rye with Caraway Seeds		1.20	72	1.0	156	B
Oroweat Soft Rye without Seeds		1.45	66	1.4	104	V
Beefsteak Soft Rye		1.20	72	0.6	150	V,II

Ratings of Breads (cont'd)

Sourdough and Italian breads

Product	Sensory index					Cost per lb.	Calories	Dietary fiber, g.	Sodium, mg.	Sensory comments
	Poor	Fair	Good	Very good	Excellent					
Francisco Extra Sourdough International		■				$.95	88	1.0	160	B
Mrs. Wright's Old Fashioned Italian		■				.60	61	0.6	116	B, F, II, JJ, KK
Taystee D'Italiano	■					1.00	60	0.9	94	B, E, F, FF, II, JJ, LL
Wonder Italian	■					.90	71	0.8	131	A, B, DD, FF, II, LL

Per slice: Calories, Dietary fiber g., Sodium mg.

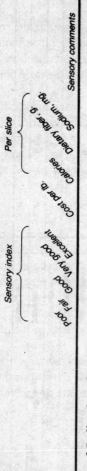

Key to Sensory Comments

A—Slightly sour.
B—Slightly crumbly.
C—Gummy texture.
D—Taste slightly sweet.
E—Very slightly cardboardlike.
F—Airy.
G—Low sweet aroma.
H—Low yeast flavor.
I—Lacks sourness.
J—Slight dairy flavor.
K—Slight eggy flavor.
L—Aroma very sweet.
M—Slightly bitter.
N—Soft crust.
O—Dense.
P—Very slightly musty.
Q—Slightly cardboardlike.
R—Very bitter.
S—Very slightly astringent.
T—Very slight rough mouthfeel.
U—Aroma moderately sweet.
V—Low grain flavor.
W—Soft.
X—Crumbly.
Y—Low sweetness.
Z—Yeasty flavor.
AA—Very slight metallic flavor.
BB—Sour.
CC—Bitter.
DD—Very slightly salty.
EE—Slightly low grain flavor.
FF—Slightly soft crust.
GG—Slightly dense.
HH—Slight grainy residue in mouth.
II—Slightly slippery mouthfeel.
JJ—Slightly low yeast flavor.
KK—Sweet aroma.
LL—Slightly musty.

Peanut Butters

A peanut-butter and jelly sandwich, in many ways, fits the requirements of the school lunchbox perfectly. It won't spoil at room temperature. It's cheap enough to lose or forget on the bus. If the sandwich falls, it doesn't fall apart. And kids like the taste of peanut butter.

Despite a flurry of "adult" brands in recent years and multigenerational interest in things like *Reese's Peanut Butter Cups,* children still eat far more peanut butter than adults do. In fact, peanut-butter sales rise when school convenes in September and fall when summer vacation arrives. Consumption apparently peaks at age seven. The favored type is smooth and creamy, kids being notoriously difficult about contrasting textures.

Adults tend to fall into the crunchy camp. But there are regional variations: West Coast folks favor chunky style, Easterners, creamy.

In addition, peanut-butter fanciers divide on the issue of whether the product should be regular or "natural." Most brands, including the best-selling ones, include partially hydrogenated vegetable oil, to keep the peanut oil from separating, and usually sweeteners and salt. (While hydrogenated oil is a saturated fat, not enough is added to increase the saturated-fat level of those products in a significant way.)

"Old-fashioned" or "natural" peanut butter is made from only ground-up peanuts, sometimes with salt. Since natural peanut butter doesn't have the added hydrogenated oil to act as an emulsifier, you have to stir in its oil when you first open the jar.

The Perfect Peanut Butter

Basically, peanut butter should taste like freshly ground, roasted peanuts. That taste isn't as simple as it sounds. As with coffee, much of the intricacy of the flavor comes from the roasting.

Peanut butter may or may not include skins, which typically contribute little papery bits to the texture and a slight bitterness and some mouth-puckering astringency to the taste. Roasting brings out the natural sweetness of the nut—a quality that can simply taste sweet, like plain table sugar, or have a more complicated sweet flavor ("sweet nuttiness") like caramelized sugar or molasses. In addition, peanuts have a certain natural saltiness. Sweeteners and salt can also be added, of course.

Then there are textural considerations, including coarseness, oiliness, and what taste testers call "adhesiveness," or how much the peanut butter sticks to other objects, such as the roof of your mouth. Creamy products should be creamy, with perhaps a hint of coarseness. Crunchy products are like creamy ones but with little chunks of peanuts.

Any of these flavor or texture qualities can be present in a perfect peanut butter, within certain ranges. But a product should be faulted if it doesn't have enough taste of roasted peanuts, say, or if it is excessively sweet or sticky. A product might also taste too salty or not salty enough.

Bad-tasting peanut butter may be rancid. Rancidity, a sign of aging and deteriorating oils, gives food a cardboard taste when slight, a fishy or painty taste when strong. It's caused by poor storage conditions, either of the peanuts before they were processed or of the peanut butter after manufacture, and is accelerated when the peanuts or the products are exposed to air, heat, or light.

Refrigeration extends the shelf life of peanut butter, especially in the summer. But peanut butter should keep at room temperature for several weeks.

Nutrition

With or without jelly, a sandwich that's been spread with peanut butter is a good lunch for a child or an adult. It provides a nice balance of protein, carbohydrates, and calories. The chart on page 128 shows how peanut butter stacks up against other sandwich standbys. Three tablespoons of peanut butter are used as a serving, not the skimpy two tablespoons most jars list on their labels.

Botanically speaking, the peanut is not a nut but a legume. It's in the same family as the bean and the pea, hence its high protein content. A peanut-butter sandwich provides about one-fourth of the daily protein requirement for an adult, more for a child.

The protein in peanut butter is also a bargain, cheaper than the protein in cheese, bologna, or tuna.

Peanut butter is also a relatively fatty food (unlike other legumes, the peanut itself is nearly half fat), with about 300 calories per three-tablespoon serving. But little of that fat is saturated. The ratio of saturated fat to total fat for peanut butter is only about 20 percent, compared with about 65 percent for American cheese and 40 percent for bologna. There shouldn't be any significant difference in total fat or saturated fat content between brands that contain added hydrogenated oil and the "natural" brands.

The differences are greater in the sugar and salt content. The products that have added sweeteners may contain plain sugar—or dextrose, corn syrup, or molasses.

"Natural" products should be only 5 to 9 percent sugars—the level that naturally occurs in peanuts.

Peanut butter without added salt contains virtually no sodium—15 or fewer milligrams per serving. But even products with added salt have fairly low sodium levels (about 180 to 250 milligrams) compared with foods such as cheese or bologna.

One worrisome aspect of peanut butter (and peanuts) is the possible presence of aflatoxin, a cancer-causing contaminant produced by certain types of mold. But products currently on the market are unlikely to exceed the limit (20 parts per billion) set by the U.S. Food and Drug Administration. The average level, in fact, is probably a great deal lower than that.

Nutrition of Peanut-Butter and Other Sandwiches

● Meets 100% or more of RDA ◕ Meets 25% of RDA ○ Meets less than 5% of RDA

	Peanut butter, 3 tbsp.[1]	American cheese, 2 oz. (with mayo)[2]	Bologna 2 oz. (with mayo)	Chunk light tuna, 2 oz. (with mayo)
Protein	◔	◔	◔	◔
Vitamin A	○	◔	○	○
Thiamin	◔	◔	◔	◔
Riboflavin	◔	◔	◔	◔
Niacin	◔	◔	◔	◔
Vitamin B$_6$	◔	○	◔	◔
Vitamin B$_{12}$	○	◔	◔	◔
Vitamin C	○	○	◔	○
Calcium	◔	◔	◔	◔
Iron	◔	◔	◔	◔
Zinc	◔	◔	◔	◔
Calories	410	413	405	290
Fat (g.)	26	27	29	13
Carbohydrates (g.)	33	28	25	24
Sodium (mg.)[3]	476	998	892	553
Cost (cents)	25	39	39	40

Pie charts based on U.S. Recommended Daily Allowances, which should meet daily dietary needs of adults and children over age four. Sandwiches are on white bread; one tablespoon of mayonnaise was used.

[1] One tablespoon of grape jelly adds about 55 calories.
[2] Values for American cheese food.
[3] For products with added salt.

As published in an **August 1987** report.

Ratings of Peanut Butter

Listed in order of sensory quality, as depicted by the sensory index. Products lose index points for lacking roasted-nut flavor and the appropriate sweetness and saltiness, as well as for defects like rancidity. Unless noted, sodium is calculated from label statement.

As published in an **August 1987** report.

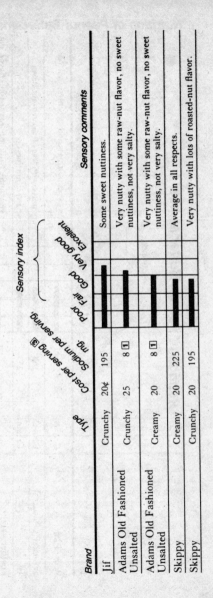

Brand	Type	Cost per serving ¢	Sodium per serving mg	Sensory index (Poor / Fair / Good / Very good / Excellent)	Sensory comments
Jif	Crunchy	20¢	195	Very good	Some sweet nuttiness.
Adams Old Fashioned Unsalted	Crunchy	25	8 ①	Good	Very nutty with some raw-nut flavor, no sweet nuttiness, not very salty.
Adams Old Fashioned Unsalted	Creamy	20	8 ①	Good	Very nutty with some raw-nut flavor, no sweet nuttiness, not very salty.
Skippy	Creamy	20	225	Good	Average in all respects.
Skippy	Crunchy	20	195	Good	Very nutty with lots of roasted-nut flavor.

129

Ratings of Peanut Butter (cont'd)

Brand	Type	Cost per serving	Sodium per serving mg. [S]	Sensory index					Sensory comments
				Poor	Fair	Good	Very good	Excellent	
Peter Pan	Crunchy	15¢	225		▮				Some sweet nuttiness and sweetness, not very sticky.
Smucker's Natural	Crunchy	20	188		▮				Very nutty with lots of roasted-nut flavor.
Jif	Creamy	15	233		▮				Some sweet nuttiness.
Featherweight Low Sodium	Creamy	50	8 [1]		▮				Not very nutty with little roasted-nut flavor, not very salty.
Peter Pan	Creamy	15	225		▮				Not very nutty but some sweet nuttiness and sweetness.
Dia-Mel Low Sodium	Creamy	35	8		▮				Not very nutty with little roasted-nut flavor, some sweet nuttiness and sweetness, not very salty.
Laura Scudder's Old Fashioned	Crunchy	25	80		▮				Very nutty with lots of roasted-nut flavor, no sweet nuttiness.
Health Valley 100% Natural Unsalted	Creamy	35	3		▮				Some raw-nut flavor and skins, not very salty.
Real Roast	Creamy	15	240		▮				Not very nutty but some sweet nuttiness.

130

Brand	Type			Comments
A&P	Crunchy	15	178 [2]	Average in all respects.
Country Pure Old Fashioned (Safeway)	Creamy	15	225	No sweet nuttiness, somewhat gritty.
Polaner Natural No Salt	Creamy	20	8	Very nutty with some raw-nut flavor and skins, no sweet nuttiness, not very salty, very coarse texture.
Lady Lee (Lucky)	Crunchy	15	210	Somewhat rancid.
Smucker's Natural	Creamy	20	188	Very nutty with lots of roasted-nut flavor, no sweet nuttiness, very coarse and somewhat gritty, very sticky.
Lady Lee (Lucky)	Creamy	15	210	Somewhat gritty.
Health Valley 100% Natural Unsalted	Crunchy	35	3	Some raw-nut flavor and skins, not very salty.
Laura Scudder's Old Fashioned Unsalted	Creamy	20	8 [1]	Some raw-nut flavor and skins, no sweet nuttiness, not very salty.
Kroger	Crunchy	15	255	Some sweet nuttiness, not very sticky, somewhat rancid.
National	Creamy	15	225	Somewhat gritty.
Country Pure Old Fashioned (Safeway)	Crunchy	15	195	Very nutty with lots of roasted-nut flavor.
Deaf Smith Arrowhead Mills No Salt Added	Creamy	25	3	Some raw-nut flavor and skins, no sweet nuttiness, not very salty, very sticky.
Pathmark	Crunchy	10	191 [2]	Somewhat rancid.

Ratings of Peanut Butter (cont'd)

Brand	Type	Cost per serving	Sodium per serving, mg.	Sensory index	Sensory comments
Pathmark	Creamy	10¢	225 [2]	Poor–Fair	Not very nutty but some sweet nuttiness, somewhat rancid.
Food Club	Creamy	15	210	Poor–Fair	Not very nutty but some sweet nuttiness, not very sticky, somewhat rancid.
Deaf Smith Arrowhead Mills No Salt Added	Crunchy	30	3	Poor–Fair	Some raw-nut flavor and skins but little roasted-nut flavor, not very salty.
Superman	Creamy	20	225	Poor–Fair	Somewhat rancid.
Nu Made (Safeway)	Crunchy	15	195	Poor–Fair	Somewhat rancid.
Real Roast	Crunchy	15	255	Poor–Fair	Somewhat rancid.
Nu Made (Safeway)	Creamy	15	225	Poor	Not very nutty, somewhat rancid.
A&P	Creamy	25	225	Poor	Not very nutty, somewhat rancid.
Cost Cutter (Kroger)	Crunchy	10	205 [2]	Poor	Not very nutty, but some sweet nuttiness, somewhat rancid.
Albertsons	Crunchy	15	180	Poor	Not very nutty; rancid.
Food Club	Crunchy	15	180	Poor	Not very nutty; rancid.

Sensory index: Poor, Fair, Good, Very good, Excellent

Brand	Type				Flavor
Albertsons	Creamy	15		225	Not very nutty; bitter, rancid.
Hazel Old Fashioned	Crunchy	20		203 [2]	Somewhat rancid, very salty.
Superman	Crunchy	15		195	Not very nutty; rancid.
Skaggs Alpha Beta	Creamy	15		210	Not very nutty, somewhat rancid.
Holsum Old Fashioned	Creamy	15		248	Somewhat rancid; bitter.
Kroger	Creamy	15		240	Not very nutty with little roasted-nut flavor, some sweet nuttiness, not very sticky; rancid.
Shurfine	Creamy	10		240 [2]	Not very nutty with little roasted-nut flavor but some sweet nuttiness, rancid, bitter.
Shurfine	Crunchy	15		189 [2]	Not very nutty; rancid, bitter.
P & Q (A&P)	Creamy	10		225	Not very nutty with little roasted-nut flavor, not very sticky; rancid.
Cost Cutter (Kroger)	Creamy	15		194 [2]	Not very nutty; rancid, bitter.
P & Q (A&P)	Crunchy	10		195	Not very nutty with little roasted-nut flavor, not very sticky; rancid, bitter.

[1] Maximum; label gives sodium as less than five milligrams per two-tablespoon serving.
[2] CU measurement.
[3] Three-tablespoon serving.

Canned Tuna

Tuna ranks as the number-one seafood in the United States. It's even a favorite among children. Kids who turn up their noses at fresh flounder and trout will usually eat tuna sandwiches without complaint. Perhaps that's because tuna isn't a very "fishy" fish. It has a relatively mild taste. And it comes in cans, free of fins and scales to remind us of its fishy past.

Flavor

Since all tuna canners fish the same oceans, why don't all canned tunas taste the same? One reason: There's more than one kind of tuna (see pages 136–37). Other differences have to do with how the fish is processed and what kind of packing medium is used.

An excellent tuna should have a not-too-overpowering fishy flavor, moderate saltiness, and a firm but flaky texture. The meat should be moist, and it shouldn't dry out as you chew.

Most water-packed brands don't measure up. This type can suffer from a pronounced dry or mealy texture, a tinny taste, excessive saltiness, sourness, or a scorched flavor.

Low-salt tuna, too, may not measure up to your expectations.

Nutrition

Canned tuna is high in a number of important vitamins and minerals. Like most fish, it's also a good source of protein, and it's relatively low in calories, fat, and cholesterol.

Most brands of tuna have nutritional labeling. But the labels don't always mention serving size; instead, they may say that the six-and-a-half- or seven-ounce cans contain a "portion." Others define a serving as only two ounces—*before* draining.

This lack of precision comes about for a reason. There is no standard serving size for tuna. The U.S. Department of Agriculture considers three ounces of drained tuna to be a typical serving. But most cans don't yield two three-ounce servings of tuna solids.

Protein Consumers Union's analyses showed that half a can of tuna has an average protein content of about 24 grams—a bit more than in a cooked, three-ounce hamburger.

Calories As dieters know, water-packed tuna has fewer calories than oil-packed. Water-packed brands average about 105 calories per half-can serving. What many dieters don't know is that, although undrained oil-packed tuna has about 240 calories per serving, *drained* oil-packed tuna weighs in at about 180 calories. If you prefer the taste of oil-packed tuna, you may think it's worth the additional 75 calories.

Fat Water-packed tuna averages 1.5 grams of fat per half-can serving. The average fat content of undrained, oil-packed tuna is about 16 grams—about 10 grams when the oil is drained off.

Cholesterol Drained or undrained, a can of tuna contains about 50 milligrams of cholesterol.

Sodium Excluding low-salt brands, tuna's sodium content is relatively high—averaging 400 milligrams per half-can serving. (Draining an oil-packed brand should reduce its sodium content by about 15 percent.)

Low-salt brands average about 55 milligrams per half-can serving.

If you're concerned about sodium, you can enjoy the benefits of low-sodium tuna without paying the premium price the low-salt brands command by simply rinsing regular tuna with tap water. A study in the *Journal of the American Dietetic Association* found that rinsing tuna under running water for three minutes reduced the sodium level in water-packed chunk light tuna by about 80 percent. Rinsing won't alter the iron content, although it will result in some loss of vitamins, especially the water-soluble B vitamins. And it will cut the calcium level in half, but since tuna is a relatively poor source of calcium in most diets, the loss is of no great concern.

HVP

Most tuna contains hydrolyzed vegetable protein (HVP), a flavor enhancer. It is on the list of additives generally recognized as safe by the FDA. But some people have an allergic reaction to it.

Recommendations

Depending on what you're making, the best tuna may be the cheapest. If you plan to mix the tuna with mayonnaise and onion in a salad or with other ingredients in a casserole, any canned tuna should do.

If you like your tuna straight, you will probably be able to detect subtle differences between types and brands. You may prefer the moister oil-packed tunas.

You may prefer the milder taste of albacore to the stronger taste of light-meat tuna. If you do, you'll usually have to pay extra for it.

Low-salt brands tend to be highest priced. If you're watching your sodium intake, you can save money by buying regular tuna and rinsing it under running water. Rinsing the tuna may diminish the taste somewhat, but that shouldn't matter much unless you eat the tuna straight.

Next to the stacks of six-and-a-half- and seven-ounce cans of tuna on your grocer's shelves, you're likely to find some 12½- and 13-ounce cans. You may think that big cans mean big savings, but that's not always true.

You can usually save money by buying a store brand instead of a national brand. However, if you do like your tuna straight, and you prefer oil-packed tuna, stick to the national brands. They are apt to be better than oil-packed store brands.

Tuna Types

There's more than one kind of tuna in the sea. And there's more than one kind on supermarket shelves.

White or Light? According to the U.S. Food and Drug Administration, a number of different fish can be called tuna. But only one, albacore, can be labeled "white meat" tuna.

White tuna has a light flesh and a characteristically mild flavor. Other tunas, such as yellowfin, bluefin, and skipjack, are darker, a bit more robust in flavor, and are labeled "light meat" tuna.

The delicate taste of white tuna isn't necessarily better than light tuna; it's a matter of preference, like the preference for light chicken meat over dark.

White and light tuna can be used interchangeably in many recipes. White meat costs more, so when a recipe calls for mayonnaise and other ingredients that will mask the delicate taste of the albacore, you might as well buy the inexpensive light tuna.

Solid or Chunk? Generally, white tuna comes in solid style and, less often, in chunk style. Light tuna comes most often in chunk, occasionally in solid style or—less expensively—in grated or flaked styles.

Solid white tuna may be labeled "fancy" or "selected." While those superlatives might seem to describe grades of tuna, there are no quality standards for canned tuna. The fancy words simply tell you that the tuna is solid rather than chunk.

Oil or Water? Water-packed tuna is flooding the market, presumably because everyone is worried about the extra calories in oil-packed tuna. Despite the popularity of water-packed brands, survey respondents usually prefer the taste of oil-packed tuna.

Soups

Soup is a comfort for many small ills, and maybe even for some larger ones. Soup is also a lifesaver for harried cooks: A soup course can add class to an otherwise ordinary dinner. It's a "light" food for the dieter, providing an interesting variety of flavors and texture without caloric overload.

Commercially prepared soup—canned, dehydrated, or frozen—is

usually quick and easy to fix, a convenience food. And the selection is vast, ranging from the familiar chicken noodle to exotic cream of asparagus, lobster bisque, and such.

Soup is also cheap. Or it can be. Some store brands cost just pennies a bowl. But you can also spend about a dollar-and-a-half a bowl.

While *Campbell's* red-and-white cans of old standards like tomato, vegetable beef, and chicken noodle still dominate supermarket shelves and sales, "gourmet" and "homestyle" versions are crowding in. In the *Campbell's* section of the shelves, the red-and-whites compete with the gold "creamy naturals," and with other lines that try to substitute for old-time homemade soups.

Lipton offers its line of dehydrated mixes that require cooking, as well as instant *Cup-a-Soup*. It offers "hearty" dried soups that are supposed to smack of home cooking, and a number of newer soups as well.

Leftover shelf space usually goes to store labels and to names such as *Crosse & Blackwell, Bookbinder's,* and *Dominique's.* The offerings of specialty-food manufacturers may turn up in other sections of the supermarket: *Knorr* mixes with gourmet foods, *Manischewitz* mixes with kosher foods, and *Progresso* canned soups with Italian foods. Salt-free soups are in the diet section, and varieties such as *Health Valley* are in the nearby health-food aisle. Soups have also penetrated the freezer section.

The good news is that, as a taste sensation, many commercial soups are very good. The bad news is that commercial soup is not such good food by itself.

Nutrition

If you rely on soup alone for lunch day in and day out, you're making significant nutritional compromises. Soup alone doesn't have what it takes to contribute a lunch's fair share to your recommended daily nutritional requirements.

As a rule of thumb, if you eat three meals a day, each meal should provide roughly one-third of the recommended daily allowance (U.S. RDA) for most nutrients. It's impractical, usually unnecessary, and probably boring to try to adhere strictly to that rule. Protein missing from one meal, for example, will probably be made up in another. A glass of orange juice at breakfast may provide all the vitamin C needed for a day. And some nutrients, like calcium, needn't be eaten every day because the body can draw temporarily on its own reserves.

But even allowing for a certain amount of dietary flexibility, commercial soups generally fall short. With most products, the data used for nutritional evaluation are right on the can or package.

Some soups—particularly the ready-to-serve or frozen products—provide 15 percent or more of the U.S. RDA for some nutrients.

Ready-to-serve chicken-noodle soups provide from 15 to 22 percent of the U.S. RDA for protein, and 15 percent of the U.S. RDA for niacin, presumably because of the chicken.

Quite a few soups offer more than 15 percent of the U.S. RDA for vitamin A. Yellow fruits and vegetables, such as tomatoes and carrots, are good sources of that vitamin. *Campbell's Chunky* vegetable is loaded with vegetables and has 127 percent of the U.S. RDA; *Campbell's Chunky* vegetable beef has 89 percent.

The calcium in most soups is negligible. But many New England chowders have between 10 and 18 percent of the U.S. RDA, either from the milk already in them (the frozen variety) or from the milk you add to them (the canned). Milk also contributes to a slightly higher protein level in those products. Label instructions on most condensed canned tomato soups call for adding "water (or milk)." Milk improves the calcium and protein content of tomato soup. Milk, however, also raises calorie content. Aside from specialty soups, the New England clam chowders as a group have the most calories, ranging all the way from 110 to 280. Calories are lowest in condensed soups and mixes, which are mostly water—ranging from about 70 to 120 calories per serving. In chunky or homestyle soups, calories range from about 100 to 150 per serving.

Like many highly processed foods, soups supply a hefty dose of sodium—from about 700 to more than 1,000 milligrams per serving. Low-sodium soups have only 20 to 60 milligrams, but the saving in sodium exacts a toll in sensory quality.

"Hearty" or "homestyle" soup generally has more solids—noodles, vegetables, meats—than regular soup. Most regular soup contains 1.6 to 2.4 ounces of solids per eight-ounce serving, whereas the chunky or homestyle varieties usually have at least three ounces. The amount of the expensive protein ingredient—the beef pieces in vegetable-beef soup, the chicken pieces in chicken noodle, the clams in chowder—is less than an ounce per serving, whether the soup is regular or chunky.

Flavor

Almost all soups have a touch of MSG flavor, common in highly processed foods. Another sign of processing that soupmakers seem unable to avoid is a yeasty taste, as well as the taste of hydrolyzed vegetable protein (HVP). Some people have allergic reactions to MSG and/or HVP.

Here are soup differences sorted out by type:

Chicken Noodle   An excellent chicken-noodle soup should taste of chicken and noodles, with perhaps a hint of celery, parsley, garlic, and onion. It should be slightly sweet, slightly salty.

The noodles and vegetables tend to be a bit too soft. These soups also leave a slightly starchy feel in the mouth. Poorer brands lack chicken flavor or, worse, taste of dehydrated chicken.

Clam Chowder   The ideal New England chowder tastes of clams, potatoes, and cream. It is relatively thick. Manufacturers use flour as a thickener, and a slight floury taste is acceptable.

Even the best chowders taste a bit too floury, and leave a starchy feeling in the mouth. A poor chowder may be too thick or too thin or have clams that are too chewy.

Manhattan chowders tend to be very good. They all have a pleasing balance of clam and tomato flavors. But all can use more herbs and spices, and all leave some starchy feeling in the mouth.

Tomato The dominant flavor in this cold-weather favorite should be tomato, of course, accented with spices. The soup should be slightly sweet, slightly salty, and moderately thick. Some brands have little tomato flavor.

Vegetable Beef The ideal vegetable-beef soup has the good flavors of vegetable, beef, and tomato. A touch of herbs and spice, plus some saltiness and sweetness, brings the primary flavors to life. The vegetables and beef are firm but not chewy.

Vegetable The perfect vegetable soup is much the same as the perfect vegetable-beef, but without the beef flavor.

Minestrone Minestrone is much like vegetable beef, too, but with the addition of beans and pasta, which affect both flavor and texture.

Low-Sodium Soup Low-sodium soup doesn't taste very good if you are accustomed to cooking with salt. But there's more to the story than just salt. The ingredients should have the correct character: tomato soup should have tomato flavor; soup with beef in it should taste of beef. People familiar with low-salt cooking know that herbs and spices can often compensate for the absence of salt, but some soup makers don't seem to heed this well-known culinary principle.

Recommendations

Although soup isn't totally "good food," it can be *tasty*. To make it better, augment it with other foods. Add a tuna sandwich and a glass of lowfat or skim milk, and you have a nutritious lunch that's fairly low in calories.

If you're concerned about sodium and like soup, you'd better make your own. Regular commercial soup is clearly too high in sodium for those on sodium-restricted diets. And low-sodium soup won't please most palates.

Ratings of Soups

Listed by types; within types, listed in order of sensory quality. Closely ranked products differ little in quality. Percent solids, sodium, and nutrition comments are for eight-ounce serving.

As published in a **March 1987** report.

● Excellent ◓ Very good ○ Good ◑ Fair ● Poor

Product	Type [1]	Cost, 8-oz. serving	Sensory Rating	Percent solids	Calories, 8-oz. serving	Sodium, 8-oz. serving, mg.	Sensory comments	Nutrition comments
Chicken noodle								
Town House Chunky (Safeway)	CR	50¢	◑	55	140	1,030	A,X,Z,aa	A,F
Kroger Chunky	CR	52	◑	55	135	1,040	A,X,Z,aa	A,B,F
Campbell's Home Cookin'	CR	65	◑	41	105	860	A,D,L,Z,aa	A,B,F
Campbell's Chunky (w/ mushrooms)	CR	55	◑	71	150	890	A,L,X,Z,aa	A,B,F
Progresso	CR	55	○	51	100	820	—	A,B,F
Myers	F	80	○	37	70	860	—	—
Campbell's	C	15	○	28	70	920	—	—
Campbell's (w/ white meat)	M	20	○	53	100	750	M	—
Thrifty Maid	C	15	○	30	70	730	C,E	—
Kroger	C	10	○	34	70	890	C	—
Lipton (w/white meat)	M	15	○	48	70	820	—	—

Product	Type [1]	Cost, 8-oz. serving	Sensory Rating	Percent solids	Calories, 8-oz. serving	Sodium, 8-oz. serving, mg.	Sensory comments	Nutrition comments
Chicken noodle (cont'd)								
Pathmark	C	15¢	○	27	70	890	C, E	—
Lady Lee (Lucky)	C	15	○	25	70	890	C, E	—
Albertsons	C	15	○	25	70	890	C, E	—
Alpha Beta	C	15	○	21	70	890	C, E	—
Town House (Safeway)	C	15	○	27	70	890	C, E	—
Cost Cutter (Kroger)	C	10	○	26	60	880	C, E	—
Knorr	M	25	○	24	60	880	—	—
Lipton Hearty (white meat)	M	25	◖	34	90	690	—	—
Lipton Cup-a-Soup (white meat)	MI	35	◖	13	65	920	C, M	—
Campbell's Noodle	M	15	◖	67	110	730	B, M	D, F
Lipton Cup-a-Soup Hearty Chicken	MI	45	◖	22	95	920	C, M	—
Mrs. Grass	M	10	◖	29	65	840	B	—
Lipton Noodle	M	10	◖	29	70	780	B, M	—
Campbell's Low Sodium	CR	55	◖	46	120	60	R, T, V, X, Z, aa	A, B, E, F
Manischewitz	C	35	◖	20	40	580	B	—
Featherweight (no salt added)	C	45	◖	26	65	50	B, E, R, T, V	—
New England clam chowder								
Hilton's	C	40 [2]	◖	19	135	900	A	—
Crosse & Blackwell	CR	$1.25	◖	34	110	760	—	—

Ratings of Soups (cont'd)

Product	Type [1]	Cost, 8-oz. serving	Sensory Rating	Percent solids	Calories, 8-oz. serving	Sodium, 8-oz. serving, mg.	Sensory comments	Nutrition comments
New England clam chowder (cont'd)								
Campbell's	C	35¢ [2]	◕	21	150	940	Y	G
Snow's	C	65 [2]	◕	19	150	720	A	A,G
C.H.B. Mariners Cove	C	30 [2]	◕	14	120	560	—	G
Doxsee	C	35 [2]	◕	12	160	1,000	Y	A
Campbell's Chunky	CR	50	○	41	215	880	A,J,N,X,aa	—
Dominique's	C	60 [2]	○	18	140	710	Y	G
Lipton International	M	$1.00	○	20	170	870	J,O	B,G
Kroger	C	30¢ [2]	○	21	140	980	—	A,G
Campbell's Soup du Jour	F	$1.65	○	38	280	1,150	A,N,O,X,aa	A,H
Myers	F	85¢	◑	30	130	740	J,N,O,X,aa	H
Tuscan Farms RSVP	F	$1.05	◑	29	145	900	J,N,O,X,aa	A
Manhattan clam chowder								
Progresso	CR	50¢	◑	37	110	1,040	X,bb	B
Crosse & Blackwell	CR	$1.30	◑	27	75	1,210	F,U,ii	C,F,H
Campbell's	C	25¢	◑	24	70	860	B,F	B
Bookbinder's	C	60	◑	18	85	970	X,ii	H
Tomato								
Andersen's	CR	45	◑	0	140	1,010	O,P,S	B
Health Valley	CR	70	○	0	120	740	O,P,X,dd	B,C

Product	Type [1]	Cost, 8-oz. serving	Sensory Rating	Percent solids	Calories, 8-oz. serving	Sodium, 8-oz. serving, mg.	Sensory comments	Nutrition comments
Tomato (cont'd)								
Lady Lee (Lucky)	C	15¢	◐	0	80	920	—	—
Kroger	C	5	◐	0	80	870	—	—
Campbell's	C	10	◐	0	90	750	—	C
Town House (Safeway)	C	15	◐	0	80	870	—	—
Hain Naturals	CR	80	◐	0	125	850	O,P,R,X, dd	—
Lipton Cup-a-Soup	MI	35	◐	0	105	870	G,O,P	—
Alpha Beta	C	10	◐	0	80	870	G	—
Cost Cutter (Kroger)	C	10	◐	0	50	870	G	—
Campbell's Low Sodium	CR	35	◑	5	135	30	R,T,V,W, cc	B,C
Featherweight (no salt added)	C	45	◑	0	65	30	G,R,T,V, W	B,H
Vegetable beef								
Campbell's Chunky	CR	65	●	62	135	900	D,H,X,aa	A,B
Campbell's Manhandler	C	25	●	29	70	820	ff	B
Town House (Safeway)	C	20	●	22	70	890	U	B
Thrifty Maid	C	20	●	25	50	750	—	—
Kroger	C	20	●	25	70	890	—	B
Featherweight (no salt added)	C	45	●	34	85	20	B,H,T,V, ii	—

Ratings of Soups (cont'd)

Product	Type [1]	Cost, 8-oz. serving	Sensory Rating	Percent solids	Calories, 8-oz. serving	Sodium, 8-oz. serving, mg.	Sensory comments	Nutrition comments
Vegetable								
Campbell's Chunky	CR	40¢	◖	54	105	820	H,Q,X,ii	B
Mrs. Grass Homestyle	M	20	○	18	35	380	—	—
Lipton Country Vegetable	M	20	○	28	80	800	A,E	B
Minestrone								
Knorr Hearty	M	30	◖	25	100	890	O,P	C
Progresso	CR	45	◖	50	120	690	H,K	B
Campbell's Vegetable (w/beef stock)	C	15	◖	28	80	770	F,I,ff	B
Manischewitz	M	10	○	26	65	210	—	E
Hain Naturals	CR	80	○	42	160	880	D,H,K,X, gg	B
Crosse & Blackwell	CR	$1.10	○	40	130	840	A,F,K,X, hh	H
Lipton Hearty	M	25¢	◖	28	100	870	I,O,P,ee	B

[1] C—Canned, condensed; CR—Canned, ready to serve; M—Mix, requires cooking;   MI—Mix, instant; F—Frozen.
[2] Prepared with milk.

Key to Sensory Comments

A—Stronger chicken, beef, or clam flavor.
B—Weaker chicken, beef, or clam flavor.

C—Dehydrated-chicken flavor.
D—Stronger vegetable flavor.

E—Weaker vegetable flavor.
F—Stronger tomato flavor.
G—Weaker tomato flavor.
H—Stronger bean flavor.
 I—Weaker bean flavor.
 J—Stronger potato flavor.
K—Weaker pasta flavor.
L—Stronger celery flavor.
M—Stronger parsley flavor.
N—Stronger floury/starchy flavor.
O—Stronger herb/spice flavor.
P—Stronger onion/garlic flavor.
Q—Weaker onion/garlic flavor.
R—No sweetness.
 S—Sweeter than most.
T—No saltiness.
U—Saltier than most.
V—Slightly bitter.
W—Sourer than most.
X—Thicker than most.
Y—Thinner than most.
 Z—Firmer meat.
aa—Chewier meat.

bb—Chewier vegetables.
 cc—Pulpy.
dd—Tomato bits.
ee—No whole beans.
 ff—Beans not chewy enough.
gg—No pasta.
hh—Pasta not firm and chewy enough.
 ii—Weaker herb/spice flavor.

Key to Nutrition Comments

A—Had at least 15% of US RDA for protein.
B—Had at least 15% of US RDA for vitamin A.
C—Had at least 15% of US RDA for vitamin C.
D—Had at least 15% of US RDA for thiamine.
E—Had at least 15% of US RDA for riboflavin.
F—Had at least 15% of US RDA for niacin.
G—Had at least 15% of US RDA for calcium.
H—Had at least 15% of US RDA for iron.

Some Specialty Soups

For those who associate chicken-noodle soup with head colds and tomato soup with grammar-school lunches, there are a number of soups marketed to more sophisticated tastes. As with other commercial soups, sodium is high, and most nutrients are in short supply. Below is a rundown, soup by soup; nutritional information is for an eight-ounce serving.

Dominique's U.S. Senate Bean Canned, ready-to-serve. 15-ounce can. 175 calories, 870 milligrams sodium.

This well-blended broth has a rich texture, but the beans are bland. Judged very good. The soup provides a bit more of the U.S. RDA for protein and iron than the average soup.

Campbell's Bean with Bacon   Canned, condensed. 11.5-ounce can. 150 calories, 860 milligrams sodium.

This soup is bland in taste and texture. Judged fair.

Campbell's Chunky Bean'n Ham   Canned, ready-to-serve. 11-ounce can. 210 calories, 840 milligrams sodium.

Not much flavor. And the soup is thick and starchy. Judged fair. Provides 65 percent of the U.S. RDA for vitamin A, and 18 percent of the RDA for protein.

Progresso Lentil   Canned, ready-to-serve. 10.5-ounce can, 135 calories, 850 milligrams sodium.

Mealy texture. Lentils and celery too soft; vegetables fibrous, and color unappealing. Judged fair. Has a bit more iron than the average soup.

Lipton International Lobster Bisque   Mix. 1.4-ounce package. 140 calories, 880 milligrams sodium.

Nice fish flavor, with well-blended spices. Rubbery lobster, though. Judged very good.

Rieber's Lobster Bisque   Mix. 2.2-ounce package. 95 calories, 1,040 milligrams sodium.

Neither lobster in flavor nor bisque in texture. Judged fair. Provides 25 percent of the U.S. RDA for vitamin C, however.

Myers Cream of Mushroom   Frozen. 14.5-ounce box. 145 calories, 860 milligrams sodium.

Slightly starchy flavor and texture. Judged very good.

Campbell's Cream of Mushroom   Canned, condensed. 10.75-ounce can. 100 calories, 820 milligrams sodium.

Not much mushroom flavor. Very starchy. Judged fair.

Lipton International California Cream of Broccoli   Mix. 1.4-ounce package. 140 calories, 810 milligrams sodium.

Well-balanced seasonings, buttery aroma. Creamy in texture, but slightly starchy. Judged very good. Provides 27 percent of the U.S. RDA for vitamin C.

Campbell's Creamy Broccoli   Canned, condensed. 10.75-ounce can. 140 calories, 860 milligrams sodium.

Little broccoli flavor. Lumpy and starchy, with overcooked broccoli. Judged fair.

Nissin Oodles of Noodles Chicken   Mix, 3-ounce package. 200 calories, 960 milligrams sodium.

Low chicken flavor, but good blend of seasonings. Lots of noodles. Judged very good.

Lipton Cup-a-Soup Lots-a-Noodles   Instant mix. 2.1-ounce package. 135 calories, 930 milligrams sodium.

Weak flavor and practically no chicken character. Noodles too soft and bland tasting. Judged fair. Provides 23 percent of the U.S. RDA for vitamin A.

Nissin Cup O'Noodles Chicken   Instant mix. 2.25-ounce package. 170 calories, 1,020 milligrams sodium.

Watery broth with weak chicken flavor and tough chicken pieces. Judged fair.

Tuscan Farms RSVP Tomato Florentine   Frozen. 14-ounce package. 60 calories, 650 milligrams sodium.

Slightly too acidic. Broth somewhat slimy and too few pasta shells. Judged good. Has 62 percent of the U.S. RDA for vitamin A.

Cottage Cheese

Curds and whey are the basic ingredients of cottage cheese. Whey is the watery part of milk that is discarded in the cheese-making process; the part that coagulates is the curd, which is the basis of *all* cheeses.

Commercial cottage cheese may still start out, as it did originally, as skim milk, but concentrated skim milk or nonfat dry milk can be used instead.

The simplest version is "dry curd" cheese. A dry-curd product contains less than ½ percent milkfat.

Anything but a dry-curd product will have had its milkfat raised by a creaming mixture. Lowfat cottage cheese may contain anything up to 2 percent milkfat. Conventional cottage cheeses (often called "creamed") contain at least 4 percent milkfat.

The creaming mixture can be (but needn't be) some sort of milk or milk product—whole, skimmed, partly skimmed, cream, or any combination of them. On the label, any milk used can be identified merely as "milk" or "skim milk." Any other ingredients (salt, thickeners, and the like) must be declared on the label.

The milk must be coagulated with rennet or another coagulating substance from a federally approved list. The cheese's ingredient list will note "enzymes" if a milk-clotting enzyme was used, or will say something like "cultured milk" if a bacterial culture was used. If acid was used to set the milk, the words to look for are "directly set" or "curd set by direct acidification." The choice of setting agent doesn't seem to affect the cheese's flavor.

Beyond those differences, cottage cheeses differ in the size of their curds. The popular "small-curd" variety contains lumps about the size of a corn kernel. There's also "large-curd" cottage cheese, with lumps about twice that size, and "chunky" cottage cheese, whose curds are larger yet. You may even find "whipped" cottage cheese in the dairy case, with virtually no lumps.

Nutrition

Dieters and the budget-conscious have long known that cottage cheese is a reasonable protein substitute for meat. The cheese's protein quality is excellent, as good as that in fish and beef. And the protein in a four-ounce serving, generally about 14 grams, provides about one-quarter of an adult's recommended daily intake (44 to 56 grams).

Furthermore, the cheese delivers its protein without meat's freight of calories. Creamed cottage cheese averages 108 calories per four-ounce serving—about half the calories in a cooked hamburger patty, some two-thirds the calories in a typical serving of tuna. Lowfat cottage cheese is only slightly lower in calories than the creamed type—ranging from about 75 to 85 calories per serving in 1-percent-fat brands, to about 85 to 110 calories in 2-percent-fat products.

You also get more calcium with cottage cheese than you do with most fish or meat. On average, cottage cheese provides 74 milligrams of calcium in a four-ounce serving.

In other respects, fish and meat provide more nutrition than cottage cheese. A typical serving of tuna or cooked hamburger supplies more of certain important nutrients, as the chart on page 152 shows. One should, of course, eat some bread or crackers and fruit or a vegetable with cottage cheese to make a better-balanced meal.

Cottage cheeses' sodium content varies widely from brand to brand. If you're on a sodium-restricted diet, check the container for information about sodium content.

Flavor

Like the milk from which it's extracted, cottage cheese is a distinctly bland dish. Ideally, the cheese should have a slightly acidic taste, as well as a hint of the fresh dairy flavors of butter, cream, and milk. The curds should be smooth, moist, and moderately chewy in texture, with enough integrity to hold their shape. Although no cheese should be rubbery or flat-out dry, a certain lack of moisture is acceptable in a dry-curd product.

Cottage cheese containers usually have an expiration date on them. But even "fresh" cheese may be moldy when you get it home, probably because it was not stored properly in the supermarket. If the cottage cheese you buy turns out to be moldy, take it back for a refund. If that happens more than a few times, ask the supermarket to change its storage practices.

Nutrition Comparison of Cottage Cheese with Tuna and Hamburger

● 100% or more U.S. RDA ◐ 25% U.S. RDA ○ 5% or less U.S. RDA

	Protein	Niacin	Riboflavin	Thiamine	Vitamin B6	Vitamin B12	Folic acid	Calcium	Phosphorus	Magnesium	Zinc	Iron	Sodium, mg.	Fat, g.	Calories
Cottage Cheese (123 g.)	◐	○	◐	○	○	◐	○	◐	◐	○	○	○	353	4.0	108
Tuna (85 g.)	●	●	○	○	◐	◐	○	○	◐	○	◐	◐	324	10.1	177
Hamburger (85 g.)	◐	◐	◐	○	◐	◐	○	○	◐	◐	●	◐	40	14.5	224

Profiles based on an average woman's recommended daily allowance of important nutrients. Serving sizes: four ounces of cottage cheese, three ounces of drained tuna or cooked hamburger.
As published in a **March 1986** report.

A Cottage-Cheese Cheesecake

*Here's a recipe that can provide a tasty ending to your dinner
without a blockbuster contribution to your waistline.*

*Make this cottage-cheese cake in a nine-inch cake pan and cut it
into 10 pieces, each of which will weigh about four ounces and
contain 190 calories. If that figure doesn't seem all that dietetic,
consider that a like weight of plain commercial cheesecake (which
will come in a smaller slice, at that) can cost you 340 calories.
Here's what you'll need:*

1 tsp. butter
2 tbsp. bread crumbs
3½ cups cottage cheese (4% milkfat)
½ cup cornstarch
½ cup + 2 tbsp. sugar
2 tsp. vanilla
1 tbsp. grated lemon rind
4 large eggs, separated

While your oven is preheating to 350°F, lightly butter the sides and
bottom of a nine-inch spring-form cake pan. Press the bread crumbs
smoothly over the butter on the bottom of the pan to line it. Beat the
cottage cheese, cornstarch, one-half cup sugar, vanilla, lemon rind,
and the egg yolks in an electric mixer until smooth.

That done, clean the mixer's beaters well and beat the egg whites
in a separate, medium-size bowl until soft peaks form. Add the two
tablespoons of sugar, a spoonful at a time. Continue beating until
the mixture is stiff, but not dry.

Fold the egg-white foam into the batter in your first bowl. Then
pour the batter into the cake pan and bake for 55 minutes. Turn the
oven off, but leave the cake in the oven to cool for another hour.
Take it out and put it on a cake rack to cool; don't chill it.

This recipe uses no salt. The sodium content nonetheless comes to 266 milligrams per four-ounce slice.

If you're counting carbohydrate grams, a slice will give you 22 grams.

Yogurts

Some historians date yogurt back to Neolithic times, when milk was left to curdle in clay pots.

Through the ages, a good deal of folklore grew up about yogurt. At various times and in various places, yogurt was thought of as an insomnia cure, a wrinkle remover, a medicine, or even a prolonger of life.

Modern yogurt makers have somewhat less exotic pitches. Today's yogurts are generally promoted as a dieter's delight, as a sort of natural health food, or both.

Helped by such pitches, yogurt is a booming dairy product. It wasn't always so. When yogurt appeared in the United States some 55 years ago, its sour-milk taste didn't make a big hit. Not until the late 1940s did the manufacturers pick up on the idea of adding fruit to yogurt. In the seventies, with the increasing emphasis on staying slim and eating healthfully, yogurt sales rocketed.

Plain yogurt is still in the dairy case, but it's not a big part of the market. The bulk of sales are flavored versions, whose sweetness matches the tastes of younger consumers.

There's a lot to choose from: yogurt flavored with strawberry, vanilla, lemon, coffee, blueberry, raspberry, cherry, apricot, and peach, among other things. Then there are different styles. There's sundae-style, with fruit at the bottom that you mix with the yogurt above. (Variants have fruit at the bottom and flavored syrup on top or throughout.) In the "Swiss" and "French" styles, the yogurt and fruit are already mixed. (The Swiss is spoonable; the French is the consistency of a "thick shake.") There's frozen yogurt on sticks and in cups, and there's a "frozen-custard" variety. There's even a drinkable yogurt that has a consistency like that of buttermilk.

Flavor

Ideally, a plain yogurt should have some astringency as well as a sweet-sour character—dairy sweetness from the fresh milk on which the yogurt is based, "yogurty" tartness from the bacterial action that converts milk to yogurt.

Fruit-flavored yogurt should taste less sour and astringent than plain, with the characteristic taste of the fruit about the same or a bit stronger than the dairy and yogurt notes.

Plain or flavored, a yogurt should have a clean, pleasant aftertaste and a slight mouthcoating. Both types should have a smooth, creamy consistency—with bits of fruit permissible in the flavored type.

Unfortunately, not every product measures up. In plain yogurt, you may find a cheesy, yeasty, or unclean sour taste. Some fruit-flavored yogurts may be chalky, floral, or even medicinal in character, or have an unpleasant aftertaste. Some have the artificially sweet taste of kids' fruit drinks.

Nutrition

Yogurt is about as nutritious as the milk from which it is made. One nutritional strong point of both is high-quality protein. Eight fluid ounces of whole milk contain about eight grams of protein; an eight-ounce serving of almost any yogurt has at least that much. Milk and yogurt are also good sources of calcium and phosphorus. Most provide about 20 percent of a woman's Recommended Daily Allowance of protein and 35 percent of calcium. Eight fluid ounces of whole milk would provide roughly the same amounts of those nutrients.

People with lactase deficiency have difficulty digesting milk. Since the lactose in yogurt is partly broken down by the fermentation process before the food is eaten, doctors sometimes recommend yogurt as a source of calcium for people with lactase deficiency.

Milk—and therefore yogurt—is deficient in some essential nutrients, notably vitamins A, C, and niacin, as well as iron. Yogurt, then, is no more a complete meal than a glass of milk is.

Nor is yogurt any more of a diet food. Eight fluid ounces of whole milk contain about 150 calories. An eight-ounce serving of plain whole-milk yogurt ranges from 150 to 210 calories. Plain lowfat yogurt is only a bit more dietetic, at 140 to 160 calories. Nonfat yogurt, at about 100, is the one dieters might choose—but at a sacrifice in flavor.

The calorie-conscious should probably give up on fruit-flavored yogurts. An eight-ounce serving ranges from approximately 220 to a hefty 280 calories (a three-ounce cooked hamburger on a bun contains only 350 calories).

Calories depend to some extent on fat content, so yogurt made from whole milk will naturally tend to have more calories than a lowfat or nonfat variety. Most whole-milk yogurts, flavored or not, will contain about 3 percent fat, on average. A typical lowfat yogurt contains about 2 percent on average, and a nonfat yogurt has little or no fat.

Calories also sneak in when sugar is added; that's why fruit-flavored yogurt bears an extra burden. First, it has the sugar that's part of the fruit itself. Then there's sugar that the manufacturer adds, perhaps to counteract any tartness in the fruit. The sugar takes the form of corn sweetener, sugar, honey, fructose, dextrose, or some combination.

Even plain yogurt generally has about twice the calories of an eight-ounce fruit salad. A glass of whole milk and an apple will provide a larger number of nutrients (and some fiber) with fewer calories than you would get with a typical strawberry yogurt.

In short: Yogurt is not a complete lunch, since it lacks some essential vitamins and minerals. It's simply a nutritious snack.

How Natural?

If you were to translate "natural" as "contains no additives," you'd mistranslate many yogurt labels. True, most plain yogurt labels make one or another claim about naturalness and, indeed, list only ingredients you might find in a homemade yogurt. But even a "natural" yogurt may contain gelatin, a stabilizer.

Other ingredients not generally thought of as natural to yogurt—even flavored yogurt—include gelatin, food starch, potassium sorbate (or sodium benzoate), sorbic acid, tragacanth, guar gum, beet juice or extract, and carmine.

Yogurt contains live yogurt cultures, "good" bacteria that convert milk into yogurt and produce acidity high enough to prevent bacterial spoilage. But even good bacteria won't protect against the growth of yeasts and molds, which can creep in on the fruit or with unsanitary processing and which can thrive in an acid environment. Some molds and yeasts can produce potentially harmful toxins.

At the least, such contamination can cause flavor to deteriorate.

How Yogurt Is Made

Russian scientist Élie Metchnikoff, winner of a Nobel prize in 1908, thought that eating yogurt prolonged life. So he ate a lot of yogurt. He died at 71.

Nonetheless, Metchnikoff's work did a lot to promote yogurt. He had noticed that native Bulgarians, for whom yogurt was a staple food, often had remarkable longevity. He managed to isolate *Lactobacillus bulgaricus*, one of the bacilli that convert milk to yogurt, from Bulgarian yogurt. He theorized that those acid-forming bacteria could replace putrefactive bacteria in the intestine, and so extend life. Only years after Metchnikoff's death did scientists realize that *Lactobacillus bulgaricus* is unlikely to become part of the intestinal flora.

It takes more than one species of bacteria to make yogurt. You start with milk (whether from cows, goats, sheep, or even camels or water buffalo doesn't matter much). To that you add *Streptococcus thermophilus*, then *Lactobacillus bulgaricus* and/or *L. acidophilus*. The milk is fermented under moderately high temperatures. Result: a good deal of lactic acid, along with other by-products that give yogurt its distinctive creamy, custardlike consistency and tangy, sweet/sour dairy flavor.

In a yogurt factory, the milk is warmed to about 140° F. Any combination of cream, skim or partially skim milk, and dry milk solids may then be added before the mixture is homogenized and pasteurized. After the milk has cooled to about 115°, it is inoculated with the starter bacteria (usually equal amounts of *Lactobacilli* and *Streptococci*). That temperature is held for three to six hours to let the culture grow and ferment, then the yogurt is refrigerated to retard fermentation.

There are two basic types of yogurt: set and stirred (or pudding-style). In set yogurt, fermentation occurs right in the retail container: The warm, inoculated mixture is poured in, allowed to ferment, and then cooled. If the product is a flavored sundae-style yogurt, fruit puree or syrup is poured in first.

Stirred yogurts are fermented in large vats, where they partially coagulate. The yogurt is then stirred back to a fluid, along with any flavoring, to fill the retail containers. In Swiss-style flavored products, a solidifying agent such as gelatin is used. French-style yogurts don't use gelatin and so are somewhat runnier.

Homemade Yogurt

Yogurt made from this recipe is lower in calories than commercial yogurt.
   Here's what you'll need:

Equipment

2-qt. double boiler
Candy thermometer
Home yogurt maker or large foam picnic chest (about 1 cu. ft.)
Seven 8-oz. plastic or glass containers with covers

Ingredients

1 qt. milk (whole or lowfat)

2 level tbsp. of room-temperature, plain lowfat yogurt containing live
bacteria (any commercial brand should do)

⅛ cup instant nonfat dry milk

Wash all the equipment in hot, sudsy water. Rinse with hot water.
Dissolve the nonfat dry milk in the whole milk or in the lowfat milk,
using the double boiler. Stir until the mixture reaches 180° F. Hold
that temperature for a minute, then allow it to drop to about 115°.
Remove about one-third of a cup of milk from the double boiler; add
the two level tablespoons of yogurt starter to that. Blend the mixture
well. Return the milk/starter combination to the double boiler, and
blend.

The next step is incubation. You can use a home yogurt-maker,
or rig up your own yogurt factory, using a foam picnic chest and
eight-ounce plastic or glass containers. To make yogurt in the picnic
chest, pour the yogurt mixture into six of the containers, cover them,
and put them in the chest around a seventh container of boiling
water. Cover the chest and set it aside for four to five hours.

After incubation, you can add any flavoring you like to your
yogurt. One-half teaspoon of vanilla extract added to each container
tones down the strong "yogurty" flavor. Dried fruit such as raisins
or apricots increases the yogurt's nutritional benefits. One-half cup
of fresh strawberries or blueberries per container adds about 40 calories; either fruit provides added nutritional value.

Whole-milk yogurt made from the above recipe contains 130 calories a serving, 10 grams of protein, 6 grams of fat, 210 milligrams
of sodium, and 330 milligrams of calcium. If you use lowfat milk,
the numbers are: 100 calories, 10 grams of protein, 2 grams of fat,
and 230 and 340 milligrams of sodium and calcium, respectively.

Quick Dinners

Frozen Entrées and Dinners

Food marketers have been heaping new products into freezer cases—new names, new packaging, new menu items—kindling the hope that truly delicious, nutritious, and quickly prepared meals are finally here.

Another hopeful sign has been the new upscale image given to frozen food. Marketers have been dressing up the latest TV dinners in formal clothes, as it were. Chicken divan, Français, picatta, cordon bleu, and cacciatore have joined chicken à la king in the freezer case. The nouveau TV dinner has been packaged with all the signals of elegance—rich colors, classy typefaces, linen and silver lurking behind the luscious-looking food in the cover photo. Instead of using the old compartmentalized trays, some lines use plastic plates.

In addition to lifting entrée ideas from a menu of continental cuisine, the makers of frozen food have sought inspiration in other types of restaurants. Lasagna and other pasta dishes are routinely included by generalists such as *Stouffer's;* lines such as *Ronzoni* are devoted solely to Italian fare. You can find Chinese, Japanese, and generic "Oriental" food throughout the freezer case, along with food from Mexican, Jewish, and other ethnic cuisines.

If entrées have been dressed up in elegance, certain lines have been dressed in slenderizing styles. The success of the *Weight Watchers* line of low-calorie dinners and desserts has led to other lines of diet dishes. Actually, the calorie count of low-calorie entrées—generally 300 calories or less per dish—doesn't differ greatly from that of the typical frozen dinner.

Today people want fast, easy meals, especially in homes in which both partners work. Among households that eat these frozen products, nearly half eat them regularly—once a week or more. If questioned closely, many will rank sensory quality secondary to convenience.

According to a Consumers Union survey, only one in five readers of *Consumer Reports* who eats frozen entrées buys them for taste. Blandness, saltiness, and a general lack of freshness are major complaints. Asked how they would rate frozen entrées, only one in 10 readers who eat the products would give them top marks. Two-thirds judge such dishes good, and one-quarter of the readers rate them only fair.

Cooking and Taste

Virtually all the entrées can be microwaved. Indeed, the microwave oven, which shortens the cooking time from 30 or 45 minutes to 10 or 12, is a primary reason for these products' popularity. As one official at a major food company put it, "Frozen foods are 'software' to the microwave's 'hardware.'"

No frozen entrée tastes much like a fresh version. Many, particularly beef dishes, taste warmed over, as if they'd been sitting all day on a restaurant steam table. Certain ingredients seem off: stringy, gristly beef; gamy chicken. Some companies stint, using cottage cheese in place of ricotta or dehydrated onions and garlic instead of fresh condiments. Salt and monosodium glutamate, instead of hyping the flavors, often add their own defects.

Some taste and texture problems are endemic to the freezing and reheating of foods, particularly with meat and fleshy fish. Small ice crystals form between the cells and puncture membranes, releasing a significant amount of fluid. When you defrost a roast, for instance, the juice left behind is evidence of just such fluid loss.

Wrapping food too loosely (some entrées are very loosely wrapped) promotes freezer burn—the food dries out as moisture evaporates off exposed surfaces. Many entrées have the dry, spongy, or tough texture and stale taste that's characteristic of freezer burn. Cooking a once-frozen dish can drive off yet more moisture.

And if an entrée, sauce, and side dish are heated on the same tray, all may not come out with the right doneness or texture. When the entrée is perfect, the vegetable or rice can be overcooked. To overcome that problem, some entrées package their rice separately, so you cook it less than the meat.

Because of freezing, meat often turns drier, tougher, and stringier than it was originally. Fish frequently becomes soft and mealy. Vegetables turn mushy: Zucchini in these products is often waterlogged and broccoli limp. Occasionally, the vegetables are tough and tasteless. Some sauces lack good consistency, tending toward starchy, pasty, gluey messes, or resembling runny canned soup.

Microwave cooking can make matters even worse, since it can result in more fluid loss than does cooking by conventional means. Further, microwave cooking is hard to control. A minute more or less can make a big difference in an entrée's taste and texture.

Another common problem is variability from sample to sample of the same product. A fish dish might run from moist and flaky to arid and stringy; a chicken dish from juicy and tender to dry and tough.

In some cases, age may be the culprit. Most times, you can't tell how old a package is. Very few brands have easily decipherable date codes on their boxes.

Rancidity and staleness in some samples may stem from poor handling—the products may have partially defrosted en route to the store's freezer case. Unfortunately, you can't tell that from looking at the package, either.

Nutrition

Good nutrition over a day, a week, or a lifetime is a juggling act. Among other things, it requires keeping fat, protein, and carbohydrates in balance as you take in the calories you need. In 1989, the National Research Council of the National Academy of Sciences set a goal that fat in the diet should account for no more than 30 percent of calories.

Such guidelines leave roughly two-thirds of the 2,000 to 2,700 calories the average adult needs in a day to be split between protein and carbohydrates. Adults need something on the order of 50 grams of protein a day, about what you find in a six-and-a-half-ounce can of tuna. That much protein would amount to less than 10 percent of a day's calories. So, ideally, more than half your calories should be consumed as carbohydrates, plentiful in fruit, vegetables, grains, and legumes. (Calorie and protein requirements depend on body weight, so men generally need more calories and protein than women do.)

You can always supplement a frozen-entrée meal with a salad or with some whole-grain bread. Both will add carbohydrates (and fiber) to the meal and tip the balance of nutrients more favorably.

You might well have to add extra food just to get enough to eat. One big complaint about these products besides the bland taste is the small portion size. Portions range considerably, from five to almost 13 ounces, and calorie content from 159 (for a lone Salisbury steak) to 450 (for a hefty portion of lasagna). If you count on each meal to provide a third or so of the day's calories, most entrées will leave you hungry for more. A typical entrée provides less than 400 calories, and the majority weigh in at under 300 calories.

Some entrées have relatively high sodium levels, sodium that comes from additives like monosodium glutamate as well as from salt. The most sodium-laden entrées give you a dose of more than 1,400 milligrams. Guidelines from the National Research Council say that 1,100 to 3,300 milligrams of sodium is sufficient and safe for most adults for an entire day.

Recommendations

If you're expecting a dish that tastes close to fresh-made from fresh ingredients, you'll be disappointed by fare from the freezer case. But if all you're expecting is a hot dish that's fairly cheap and quick to prepare, you'll be more easily satisfied. If you choose wisely, you can find entrées that combine respectable taste, reasonable price, and solid nutrition.

Some entrées' shortcomings—dryness, toughness, freezer burn, and mushy side vegetables—are probably unavoidable in frozen food. Until food technologists can surmount those problems, hope for good-tasting, low-effort meals lies elsewhere than in the super-market freezer case.

Ratings of Frozen Entrées

Listed by types; within types, listed in order of overall sensory quality, as depicted by the sensory index; if scores are equal, listed alphabetically. Except as noted, all packages contain one serving and may be heated in conventional or microwave oven.

As published in a **May 1988** report. Prices have been updated to December 1989.

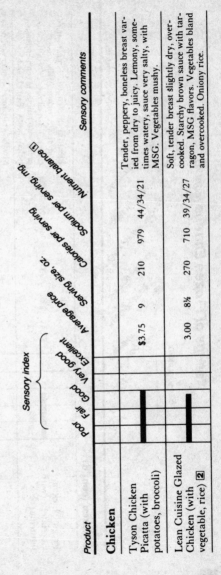

Product	Sensory index Poor / Fair / Good / Very good / Excellent	Average price	Serving size oz.	Calories per serving	Sodium per serving mg	Nutrient balance [1]	Sensory comments
Chicken							
Tyson Chicken Picatta (with potatoes, broccoli)	Fair–Good	$3.75	9	210	979	44/34/21	Tender, peppery, boneless breast varied from dry to juicy. Lemony, sometimes very salty, sauce watery, with MSG. Vegetables mushy.
Lean Cuisine Glazed Chicken (with vegetable, rice) [2]	Fair–Good	3.00	8½	270	710	39/34/27	Soft, tender breast slightly dry, overcooked. Starchy brown sauce with tarragon, MSG flavors. Vegetables bland and overcooked. Oniony rice.

Ratings of Frozen Entrées (cont'd)

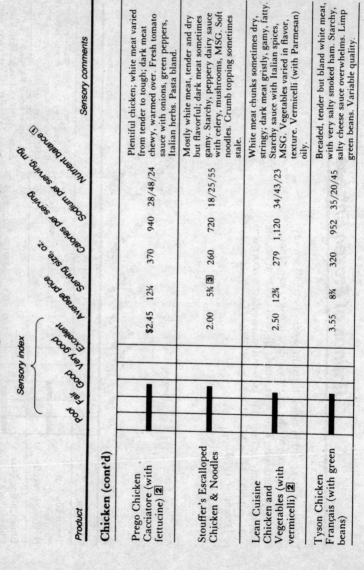

Product	Sensory index (Poor · Fair · Good · Very good · Excellent)	Average price	Serving size, oz.	Calories per serving	Sodium per serving, mg.	Nutrient balance [1]	Sensory comments
Chicken (cont'd)							
Prego Chicken Cacciatore (with fetucine) [2]		$2.45	12¾	370	940	28/48/24	Plentiful chicken; white meat varied from tender to tough; dark meat chewy, warmed over. Fresh tomato sauce with onions, green peppers, Italian herbs. Pasta bland.
Stouffer's Escalloped Chicken & Noodles		2.00	5¾ [3]	260	720	18/25/55	Mostly white meat, tender and dry but flavorful; dark meat sometimes gamy. Starchy, peppery dairy sauce with celery, mushrooms, MSG. Soft noodles. Crumb topping sometimes stale.
Lean Cuisine Chicken and Vegetables (with vermicelli) [2]		2.50	12¾	279	1,120	34/43/23	White meat chunks sometimes dry, stringy; dark meat gristly, gamy, fatty. Starchy sauce with Italian spices, MSG. Vegetables varied in flavor, texture. Vermicelli (with Parmesan) oily.
Tyson Chicken Français (with green beans)		3.55	8¾	320	952	35/20/45	Breaded, tender but bland white meat, with very salty smoked ham. Starchy, salty cheese sauce overwhelms. Limp green beans. Variable quality.

Budget Gourmet French Recipe Chicken and Vegetables	2.00	10	270	830	34/30/37	Usually dry chicken chunks, with gamy, chewy dark meat. Tomato sauce more like oily broth, with pepper, thyme. Mushy vegetables.
Stouffer's Chicken à la King (with rice)	1.95	9¾	320	840	24/46/31	Plentiful chicken with dry, tender white meat and fatty, gristly dark meat. Starchy, salty sauce like cream of celery soup with MSG. Soft vegetables. Fluffy, salty rice.
International Entrée Chicken Cordon Bleu	3.75	6 [3]	339	811	34/26/40	Tender but bland white meat. Soggy, corn-flavored breading oily, sometimes gummy. Cheese chalky and Canadian bacon tough. Very smoky, salty.
Swanson Entrées for Two Chicken Duets (with broccoli and stuffing)	3.95	6 [3]	310	630	26/23/49	Tender but bland chicken seemed texturized. Too much breading, sometimes rancid tasting from oil. Runny stuffing, like cream of mushroom soup; little broccoli.
Benihana Sweet and Sour Chicken (with rice) [2]	2.55	11	375	972	28/54/17	Chicken usually dry, with gamy dark meat. Soy-based sauce very sweet, with MSG. Vegetables slightly crunchy to mushy. Starchy, dry rice.
Freezer Queen Chicken à la King (with rice) [2]	1.25	9½	295	434	31/49/21	Dry, pasty white meat; gamy, chewy dark meat. Thick, starchy, salty sauce with lots of celery flavor, MSG. Mushy vegetables. Hard, dry rice.
Weight Watchers Chicken à la King [2]	2.30	9	230	859	45/26/27	Bland white meat and gamy, dry dark meat. Thick, starchy sauce with lots of celery, pepper, MSG. Mushy vegetables.

Ratings of Frozen Entrées (cont'd)

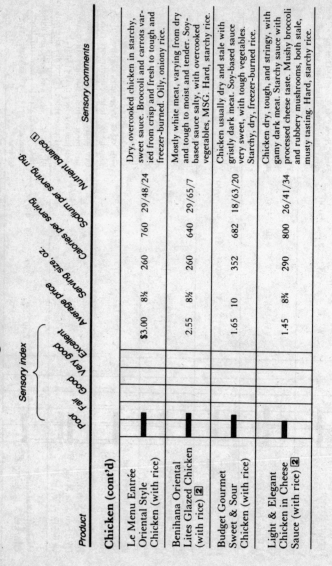

Product	Sensory index Poor Fair Good Very good Excellent	Average price	Serving size, oz.	Calories per serving	Sodium per serving, mg	Nutrient balance [1]	Sensory comments
Chicken (cont'd)							
Le Menu Entrée Oriental Style Chicken (with rice)	Poor	$3.00	8¾	260	760	29/48/24	Dry, overcooked chicken in starchy, sweet sauce. Broccoli and carrots varied from crisp and fresh to tough and freezer-burned. Oily, oniony rice.
Benihana Oriental Lites Glazed Chicken (with rice) [2]	Poor	2.55	8¾	260	640	29/65/7	Mostly white meat, varying from dry and tough to moist and tender. Soy-based sauce salty, with overcooked vegetables, MSG. Hard, starchy rice.
Budget Gourmet Sweet & Sour Chicken (with rice)	Poor	1.65	10	352	682	18/63/20	Chicken usually dry and stale with gristly dark meat. Soy-based sauce very sweet, with tough vegetables. Starchy, dry, freezer-burned rice.
Light & Elegant Chicken in Cheese Sauce (with rice) [2]	Poor	1.45	8¾	290	800	26/41/34	Chicken dry, tough, and stringy, with gamy dark meat. Starchy sauce with processed cheese taste. Mushy broccoli and rubbery mushrooms, both stale, musty tasting. Hard, starchy rice.

Banquet Family Entrée Chicken and Dumplings						1.80	7 4	280	872	17/40/45	Like chicken pot pie, in raw, doughy crust. Cubes of stale, stringy, mostly dark meat in starchy, salty sauce; lots of MSG. Tasted like dishwater.
Beef											
Prego Beef Marsala (with noodles) 2						2.65	11¼	390	850	28/36/35	Beef chunks chewy, stringy, fatty with stale, warmed-over flavor. Runny sauce. Mushrooms tasted canned. Noodles soft and oily.
Stouffer's Green Pepper Steak Chinese Style (with rice)						2.80	10½	340	1,470	26/45/29	Tough, dry, chewy beef tasted bland and warmed over. Tomatoey sauce very salty, with MSG. Soft, mushy green pepper. Very salty rice.
Lean Cuisine Oriental Beef (with rice) 2						2.75	8⅝	270	1,150	30/44/27	Sliced bland beef, texture varying from chewy to tender. Teriyaki-style sauce salty, with MSG and over-cooked vegetables. Very salty rice.
Swanson Salisbury Steak in Gravy (with macaroni and cheese)						1.60	10	410	970	21/9/70	Beef tasted like hot dog, with garlic, smoke flavors. Starchy, salty gravy with dried onion, garlic. Macaroni noodles soft in gluey cheese sauce.
Weight Watchers Beef Salisbury Steak Romana (with noodles)						2.40	8¾	300	1,085	33/32/36	Gristly beef, slight warmed-over flavor. Stewed-tomato sauce with dehydrated onion and garlic but fresh mozzarella. Waterlogged squash. Buttery, oily noodles, dry at edges, with parsley.

Ratings of Frozen Entrées (cont'd)

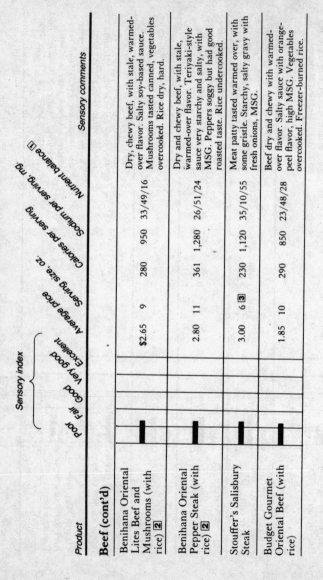

Product	Sensory index (Poor / Fair / Good / Very good / Excellent)	Average price	Serving size, oz.	Calories per serving	Sodium per serving, mg	Nutrient balance [1]	Sensory comments
Beef (cont'd)							
Benihana Oriental Lites Beef and Mushrooms (with rice) [2]	Poor	$2.65	9	280	950	33/49/16	Dry, chewy beef, with stale, warmed-over flavor. Salty soy-based sauce. Mushrooms tasted canned, vegetables overcooked. Rice dry, hard.
Benihana Oriental Pepper Steak (with rice) [2]	Poor	2.80	11	361	1,280	26/51/24	Dry and chewy beef, with stale, warmed-over flavor. Teriyaki-style sauce very starchy and salty, with MSG. Peppers soggy but had good roasted taste. Rice undercooked.
Stouffer's Salisbury Steak	Poor	3.00	6 [3]	230	1,120	35/10/55	Meat patty tasted warmed over, with some gristle. Starchy, salty gravy with fresh onions, MSG.
Budget Gourmet Oriental Beef (with rice)	Poor	1.85	10	290	850	23/48/28	Beef dry and chewy with warmed-over flavor. Salty sauce with orange-peel flavor, high MSG. Vegetables overcooked. Freezer-burned rice.

Product		Price		Calories	Sodium	Pct.	Comments
Budget Gourmet Sirloin of Beef in Herb Sauce (with noodles)	▮	2.00	10	290	920	29/35/34	Skimpy, bland beef with warmed-over flavor, variable texture. Herb sauce starchy, oily. Noodles often starchy, mushy, oily. Sometimes freezer-burned.
Le Menu Entrée Beef Burgundy (with noodles)	▮	3.70	7¾	310	600	32/14/55	Chunks of soft, stringy, fatty beef with smoky, scorched taste. Wine sauce very salty. Soft, oily noodles. Overall, greasy and variable in quality.
On-Cor Deluxe Entrée Gravy and 6 Salisbury Steaks	▮	2.65	8 [4]	296	1,061	22/18/61	Meat tasted charred and like cereal, with crumbly texture and bits of gristle. Starchy, oily brown gravy with dried onion and garlic, salt, MSG.
Light & Elegant Beef Stroganoff (with noodles) [2]	▮	1.55	9	260	790	37/42/21	Beef thinly sliced, tough, overcooked. Winey sauce tasted like canned mushroom soup, very salty with MSG. Mushy peas, noodles.
Budget Gourmet Pepper Steak (with rice)	▮	1.75	10	267	628	25/57/20	Skimpy, thin-sliced beef with tough, chewy texture, warmed-over flavor. Thick, starchy tomato-onion sauce. Overcooked green pepper. Mushy rice, often with off-taste. Often freezer-burned.
Freezer Queen Gravy and Salisbury Steak [2]	▮	.60	5	159	638	20/18/62	Meat tasted more like cereal than beef, with crumbly texture. Starchy, brothlike gravy, with salt and MSG.
Banquet Cookin' Bag Gravy and Salisbury Steak [2]	▮	.65	5	190	590	19/17/66	Meat tasted more like cereal than beef, with crumbly texture, some gristle. Gelatinous gravy was salty, oily, starchy. Often stale.

Ratings of Frozen Entrées (cont'd)

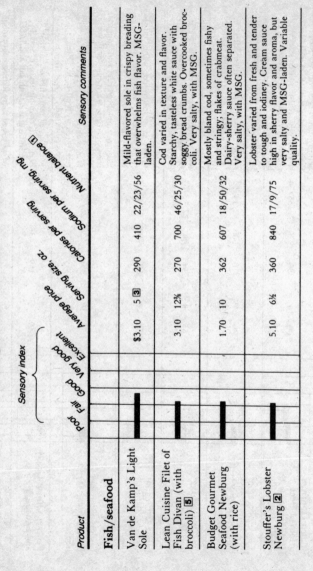

Product	Sensory index (Poor · Fair · Good · Very good · Excellent)	Average price	Serving size, oz.	Calories per serving	Sodium per serving, mg	Nutrient balance □	Sensory comments
Fish/seafood							
Van de Kamp's Light Sole		$3.10	5 ③	290	410	22/23/56	Mild-flavored sole in crispy breading that overwhelms fish flavor. MSG-laden.
Lean Cuisine Filet of Fish Divan (with broccoli) ⑤		3.10	12½	270	700	46/25/30	Cod varied in texture and flavor. Starchy, tasteless white sauce with soggy bread crumbs. Overcooked broccoli. Very salty, with MSG.
Budget Gourmet Seafood Newburg (with rice)		1.70	10	362	607	18/50/32	Mostly bland cod, sometimes fishy and stringy; flakes of crabmeat. Dairy-sherry sauce often separated. Very salty, with MSG.
Stouffer's Lobster Newburg ②		5.10	6½	360	840	17/9/75	Lobster varied from fresh and tender to tough and iodiney. Cream sauce high in sherry flavor and aroma, but very salty and MSG-laden. Variable quality.

Product	Price					Comments
Mrs. Paul's Light Seafood Fish Dijon (with asparagus)	2.80	9¾	280	650	36/16/48	Haddock or cod pieces varied in taste and texture. Sauce tasted like mayonnaise and mustard. Stringy, off-flavored asparagus. Variable quality.
Gorton's Light Recipe Shrimp Scampi	3.30	6	350	420	22/17/62	Shrimp varied from flavorful and tender to tough and iodiney. Stale, soggy crumb topping; lots of oil and dehydrated garlic.
Lean Cuisine Filet of Fish Jardinière (with souffléed potatoes) [5]	3.00	11¼	280	710	43/26/32	Bland cod in starchy white sauce tasted fishy and like dehydrated onion; very salty, with MSG. Dehydrated whipped potatoes, bits of green beans, carrots.
Benihana Oriental Lites Shrimp and Cashews (with rice) [2]	2.65	9	260	700	17/63/21	Shrimp often iodiney, with soft cashews and vegetables. Starchy sauce with onion, garlic, ginger, salt, MSG.
Mrs. Paul's Light Seafood Entrée Fish Mornay (with broccoli)	2.75	10	230	665	43/19/39	Tasteless cod varied from flaky and moist to stringy and dry. Sauce tasted of processed cheese, dried onion and garlic. Mushy broccoli.
Benihana Shrimp with Lobster Sauce (with rice) [2]	2.75	11	312	976	26/54/20	Tough shrimp varied from fresh to iodiney. Pork and egg sauce gelatinous and starchy, very salty, with MSG. Pork bordered on rancid.
Weight Watchers Filet of Fish au Gratin (with broccoli)	2.60	9¾	210	910	48/23/30	Cod tasted fishy with stringy, tough texture. Cheese sauce pasty. Mushy broccoli in garlic butter.

Ratings of Frozen Entrées (cont'd)

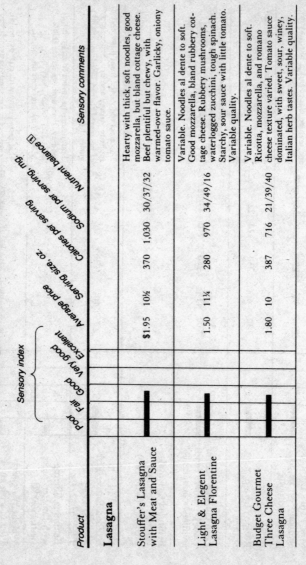

Product	Sensory index (Poor–Fair–Good–Very good–Excellent)	Average price	Serving size, oz.	Calories per serving	Sodium per serving, mg	Nutrient balance ☐	Sensory comments
Lasagna							
Stouffer's Lasagna with Meat and Sauce	Fair	$1.95	10½	370	1,030	30/37/32	Hearty with thick, soft noodles, good mozzarella, but bland cottage cheese. Beef plentiful but chewy, with warmed-over flavor. Garlicky, oniony tomato sauce.
Light & Elegent Lasagna Florentine	Fair	1.50	11¼	280	970	34/49/16	Variable. Noodles al dente to soft. Good mozzarella, bland rubbery cottage cheese. Rubbery mushrooms, waterlogged zucchini, tough spinach. Starchy, sour sauce with little tomato. Variable quality.
Budget Gourmet Three Cheese Lasagna	Fair	1.80	10	387	716	21/39/40	Variable. Noodles al dente to soft. Ricotta, mozzarella, and romano cheese texture varied. Tomato sauce dominated, with sweet, sour, winey, Italian herb tastes. Variable quality.

Product	Price		Calories	Sodium (mg)	%cal protein/carb/fat	Comments
Celantano Lasagna	2.35	8 [3]	320	410	18/38/45	Soft, thin egg noodles with lots of fresh ricotta, some mozzarella. Sweet, sour tomato sauce with fresh onion; peppery aftertaste.
Budget Gourmet Lasagna with Meat Sauce	1.75	10	290	890	25/44/31	Noodles varied from al dente to soft. Little cheese flavor; veal tasted like spicy, peppery, warmed-over sausage. Runny, stewed tomato sauce.
Lean Cuisine Zucchini Lasagna	2.00	11	260	975	32/43/24	Soft, starchy noodles with cottage cheese and tough, bland mozzarella. Waterlogged zucchini sometimes musty. Starchy, stewed tomato sauce.
Stouffer's Vegetable Lasagna [5]	2.00	10½	450	910	23/26/50	Soft noodles with ricotta, Parmesan, mild and chewy mozzarella. Starchy, salty white sauce with onion, garlic but little spinach or carrot flavors. Crumb topping often slightly rancid.
Weight Watchers Italian Cheese Lasagna	1.90	12	360	1,420	21/39/40	Noodles varied from al dente to soft. Little flavor from cheeses. Tomato sauce overwhelmed. Sometimes slightly scorched or bitter.
Weight Watchers Lasagna	2.30	12	360	1,039	27/44/28	Noodles varied from al dente to soft. Amount of meat varied, tasted warmed over. Lots of ricotta, but spicy tomato sauce predominates. Slightly scorched but hearty flavor.
Ronzoni Meat Lasagna	1.95	10½	330	610	30/29/41	Noodles varied from al dente to soft, but edges tough. Stale cheese. Lots of tough ground beef with warmed-over flavor. Not much sauce.

Ratings of Frozen Entrées (cont'd)

Lasagna (cont'd)

Product	Sensory index Poor / Fair / Good / Very good / Excellent	Average price	Serving size, oz.	Calories per serving	Sodium per serving, mg.	Nutrient balance [1]	Sensory comments
Banquet Family Entrée Lasagna with Meat Sauce		$2.95	7 [4]	270	814	22/44/33	Thick, gummy noodles and skimpy, gristly beef with little cheese flavor. Starchy, salty sauce had little tomato flavor. Variable quality.
On-Cor Deluxe Entrée Lasagna		3.00	8 [4]	248	841	20/53/25	Thick, soft noodles with little mozzarella and few blobs of tough, bland cottage cheese. Tough, gristly meat. Starchy, thick sauce with little tomato flavor.

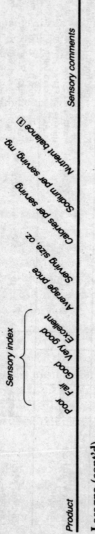

[1] The percentage of calories from protein/carbohydrates/fat. Numbers may not add to 100% because of rounding off.

[2] Boil-in bag; may be heated in microwave or in water.

[3] Two servings per package.

[4] Four servings per package.

[5] May be heated in conventional oven only.

Frozen Pot Pies

A pot pie, ready for heating in the oven, makes a convenient center-piece of a meal. No labor or time-consuming preparation is necessary, but cooking does take a while, especially if you want the top crust to turn out crispy and browned.

The most popular varieties of pot pies are beef, chicken, turkey, and vegetable with beef. Most weigh only seven or eight ounces, although the heftiest, *Swanson Hungry-Man* pies, are a pound apiece. Lightweight or not, some pies taste very good.

Ingredients

Regulations of the U.S. Department of Agriculture governing minimum amounts of meat in frozen pot pies don't encourage very generous allotments. For beef and poultry pies, processors must provide that only 25 percent by weight is raw beef or that 14 percent is cooked poultry (the discrepancy between those percentages presumably being counterbalanced by weight lost as the beef cooks). For pies categorized as vegetable with beef, processors need contribute only 12 percent raw beef by weight. USDA standards don't specify that the meat be prepared in any special way.

A pot pie should live up to the following standards: a meat flavor that's distinct and appropriate for beef or poultry. The meat is tender (though it can be a little chewy) and taken from whole, unprocessed muscle tissue. It shows no textural defects, such as gristle or tiny, hard particles (signifying, perhaps, ground-up bone). And it is free of flavor defects, such as the other "protein flavors" (suggesting the presence of soy protein or organ meats).

The vegetables in an excellent pie should be identifiable by flavor, rather than having their flavors submerged in gravy, and they should be at least moderately firm. The gravy may have its own particular balance of meat, vegetable, and spice flavors, but those tastes must be no more than moderately intense. The pie crust should be tender, flavorful, and slightly salty.

The best frozen pies fall down on only a few points: by missing distinctive flavors and firmness in the vegetables and by lacking sufficient flavor in the crust.

A poor pie gets that way mostly because of the quality of the meat. That component may be "restructured" meat—poultry bits mixed with a soy-protein binder or beef scraps pressed into molds and cut into spongy cubes that retain little of the meat's texture or taste. In a low-quality pie, other ingredients suffer, too. The vegetables may be small, soft cubes swimming in gravy.

Unlike many food packages in the supermarket freezer case, potpie boxes barely acknowledge the existence of the microwave oven. Cooking crust—like any browning—poses difficulties for microwaves, and foods that are meant to be browned or baked often end up with a tough, chewy texture. Nevertheless, more and more companies are offering the option of microwaving for these products. After all, the microwave is quite a bit faster than the conventional oven.

Nutrition

A pot pie's fat content is generally higher than seems warranted for the calories it contains. Calorie content varies from about 300 for some small seven-ounce pies to about 700 for a 16-ounce pie. (Typical daily allotments for calories are 2,000 for women and 2,700 for men.)

Inasmuch as pot pies are often represented as meals in themselves—containing, as they do, meat, vegetables, and breadstuff—they ought to present a fairly balanced nutritional profile. As the graph on the following page shows, a good chicken pie has a respectable profile.

In addition to fat, a few nutrients stand out. Pot pies generally provide more than their calories' share of protein—from about 10 grams in a typical small pie to about 30 grams in a large one. (The

U.S. Recommended Daily Allowance for protein is 45 grams.) As might be expected of a processed food, pot pies contain a lot of sodium; more than 800 milligrams is typical. Vitamin A is abundant in pies that contain carrots (which most do).

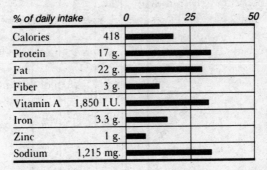

Frozen Chicken Pot Pie Nutrition

% of daily intake		0	25	50
Calories	418			
Protein	17 g.			
Fat	22 g.			
Fiber	3 g.			
Vitamin A	1,850 I.U.			
Iron	3.3 g.			
Zinc	1 g.			
Sodium	1,215 mg.			

Profile based on an average woman's daily dietary needs: calories, 2,000; protein, 45 g.; fat, 67 g.; fiber, 20 g.; vitamin A, 5,000 I.U.; iron, 18 mg.; zinc, 15 mg.; sodium, 3,300 mg. Recommended amounts for an average man are higher for calories, protein, and fat; for children, lower.

As published in a **January 1990** report.

Ratings of Frozen Pot Pies

Listed by types; within types, listed in order of overall sensory quality.

As published in a **January 1990** report.

Product	Sensory index (Poor / Fair / Good / Very good / Excellent)	Price	Size, oz.	Cost per oz.	Calories	Sodium, mg	Sensory comments
Beef							
Stouffer's	Very good	$2.23	10	22¢	522	1,485	Flaky, tender crust; tender beef; chunks of fairly flavorful vegetables, including onion.
Swanson Hungry-Man	Good	2.19	16	14	679	1,807	Chewy, slightly stringy beef; chunks of fairly flavorful vegetables, including celery; thin gravy.
Swanson Original Style	Good	.85	7	12	389	823	Chewy, slightly stringy beef; chunks of vegetables.
Empire	Fair	1.98	8	25	504	841	Tough crust; flavorful but slightly chewy and stringy beef with gristle; lots of vegetable chunks; thin, sparse gravy; less salty than most.
A&P	Poor	.48	8	6	425	1,270	Spongy cubes of restructured beef with little flavor; very few cubes of vegetables; thin gravy.

						Comments
Kroger		.51	7	7	424	1,098	Spongy cubes of restructured beef with little flavor; very few cubes of vegetables; thin gravy.
Dining Treat		.44	7	6	418	1,046	Spongy cubes of restructured beef with little flavor; very few cubes of vegetables; thin gravy.
Banquet Supreme Microwave		.79	7	11	345	1,013	Hard, overcooked top crust with part of the filling, including meat and vegetables, baked onto its underside.
Chicken							
Swanson Homestyle Recipe		1.95	9	22	418	1,215	Biscuitlike crust; tender chunks of white meat; lots of firm, fairly flavorful vegetables including broccoli; thick gravy full of vegetable and spice flavor.
Stouffer's		1.91	10	19	533	1,352	Flaky, tender crust; tender chunks of white and dark meat; chunks of firm, fairly flavorful vegetables; gravy full of vegetable and dairy flavor; less salty than most.
Swanson Hungry-Man		1.73	16	11	718	1,676	Chewy chunks of white and dark meat; chunks of fairly flavorful vegetables, including celery.
Swanson Original Style		.81	7	12	451	835	Tender top crust; tender chunks of white and dark meat, but not much of it; chunks of flavorful vegetables including red pepper/pimento.
A&P		.48	8	6	377	846	Spongy cubes of restructured meat with protein flavors other than poultry; cubes of vegetables.

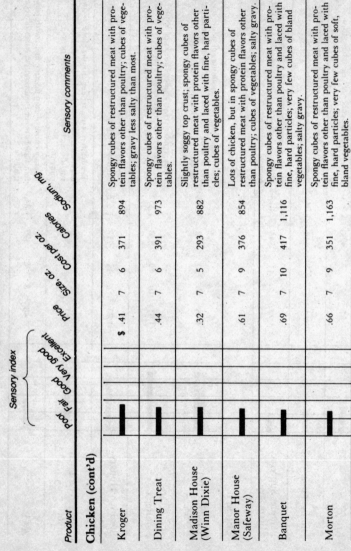

Ratings of Frozen Pot Pies (cont'd)

Product	Sensory index (Poor / Fair / Good / Very good / Excellent)	Price	Size, oz.	Cost per oz.	Calories	Sodium, mg	Sensory comments
Chicken (cont'd)							
Kroger		$ .41	7	6	371	894	Spongy cubes of restructured meat with protein flavors other than poultry; cubes of vegetables; gravy less salty than most.
Dining Treat		.44	7	6	391	973	Spongy cubes of restructured meat with protein flavors other than poultry; cubes of vegetables.
Madison House (Winn Dixie)		.32	7	5	293	882	Slightly soggy top crust; spongy cubes of restructured meat with protein flavors other than poultry and laced with fine, hard particles; cubes of vegetables.
Manor House (Safeway)		.61	7	9	376	854	Lots of chicken, but in spongy cubes of restructured meat with protein flavors other than poultry; cubes of vegetables; salty gravy.
Banquet		.69	7	10	417	1,116	Spongy cubes of restructured meat with protein flavors other than poultry and laced with fine, hard particles; very few cubes of bland vegetables; salty gravy.
Morton		.66	7	9	351	1,163	Spongy cubes of restructured meat with protein flavors other than poultry and laced with fine, hard particles; very few cubes of soft, bland vegetables.

Ozark Valley	.38	7	5	319	1,066	Spongy cubes of restructured meat with protein flavors other than poultry and laced with fine, hard particles; very few cubes of soft, bland vegetables; lots of brown gravy.

Turkey

Stouffer's	1.88	10	19	505	1,213	Flaky, tender crust; tender chunks of white and dark meat; chunks of fairly flavorful vegetables including celery; gravy full of dairy flavor.
Swanson Hungry-Man	1.79	16	11	739	1,539	Chewy chunks of white and dark meat, chunks of fairly flavorful vegetables including celery.
Swanson Original Style	.78	7	11	429	924	Chewy and stringy chunks of white and dark meat with faint warmed-over flavor; chunks of vegetables.
A&P	.50	8	6	390	1,000	Spongy cubes of restructured meat with faint warmed-over flavor and protein flavors other than poultry and laced with fine, hard particles; cubes of vegetables.
Ozark Valley	.40	7	6	321	994	Spongy cubes of restructured meat with protein flavors other than poultry and laced with fine, hard particles; very few cubes of soft vegetables.
Banquet	.69	7	10	431	1,120	Spongy cubes of restructured meat with protein flavors other than poultry and laced with fine, hard particles; very few cubes of soft vegetables.

Ratings of Frozen Pot Pies *(cont'd)*

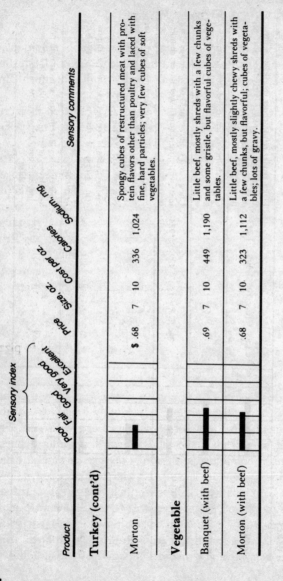

Product	Price	Size, oz.	Cost per oz.	Calories	Sodium, mg	Sensory comments
Turkey (cont'd)						
Morton	$ .68	7	10	336	1,024	Spongy cubes of restructured meat with protein flavors other than poultry and laced with fine, hard particles; very few cubes of soft vegetables.
Vegetable						
Banquet (with beef)	.69	7	10	449	1,190	Little beef, mostly shreds with a few chunks and some gristle, but flavorful cubes of vegetables.
Morton (with beef)	.68	7	10.	323	1,112	Little beef, mostly slightly chewy shreds with a few chunks, but flavorful; cubes of vegetables; lots of gravy.

Sensory index: Poor / Fair / Good / Very good / Excellent

Frozen Pizza

Frozen pizza is easy to prepare, cheap, and reasonably nutritious.

Never mind that frozen pizza isn't the same thing as a fresh slice hot from a pizzeria oven; children may not care all that much. But grown-ups do.

It isn't all that easy to compare frozen pizza with fresh. Pizzeria pizzas can vary enormously in just one neighborhood. The spread gets wider still from city to city and from region to region.

Brands and types of frozen pizza also vary from place to place. Many manufacturers are regional and focus on the kinds of pizza the locals seem to like. Even national brands tilt their distribution to accommodate local taste. Easterners buy more plain-cheese pizza than any other type; maybe they like to toss on their own toppings before cooking. Midwesterners prefer sausage-topped pizza. Pepperoni pizza (as well as pizza "with everything") finds most favor in the South and West. Specialized pizzas—with beef, Mexican toppings, or Canadian bacon—also have local but loyal followings.

Pizza Basics

There are several essential components that are important to pizza quality:

Cheese Freezing doesn't help pizza's cheese component at all. Mozzarella, the basic pizza cheese, is normally bought fresh and must be consumed quickly. It just doesn't keep or freeze well. The distinctive mild mozzarella flavor shifts toward a cruder "cheesiness" when frozen, while the soft, stringy texture becomes a drier, crumblier ropiness. Maybe that's why most makers use a low-moisture, part-skim mozzarella cheese in their frozen cheese pizzas.

Sausage and pepperoni pizzas often stray even further with mozzarella cheese; most of it is replaced with a low-moisture, part-skim mozzarella-cheese substitute. The substitute is formulated from casein (a constituent of milk), soybean oil, and a string of additives whose description on the pizza label can be almost as long as all the rest of the pizza ingredients combined.

The best cheese consistency in frozen pizza is stringy and somewhat elastic; the worst is chewy or crumbly.

Tomato Sauce Sauces, too, suffer in freezing—their subtle blend of distinct flavors drifts toward a murky garlic-tomato fog. The traditional sauce spices, oregano and basil, just make the fog denser if used generously. Olive oil in the sauce suffers the same fate. Not surprisingly, then, spices and herbs rarely come through as individual flavor notes.

Frozen pizza is likely to be only moderately spicy. Manufacturers doubtless know that children don't usually like spicy food.

A flavorful sauce combines fresh and cooked tomato flavors successfully. A good sauce should also have body—not too thin or too pasty, too dry or too wet.

Meat Toppings Both regular sausage and pepperoni sausage are spicy meat products; in the classic Italian versions, pork is the meat used. Pepperoni, a dry sausage, is spicier and firmer than regular sausage, so its presence is more pronounced amid the cheese and tomato sauce on a pizza.

A pizza eater would be hard-pressed to identify the kind of meat used in the sausage in a pizzeria product, much less in a frozen pizza. Pepperoni products typically contain beef as well as pork. Using beef in addition to pork doesn't seem to have an effect on frozen pizzas' taste; the differences from one brand to another are submerged under the spice flavors and sauces.

Crust A pizza fresh from the oven summons you with the aroma of the toppings mingling with the delightful fragrance of toasty crust. Unlike the other pizza ingredients, dough keeps well in freezing. If properly cooked, frozen dough can be a match for fresh. But pizzeria ovens can run above 600° F, and the fresh pizzas are cooked directly on the oven's hot floor: You can't do that in your kitchen oven.

Consequently, the makers of frozen pizza have developed a dough that can be cooked in its frozen state in a kitchen oven. The crust doesn't exactly match a crust made from fresh yeast dough—a thin crispy bottom layer supporting a thin yeast-bread layer. But many makers have come up with a reasonable approximation.

In general, crusts are somewhat crackerlike or biscuitlike. They become crispy nearly all the way through when you cook them. Some makers partially cook the crust before adding the toppings and freezing, apparently trying for a more uniformly crispy/chewy character in the finished product.

Nutrition

An appropriate snack or lunch portion is about six ounces—roughly the weight of a generous slice in a neighborhood pizzeria.

As a snack or part of a quick meal, pizza fits nicely into a well-balanced diet. It's not low-calorie food, of course, but with its calories it also contributes very respectably to nutrition. For instance, it supplies a fair amount of vitamins A and C as well as iron. Pizzas with a fairly thick crust are a decent source of the B vitamins—niacin, thiamin, and riboflavin.

Pizza is also a good source of protein. On average, a slice of meat-topped pizza contains about 20 grams, more than one-third of most people's Recommended Daily Allowance (RDA).

Cheese pizza contains a lot of calcium, averaging about 422 milligrams a slice, one-half of most people's RDA. Meat pizza contains less calcium, averaging about 280 milligrams—35 percent of the RDA.

If you can stop at a single slice, a portion of pizza won't do undue damage to your waistline. On average, expect around 450 calories from a serving of frozen pizza, regardless of its type.

Your best chance of finding nutritional balance lies with a cheese pizza. That type escapes the extra fat content of meat topping, and it provides more calcium.

Sodium-aware people should note that frozen pizza averages about 1,000 milligrams per slice. That's about the amount in a half-teaspoon of table salt.

Recommendations

You have to make a trip out to get a fresh pizza, not just take a stroll to the freezer. You can't evade that inconvenience by buying fresh pizzas and freezing them, either; the results can be disappointing.

Keep an eye on the weekly food ads. Frozen pizza is often on sale at prices that make it a bargain among processed foods. You may find a high-rated brand marked down to a level that's downright cheap.

Spaghetti

"Pasta" is a term that covers a wide variety of noodles and other wheat products such as linguine, ravioli, manicotti, cannelloni, tortellini, lasagna, ziti, and others. But spaghetti is the most common pasta product, at least in the United States.

We included 30 brands of regular spaghetti in our tests. Some brands of spaghetti are imported, some not. A few carry a gourmet price. Fresh pasta usually isn't spaghetti—it's more commonly in one of the flat shapes. The main difference between fresh and regular is perishability. The fresh has a high moisture content and lasts only a few days or, in a semi-dried form, up to three months.

There are also untraditional spaghettis made with whole wheat, spinach flavoring, or both (see pages 192–193).

Flavor and Texture

Spaghetti is basically bland; it has the mild flavor of its principal ingredient, wheat.

Whereas pasta's taste is simple, its texture is not. Manufacturers' cooking instructions call for "al dente," or "firm." That firmness—"to the tooth," in Italian—is the easiest aspect of texture for most people to evaluate, by gauging how much force is required to bite through a food. Less easy to discern is the pasta's "bounce," or resilience: When you bite down, the strands are supposed to resist your teeth a little. As you chew, the strands should break into smaller and smaller pieces. Spaghetti shouldn't "chew down" like bread into a mushy mass, nor pack into your teeth ("toothpack") as crackers do. It shouldn't leave a starchy feeling in your mouth, nor leave coarse, gritty, or grainy particles.

Much of what determines the texture is the type of wheat used and how it's ground. Most pasta, including spaghetti, is made from semolina, which is coarsely ground durum wheat. That's the "hardest" type of wheat, called hard because its high gluten content allows it to make a very stiff, strong dough.

Manufacturers may also add a small percentage of flour or farina, which are softer and starchier and so tend to make a softer spaghetti. Manufacturers, however, have discovered that a coating of egg white on pasta allows it to absorb more water without becoming too soft.

As for fresh spaghetti, the main ingredient is durum flour, which has a much finer texture than semolina. The substitution is common in fresh-pasta recipes because pasta machines often have difficulty handling stiff semolina dough. In any case, fresh pasta is likely to be expensive. If the label lists semolina, you have a better chance of getting a pasta that'll cook up firm. If the label also lists an expiration date, you'll be better able to gauge the pasta's freshness.

Nutrition

Spaghetti's calories carry more than their share of protein (although it's not complete protein)—nearly one-third the recommended daily need with only 21 percent of the daily need for calories. Along with that comes nearly one-fifth of a day's iron, riboflavin, and niacin plus one-third of a day's thiamin. And unlike many foods, spaghetti provides calories that don't carry excess baggage in the form of too much fat or sodium.

If you add tomato sauce and cheese, the profiles still look good. The tomato sauce adds vitamins A and C. Cheese adds fat and sodium, but the total fat remains low. Ground beef adds extra iron and increases the quantity and quality of the protein. It also adds fat, but not too much for the calories.

An oil-based or cream-based sauce boosts the fat and the calories considerably.

Plain Spaghetti
(10 ounces cooked)

% of daily intake		0	25	50	75	100
Calories	420					
Protein	14 g.					
Total fat	1 g.					
Calcium	31 mg.					
Iron	3 mg.					
Vitamin A	0 I.U.					
Thiamin	0.5 mg.					
Riboflavin	0.3 mg.					
Niacin	4 mg.					
Vitamin C	0 mg.					
Sodium	3 mg.					

Profile based on an average woman's daily dietary needs: Quotas for an average man are greater for calories, protein, and fat; for children, lower. Data from USDA.

As published in an **August 1988** report.

Spaghetti with Tomato Sauce
(6 ounces tomato sauce and cheese)

% of daily intake		0	25	50	75	100
Calories	520					
Protein	18 g.					
Total fat	5 g.					
Calcium	94 mg.					
Iron	5 mg.					
Vitamin A	1,678 I.U.					
Thiamin	0.6 mg.					
Riboflavin	0.5 mg.					
Niacin	6 mg.					
Vitamin C	.17 mg.					
Sodium	1,031 mg.					

Spaghetti with Meatballs
(6 ounces tomato sauce and cheese, 4 ounces ground beef)

% of daily intake		0	25	50	75	100
Calories	801					
Protein	47 g.					
Total fat	24 g.					
Calcium	69 mg.					
Iron	8 mg.					
Vitamin A	1,709 I.U.					
Thiamin	0.7 mg.					
Riboflavin	0.6 mg.					
Niacin	13 mg.					
Vitamin C	22 mg.					
Sodium	1,136 mg.					

Ingredients

Pasta's ingredients are simple—basically wheat and water. Most labels list durum semolina and the nutrients that are added to enriched wheat—thiamin, riboflavin, niacin, and iron.

Labels may also show ingredients such as disodium phosphate (to decrease cooking time) and glyceryl monostearate (to reduce foaming).

Because spaghetti has what's called a federal standard of identity, the label doesn't have to tell you everything. There can be egg white, added salt, or gluten (wheat protein) to improve texture and cohesiveness.

Two manufacturers advertise the protein content of their products. One product is *Prince Superoni* (a more recent version of which is *Prince Natural Superoni*). The spaghetti delivers about 50 percent more protein than the average.

Buitoni High Protein spaghetti contains wheat germ, which adds protein. More important, the product plays a little trick with water. It's formulated to be cooked for a shorter time than most. So the cooked spaghetti contains less water and more spaghetti—and therefore more protein and calories—per serving than usual.

Although pasta is not a high-calorie food (averaging about 365 calories per 10-ounce serving), it has an undeserved reputation for being fattening—perhaps because it's associated with rich sauces and large servings. That opens a promotional opportunity for *Prince Light,* which delivers one-third fewer calories by playing the water trick in reverse.

Prince Light is meant to be cooked longer than the 10 to 14 minutes for other brands. The longer cooking time allows it to absorb extra water, so there's less spaghetti per serving, hence fewer calories—but less protein and other nutrients.

Flavored Spaghetti

Spaghetti doesn't have to be made entirely of wheat. You can find pasta made with whole wheat, spinach, or tomato. More exotic varieties include artichoke, wheat germ, bran, red chili, buckwheat, garlic/parsley, basil, and broccoli.

Flavored spaghetti can be expensive—often more than twice as much as regular supermarket brands.

From a sensory point of view, flavored spaghetti may not live up to your expectations. The consistency tends to be too chewy and sticky, with no bounce but with plenty of toothpack.

Protein and calorie contents should be about the same as for the regular products.

Ratings of Spaghetti

Listed in order of overall sensory quality, as depicted by the sensory index. Unless noted, all the products are slightly sticky, slightly too chewy, slightly bouncy, and have slight toothpack. Serving size is 10 ounces of cooked spaghetti (about four ounces dry), a main serving.

As published in an **August 1988** report.

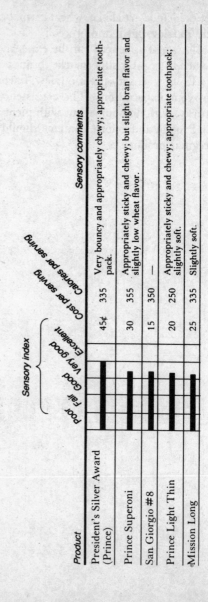

Product	Sensory index (Poor, Fair, Good, Very good, Excellent)	Cost per serving	Calories per serving	Sensory comments
President's Silver Award (Prince)		45¢	335	Very bouncy and appropriately chewy; appropriate toothpack.
Prince Superoni		30	355	Appropriately sticky and chewy; but slight bran flavor and slightly low wheat flavor.
San Giorgio #8		15	350	—
Prince Light Thin		20	250	Appropriately sticky and chewy; appropriate toothpack; slightly soft.
Mission Long		25	335	Slightly soft.

Brand			Comments
Town House (Safeway)	15	355	—
Prince	15	360	Appropriately sticky.
Golden Grain	20	325	Slightly soft.
Ronzoni #8	20	345	—
American Beauty	20	375	Slightly soft.
Lady Lee (Lucky)	15	335	Slightly soft.
Luxury #4	20	365	Slightly soft.
Sidari #144	15	370	—
La Rosa #8	15	340	Slightly soft.
Kroger	15	355	Appropriately sticky.
A&P #6	15	380	—
Spigadoro #3	15	355	Too sticky.
Pathmark #8	15	410	High toothpack.
Merlino's Long	25	350	Too sticky; slightly soft and slightly too gummy.
De Cecco #12	30 —	380	High toothpack.
Creamette	10	370	High toothpack.
Skinner	25	380	High toothpack and no bounce; slightly too gummy.
No Frills #8 (Pathmark)	10	370	High toothpack and no bounce; slightly too gummy.
Buitoni High Protein	50	480	High toothpack and no bounce; slightly too gummy; slight bran and whole-wheat flavors; slightly low wheat flavor.
R F (Ravarino & Freschi)	25	390	High toothpack and no bounce; slightly too gummy.
Da Vinci	25	405	High toothpack and no bounce; slightly too gummy.

Ratings of Spaghetti *(cont'd)*

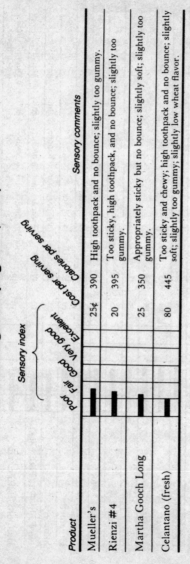

Product	Sensory index					Cost per serving	Calories per serving	Sensory comments
	Poor	Fair	Good	Very good	Excellent			
Mueller's		▮				25¢	390	High toothpack and no bounce; slightly too gummy.
Rienzi #4		▮				20	395	Too sticky, high toothpack, and no bounce; slightly too gummy.
Martha Gooch Long		▮				25	350	Appropriately sticky but no bounce; slightly soft; slightly too gummy.
Celantano (fresh)		▮				80	445	Too sticky and chewy; high toothpack and no bounce; slightly soft; slightly too gummy; slightly low wheat flavor.

Spaghetti Sauces

Not so very long ago, most people made their spaghetti sauce from scratch. Not anymore. Manufacturers have convinced about two-thirds of the home sauce-makers to buy their convenient prepared spaghetti sauces.

Ingredients

Most commercial sauces list tomato paste as the main ingredient, although many also contain some tomato solids and skins, and bits of onion. Mushroom sauces contain slices and pieces of mushroom. But the meat and meat-flavored sauces consist of very little meat—possibly less than 3 percent by weight.

By way of comparison, homemade meatless sauces, when drained, contain from seven to nine ounces of tomato solids and skins, onion and other vegetable bits. The recipe for homemade meat sauce (see page 199) contains 10 ounces of drained solids.

Flavor

An excellent spaghetti sauce is a red to red-orange color and has a moderately thick consistency. It also has a distinct fresh-tomato flavor. Somewhat spicy, it carries a hint of herbs, typically oregano and basil. A good meat sauce should have some fresh-meat flavor and aroma; mushroom sauce should taste of mushrooms.

Homemade sauces usually live up to those expectations. Most especially, they tend to have a strong, clear, fresh-tomato flavor.

Many commercial sauces lack that fresh-tomato flavor and are rather bland. Mushroom, meat, and meat-flavored sauces tend to lack the flavor associated with their types. Many meatless sauces are overly sweet or too thick and gummy.

Spaghetti sauce should be thick enough to coat the pasta, though.

The thinnest commercial sauces are similar in consistency to a slightly thickened tomato soup.

Nutrition

A meatless spaghetti sauce over pasta, sprinkled with Parmesan and served with a salad, is a relatively nutritious main dish that's not especially high in calories. Such a meal would provide about one-third of a person's recommended daily allowance for various nutrients, including protein. And it would contain much less fat and more carbohydrate than a meal of beef, potatoes, and a green vegetable.

A three-quarters-cup serving of an average meatless product contains 145 calories, three grams of protein, five grams of fat, and 21 grams of carbohydrate. The homemade meatless sauces on pages 199–200 are lower in fat than most commercial products and contain fewer calories (105 per serving).

Commercial sauces also tend to be high in sodium, providing an average of 800 milligrams per serving. The homemade sauces contain an average of 525 milligrams of sodium.

In the old days, simmering a sauce in an iron pot supposedly helped add iron to the daily diet. It does. Consumers Union's testers checked the iron content of a meatless sauce before and after simmering it in a cast-iron pot for three minutes or so. Before simmering, the sauce contained about two milligrams of iron per three-quarters-cup serving. After cooking, the iron content had doubled.

Recommendations

If you want an excellent homemade sauce, try one of the recipes that follow. The sauces have a zesty fresh-tomato-and-herbs taste, and the sauce with meat has the added richness of good meat flavor. The recipes are easy to make.

If you prefer the convenience of a commercial sauce, take your favorite brand and dress it up yourself. Using the sauce as a base, add fresh vegetables, meat, and mushrooms as desired.

Homemade Spaghetti Sauce

These spaghetti sauces are easy to make. You can make the basic recipe plain or dress it up with mushrooms or meat. If you like a zestier sauce, you can make the marinara recipe. Both recipes yield six servings of three-quarters-cup each.

Basic recipe

3 tbsp. olive oil
One 28-oz. can *Redpack* concentrated crushed tomatoes
One 15-oz. can *Contadina* tomato sauce
1 tbsp. minced dehydrated onion
½ tsp. minced dehydrated garlic
½ tsp. dried basil
¼ tsp. black pepper
1 tsp. oregano
½ tsp. dried parsley

Heat the olive oil in a six-quart saucepan over medium heat. Add the crushed tomatoes and tomato sauce. Add the remaining ingredients. Blend in thoroughly. Simmer for 30 minutes over low heat, stirring often.

For mushroom sauce, sauté one drained four-and-a-half-ounce container of mushrooms in the olive oil. Continue as for basic sauce.

For meat sauce, brown one-half pound of ground beef in a pan. Drain off fat; add to basic sauce during last 10 minutes of simmering.

Marinara recipe

3 tbsp. olive oil
1 small onion, chopped
1 celery stalk, chopped

½ medium green pepper, chopped
1 28-oz. can *Redpack* Italian-style whole tomatoes in sauce
1 15-oz. can *Contadina* tomato sauce
½ tsp. minced dehydrated garlic
½ tsp. dried basil
¼ tsp. black pepper
1 tsp. oregano
½ tsp. dried parsley

Heat the olive oil in a six-quart saucepan over medium heat. Add the fresh onion, celery, and green pepper, and sauté until transparent. Add the tomato products and stir thoroughly. Add the remaining ingredients. Simmer the sauce for 30 minutes, stirring frequently.

Fresh Chicken

Fried, roasted, or stewed chicken, chicken soup, and all manner of other chicken dishes freeze well. Once frozen, cooked chicken becomes a very fast food, easily thawed in a microwave oven, a conventional oven, or on a cooktop.

Chicken is wholesome and (if you don't eat the skin) low in fat. These factors probably contributed to poultry having passed beef in popularity.

Chicken's reputation as a cheap meat has helped its popularity, too. In the supermarket, whole chicken and some cut-up parts are cheaper per pound than beef. But chicken's success also owes a good deal to clever marketing and food engineering.

Chicken is a relative novelty in the nation's meat markets. As recently as the 1920s, farmers valued chickens mainly for eggs; a chicken came to table only when her egg-laying days were done. Mrs. Wilmer Steele of Ocean View, Delaware, is generally credited with starting the chicken-as-meat industry in 1923, when she began to sell live chickens for eating. She got 62 cents a pound, feathers and all—a hefty price, in view of the dollar's buying power back then.

Once, the chicken that came to market was a free-range bird that pecked for her livelihood in the nation's barnyards. Today's chicken is a factory product, and the factory is no spa. The chicken lives out her short life in a cramped cage, eating feed laced with antibiotics and added nutrients, her beak snipped so she can't peck her cage-mates. Where once she took 16 weeks to reach two pounds, she now plumps up to four pounds in less than eight weeks. And the seasonal breeding that produced "spring chickens" has given way to year-round production.

Modern mass-produced chicken isn't always a nameless commodity product, though. About 50 percent of chicken sold in the United States carries a brand name. Frank Perdue of Perdue Farms created the market for brand-name fowl in the 1970s. Perdue's ads ("It takes a tough man to make a tender chicken") have helped sell truckloads of chicken in the Eastern and Central states and have made him a star in the bargain. Other producers soon entered the Star Wars—*Paramount* with Pearl Bailey and *Holly Farms* with Dinah Shore.

In a Consumers Union survey, the respondents said they were somewhat more likely to buy brand-name chicken than a store brand. Many cited quality as the reason.

Flavor

After cooking in a 375° F oven, a chicken breast should be slightly sweet, with the mild yet not-quite-bland mix of tastes and aromas that identifies white meat. Thighs need to have the stronger, more intense and meaty flavor that's characteristic of dark meat. A hint of salt and fat is all right for both sorts of meat. High-quality chicken should be very tender and juicy and keep its juiciness as it is chewed. There shouldn't be bitterness, rancidity, undue saltiness, stringiness, or other inappropriate traits.

The quality of the skin varies broadly. And a brand name—even an extensively promoted one—often isn't a useful guide to uniform high quality.

Free-range chicken, dear to the nostalgic memories of gourmets, is likely to prove quite flavorful. But the breasts may be no tastier than some brand-name and supermarket breasts. And free-range breasts are stunningly expensive—more than double to triple the price of other breasts.

Don't rely on a grade level to help you find the best chicken. Any chicken parts you buy are likely to be Grade A, whether the label says so or not. Grade B and C chickens usually end up as frozen pot pies, chicken-noodle soup, and the like. In any event, a Grade A sticker simply means that the chicken meets federal standards for looks and fleshiness; it's no guarantee of tenderness or tastiness.

Nutrition

Chicken doesn't contain much fat, so it delivers protein and other nutrients rather efficiently in terms of nutrients per calorie. To see what we mean, compare chicken, hamburger, and pork.

On average, you get 23 to 31 grams of protein from a three-and-a-half-ounce cooked serving of pork, hamburger, or chicken—more than 50 percent of an adult female's recommended daily protein allowance (and more than 40 percent of a man's).

Much of the fat in pork or beef is distributed throughout the muscle, where it helps tenderize the meat. In chicken, much of the fat is concentrated in or right underneath the skin. To reduce the calorie count of a chicken portion (or to reduce your fat intake), just don't eat the skin.

Chicken has other nutritional benefits. The fat it contains is higher in polyunsaturates than the fat in red meat—a possible advantage for people with overly high blood-cholesterol levels. Chicken is also a very good source of niacin, and it provides a significant amount of riboflavin, vitamin B_6, and phosphorus.

Economy

Despite its reputation, chicken isn't necessarily all that cheap when you consider cooking losses and inedible parts. Chicken breasts lose about 20 percent of their raw weight in cooking and almost 20 percent more when you discard the bones from the cooked meat. With thighs, you get only about 50 percent of the original weight. So the cost per pound of chicken you can actually eat is roughly twice the cost of the raw breasts or thighs. As a result, chicken often turns out to be no cheaper than hamburger.

Hamburger, too, slims down in cooking—by almost one-third of its raw weight. Even so, it's often considerably cheaper on your plate than chicken breasts or thighs. Only whole chicken or store-brand thighs beat hamburger in cost per serving; you often pay a premium for cut-up chicken. Brand-name chicken parts generally command a price premium over supermarket brands. And there isn't always more edible meat on brand-name bones to justify the extra money.

Some brand-name chicken parts, notably *Perdue* and *Empire* breasts, are indeed meatier than some supermarket parts. But certain supermarket brands provide more cooked meat than some brand-name parts. In any event, buxomness alone doesn't make a chicken a good buy; the meatiest parts are neither the cheapest per portion nor the tastiest.

Sanitation

Salmonella bacteria cause salmonellosis, an illness whose effects can range from a mild upset stomach to violent gastrointestinal distress. It can be lethal if a victim is very young or very old. Salmonellosis is one of the major food-borne illnesses, and poultry is a major source of it. (See also "Salmonella from Eggs," p. 49.)

Even contaminated chicken, however, won't threaten your health if you handle the chicken properly—salmonella bacteria are killed during cooking. Your risk arises from improperly cooked poultry and the bacteria left by the uncooked poultry on a cutting board, utensil, or platter, which could contaminate the cooked chicken or other foods. Immediately after preparing raw chicken, clean utensils and surfaces thoroughly. And cook the bird completely.

Storage

If chicken isn't well iced and delivered quickly to market, or if it languishes in a showcase, it will develop off-flavors, off-odors, and other signs of spoilage. Your meal may not prove appetizing unless you pick a reasonably fresh product.

Chicken labeling that gives a "sell by" date is your only possible guide to freshness. Unfortunately, no federal regulations state how far in advance this date may be set, or even that it be provided. At least one company has said it sets sell-by dates 10 days beyond the date of a chicken's slaughter. But other companies may set a longer interval. When you shop for chicken, you may find samples still in showcases after their sell-by dates. Some may not carry a sell-by date at all.

Recommendations

Buying a brand-name bird won't guarantee superior taste or even consistent quality. But you're apt to pay a premium price for the brand name.

When you shop for chicken, just compare the purchase price of your alternatives. Once you've identified the cheapest brand per pound, select the breasts or thighs that look plump.

To find the freshest chicken, select the package with the latest sell-by date. If you're going to freeze the bird, be sure to rewrap it in freezer wrap. Chicken will then keep in the freezer for about six months without much loss in quality.

CHICKEN
Store Brands Versus Name Brands

Samples within a brand tend to vary in quality. The dots on the chart show how Consumers Union scored each sample. Only certain brands offered reasonably consistent quality. Listed alphabetically.

As published in a **February 1989** report.

Worse ←————→ Better

		Worse				Better
Store brands		●	◑	○	◐	⊙
Associated Stores	Breasts				•	•••••
	Thighs	•		•••	••	•
Gold-n-Fancy (Waldbaum's)	Breasts		•		•••••	
	Thighs			•	•••	••
Lobel's (free range)	Breasts				•••	•••
Sugar Plum (Food Emporium)	Breasts				••••	•••
	Thighs			•	•••	•••
Name brands						
Cookin' Good	Breasts				•••	•••
	Thighs				•••	•••
Cookin' Good (whole birds)	Breasts			•	••••	••
	Thighs			•	••••••	
Country Pride	Breasts			••	••••	
	Thighs			••	•••	••
Empire (kosher)	Breasts			•	•••••	
	Thighs			•	••••	••
Empire (kosher, whole birds)	Breasts			•	••••••	
	Thighs			•	•••••	•
Holly Farms	Breasts			•	••••	•
	Thighs			•	••	•••
Perdue Oven Stuffer	Breasts			••••	••	•
Perdue Prime Parts	Breasts		•	•••	••	•
	Thighs			•	••••••	
Perdue (whole birds)	Breasts				•••	•••
	Thighs			•	••••	•

Hamburger

Fast-food establishments account for a great deal of hamburger consumption in the United States. But ground meat is still served regularly, in one form or another, in a very high percentage of households. The varieties of ground beef available at supermarkets vary substantially in price because price and fat content have a close relationship. The cheaper the hamburger meat, the higher the fat content. Sometimes the package label states fat content. Sometimes it doesn't. Packages labeled "ground beef" (with a maximum percentage of fat or a minimum amount of lean stated on the label) are generally the cheapest per pound and contain the highest percentage of fat.

The next cheapest type may be labeled "ground chuck," "lean beef," "ground beef, 80 percent lean," or "ground beef, does not exceed 22 percent fat."

More expensive ground beef will be labeled "ground round," "extralean beef," or "ground beef, 16 percent fat." The most expensive is usually "ground sirloin."

"Hamburger meat" and "ground beef" are designations one tends to use interchangeably, but there is a difference. "Hamburger meat" is ground beef to which seasonings and beef fat may have been added while the meat was being ground. "Ground beef" is just that, without any extras (but seasonings may be present if they are identified on the label).

Prepackaged ground beef is often red on the outside and a grayish shade inside. That's the result of the oxymyoglobin in meat. This natural pigment combines with oxygen when exposed to air, and turns red.

Freshness

When you buy ground beef, make sure the plastic film on the package isn't torn. Choose a package that feels cold, and make it one of the last items you select before going to the checkout counter.

Refrigerate ground beef as soon as possible after you buy it. Store the meat in the coldest part of the refrigerator, in its original transparent plastic film wrapping. If the meat has been wrapped in butcher paper, rewrap it in plastic film. If you don't plan on cooking the beef within a couple of days, freeze the package. It should keep for a couple of weeks. For longer storage, wrap the meat in tightly sealed aluminum foil, freezer paper, or plastic bags. If your freezer operates at 0° F, the meat should keep quite well for as long as three months. You can keep track of storage time by marking each package with the date it was placed in the freezer.

When you get around to thawing frozen ground beef, move the package from the freezer to the refrigerator. That will result in slow but safe thawing, because the meat will remain cold. For quick thawing, place the meat in a watertight wrapper in cold water or defrost it in a microwave oven; then cook it as soon as it is thawed.

Safety

Authorities advise against eating or tasting raw ground beef because of the possibility of bacterial contamination. As for eating rare hamburgers, the inside shouldn't be raw; it should be at least brownish pink in color.

Recommendations

A cooked quarter-pounder ground from sirloin contains about 15 percent fat. Ground round and ground chuck have more fat, about 17–18 percent. "Ground beef" contains the most fat, about 20 percent.

The calorie count doesn't vary much from one kind of beef to the next. After cooking, a quarter-pound of ground raw meat runs 200 to 210 calories. Ground sirloin's protein content (about 22 grams) isn't much higher than the 19 grams in a ground beef burger.

It makes sense to buy hamburger by price. When you pay extra to get ground round or sirloin, you don't necessarily get significantly leaner beef. Nor do you get much more cooked yield or protein for your money. And you don't save calories in any significant way.

The only circumstance in which it might be wiser to pay extra for leaner meat is when the dish you're cooking will contain the fat that would be rendered out if you were cooking burgers.

For ordinary baking and grilling, buy either low-priced ground beef or, if you find that a bit chewy or too bland, ground chuck. And note that if a burger is going to be "dressed" with ketchup or other condiments, and if a meat loaf will be doused with sauce, the cheapest meat isn't likely to taste noticeably different from the next-cheapest.

Canned Tomatoes

The tomatoes you buy in cans often make better sauces and condiments than do fresh tomatoes. Unlike the Florida winter crop that provides most of the out-of-season fresh tomatoes in supermarkets, California processing tomatoes are allowed to ripen fully red before picking. All the luscious tomato aroma and flavor is held in by their sun-ripened red skins, and canners don't let it go to waste.

At canneries near the fields, the skins are removed by scalding the tomatoes with steam and running them through an abrasive device. After skinning and coring, the tomatoes are sorted. The best-looking ones are quickly popped into cans as whole tomatoes. The next-best are destined to be stewed tomatoes, and the remainder wind up as crushed tomatoes—or as puree, sauce, or paste.

Once each can of tomatoes has its allotment of fruit, some tomato juice or puree extracted from the skins and cores is poured into the can to fill it up. Salts, acid, and other enhancers of flavor, color, and texture are added, either dry or mixed in with the juice. Then the cans are sealed and passed through retorts, which are room-size pressure cookers that cook and commercially sterilize the contents of the cans.

The process is swift enough to leave intact a good share of the fresh fruit's vitamins and minerals, and also to avoid the musty, fermented quality that can arise when tomatoes sit too long in a pile.

Taste and Texture

There are obvious differences in size, shape, and cut among crushed tomatoes, peeled, whole tomatoes, and pear-shaped (Italian style) tomatoes. But the three types of tomato product don't differ much in flavor. Some of the crushed tomatoes contain bits of skin, stem, and green core.

Although canned tomatoes don't equal the excellent flavor expected of lightly stewed ripe garden tomatoes, the general level of quality is high. Differences in flavor and texture seem to relate more to the additives than to the tomatoes themselves.

Take the tomatoes' texture. Mushy softness is a sign of overripe or overcooked tomatoes, and spongy toughness is a sign of green tomatoes. But if calcium salts are added to the can, the tomatoes tend to stay firmer. Products whose label states that no calcium is added are likely to be slightly soft. (That softness may actually be a virtue, if you're making sauce and don't want big firm chunks.)

Most canners add table salt. Salt brings out the tomatoes' flavor, that slightly tart balance of natural acids and fruit sugars. And it can help mask off-notes such as bitterness and greenness.

Many no-salt-added products are imports, perfectly suitable for recipes in which the tomatoes will be further seasoned.

Nutrition

Tomatoes provide a major share of some important nutrients in the American diet. That's because tomatoes are consumed in such volume—fresh, canned, in soups, sauces, ketchup, and juice.

Vitamin C is the most important contribution. The canning process reduces the fruit's vitamin C content somewhat, but a half-cup serving of canned tomatoes still provides about 25 percent of an adult's Recommended Daily Allowance—a significant amount if your diet is short on citrus products.

Canned tomatoes are also rich in vitamin A. One serving provides about 15 percent of the RDA, making tomatoes a good food to serve in meals that omit yellow or leafy green vegetables.

Because tomatoes have inconsequential amounts of protein, fats, and carbohydrates, they also have very few calories. There are only about 25 calories in a half-cup serving. That means tomatoes can have a prominent place in a weight-loss regimen.

Those who are concerned about their sodium intake should note that a serving of even the most sodium-laden product contains less than one-eighth teaspoon of salt. If the tomatoes are going into a soup or sauce, you may wish to start with no-salt-added tomatoes, the better to adjust the seasonings yourself.

Tomato Tips

Tomato sauce is much the same as puree, but with the addition of flavorings such as peppers, herbs, and spices. Tomato sauce and tomato puree can usually be substituted for each other. Tomato paste has been cooked down until it contains more than 24 percent tomato solids. To substitute paste for puree, use half the quantity specified and make up the difference with any liquid suitable for the recipe.

Recommendations

Tomatoes are worthy of being eaten plain, and they're part of an endless stream of recipes for sauces, casseroles, and soups. They contain some important nutrients while being blessed with few calories. And canned tomatoes are cheap year round—much cheaper than fresh tomatoes in any season.

If you're using the tomatoes in a recipe, buy by price. If you're going to eat them as a side dish, choose a higher-quality product.

Ratings of Canned Tomatoes

Listed by types; within types, listed in order of sensory index. Brands with identical scores are listed alphabetically. Except as noted, all have the appropriate level of saltiness (moderate), sourness (slight), and sweetness (very slight). Differences between closely ranked products are slight.

As published in a **July 1989** report.

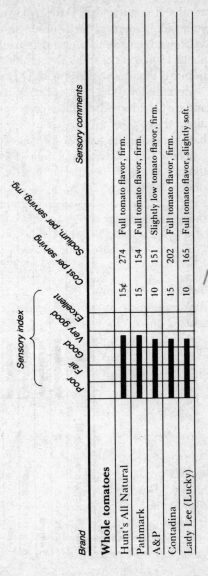

Brand	Sensory index (Poor / Fair / Good / Very good / Excellent)	Cost per serving	Sodium, per serving, mg	Sensory comments
Whole tomatoes				
Hunt's All Natural		15¢	274	Full tomato flavor, firm.
Pathmark		15	154	Full tomato flavor, firm.
A&P		10	151	Slightly low tomato flavor, firm.
Contadina		15	202	Full tomato flavor, firm.
Lady Lee (Lucky)		10	165	Full tomato flavor, slightly soft.

Ratings of Canned Tomatoes (cont'd)

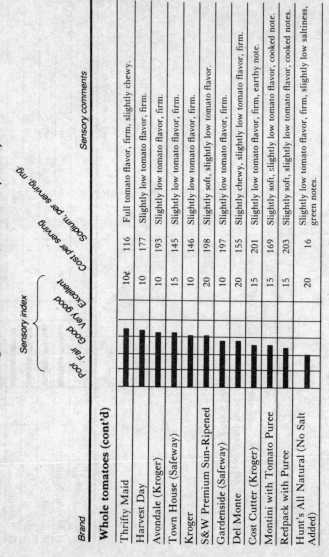

Brand	Sensory index (Poor, Fair, Good, Very good, Excellent)	Cost per serving	Sodium per serving, mg	Sensory comments
Whole tomatoes (cont'd)				
Thrifty Maid		10¢	116	Full tomato flavor, firm, slightly chewy.
Harvest Day		10	177	Slightly low tomato flavor, firm.
Avondale (Kroger)		10	193	Slightly low tomato flavor, firm.
Town House (Safeway)		15	145	Slightly low tomato flavor, firm.
Kroger		10	146	Slightly low tomato flavor, firm.
S&W Premium Sun-Ripened		20	198	Slightly soft, slightly low tomato flavor.
Gardenside (Safeway)		10	197	Slightly low tomato flavor, firm.
Del Monte		20	155	Slightly chewy, slightly low tomato flavor, firm.
Cost Cutter (Kroger)		15	201	Slightly low tomato flavor, firm, earthy note.
Montini with Tomato Puree		15	169	Slightly soft, slightly low tomato flavor, cooked note.
Redpack with Puree		15	203	Slightly soft, slightly low tomato flavor, cooked notes.
Hunt's All Natural (No Salt Added)		20	16	Slightly low tomato flavor, firm, slightly low saltiness, green notes.

Product			Comments
Nutradiet (No Salt Added)	25	23	Slightly low tomato flavor, firm, slightly low saltiness, green notes.
Pride of the Farm	10	67	Slightly soft, low tomato flavor, various off-notes; earthy, fermented, plastic.
Pine Cone	10	85	Slightly soft, low tomato flavor, slightly low saltiness, various off-notes; earthy, fermented, plastic.
Kroger (No Salt Added)	15	20	Low tomato flavor, firm, slightly low saltiness, green notes, earthy off-note.

Italian-style tomatoes

Product			Comments
Hunt's All Natural	15	294	Full tomato flavor, firm, slightly chewy.
Pope Imported from Spain	10	175	Slightly low tomato flavor, firm.
Contadina	20	215	Full tomato flavor, firm, slightly chewy.
Progresso Italian Imported	15	35	Slightly soft, slightly low tomato flavor, slightly low saltiness.
Cento Imported Italian [1]	10	33	Slightly soft, slightly low tomato flavor, slightly low saltiness.
Rienzi Italian Imported [1]	10	30	Slightly soft, slightly low tomato flavor, slightly low saltiness.
Rienzi with Puree Imported [1]	15	30	Slightly soft, slightly low tomato flavor, slightly low saltiness.
Pope Italian Imported [1]	15	42	Slightly soft, slightly low tomato flavor, slightly low saltiness.

Ratings of Canned Tomatoes *(cont'd)*

Brand	Sensory index	Cost per serving	Sodium, per serving, mg	Sensory comments
Crushed tomatoes				
Redpack Ready-to-Use	Very good	15¢	195	Full tomato flavor.
Progresso with Puree	Very good	15	185	Full tomato flavor.
Montini Concentrated	Very good	15	148	Full tomato flavor, cooked notes, some skins and stems.
Pope Concentrated	Very good	15	234	Full tomato flavor, some skins and stems.
Contadina with Puree	Good	15	293	Full tomato flavor, lots of skins and stems.
Rosa	Fair	10	109	Slightly low tomato flavor, cooked notes, some skins and stems.
Rienzi in Puree Imported [1]	Fair	15	33	Slightly low tomato flavor, slightly low saltiness, green notes.

Sensory index scale: Poor, Fair, Good, Very good, Excellent

[1] According to ingredients list, no salt added.

Hot Dogs

Hot dogs are low in protein and high in fat and sodium. You can buy a hot dog that has a little less fat than most, but you'll probably sacrifice some of what makes a good hot dog taste great.

If you're prudent about restricting the amount of fat in your diet, you shouldn't eat hot dogs. And maybe you shouldn't eat them in any case.

Ingredients

Hot dogs are mostly water and fat. Descendants of the sausage, they're made of odds and ends of meat ground with water and spices, pumped into casings, cooked, and cured.

Hot-dog meat can be almost anything. Most hot dogs are made with beef or a combination of beef and other meats. Some are made with chicken or turkey. A few add chili or cheese.

Hot dogs have a poor reputation not only because of their high fat content but also because their finely ground texture can disguise almost any kind of meat—and, some years ago, routinely did. Now, under U.S. Department of Agriculture regulations, lips, snouts, and other assorted animal parts can be used only if they are indicated in the product's name and in the ingredients list. That type of hot dog is rare today.

The main hot-dog ingredient these days is the scraps and trimmings of muscle meat—that is, meat that was once attached to the skeleton of the animal.

The average cooked hot dog is a little over half water. Most of that is water that's found naturally in meat. But the USDA allows manufacturers to add up to 10 percent water, usually in the form of ice to keep the meat cool while it's being ground.

The USDA also lets manufacturers make hot dogs with up to 30 percent fat, the amount in a well-marbled steak. Fifty-five years ago, hot dogs were only about 20 percent fat. Nowadays, most contain between 25 and 30 percent fat, but a fair number of poultry hot dogs have 20 percent fat or less.

With so much water and fat, it's no surprise that there isn't a lot of protein in a hot dog.

Labeling

If you want to know *exactly* what's in the hot dogs you're eating, read the label, where ingredients must be listed in descending order by weight. If a hot dog is made from only one kind of meat or poultry, that must be part of the product name: "beef franks," "turkey wieners."

"Meat" franks are predominantly beef and pork, although they may contain up to 15 percent poultry meat. Here the descending-order rule doesn't always hold. If the label lists "beef, pork," you know the hot dogs contain more beef than pork. But if the ingredients list starts out "beef and pork," you can't be sure; an "and" instead of a comma between the two main meats invokes what's called the 70/30 rule. The USDA passed the rule to allow manufacturers to get meat for their mixed-meat hot dogs as cheaply as possible without having to change the label every time they changed the formula. The "70" means that the two meats must together make up at least 70 percent of the meat. The "30" means that the exact amounts can be juggled, as long as neither meat is less than 30 percent of the meat in the hot dog.

Manufacturers can use the words "lowfat" or "lean" or "lite" on the hot-dog label, but the words must be accompanied by an explanation. For example: "This product contains no more than 20 percent fat whereas the USDA standard for franks allows 30 percent fat."

The USDA lets processors add up to 3.5 percent nonmeat and nonwater ingredients. Those are usually binders, such as calcium-reduced dried skim milk. In addition, manufacturers can add small amounts of preservatives and flavorings, which make up the rest of the ingredients you see on a label. Likely to be on the list: salt, sweeteners such as corn syrup or dextrose, ascorbic acid (vitamin C) or one of its derivatives such as sodium erythorbate or sodium ascorbate, and nitrite.

Of these, nitrite is by far the most controversial. Nitrite preserves meat and gives it its characteristic flavor and color. Federal rules require the use of nitrite or its chemical precursor, nitrate, in all cured meats—including bacon, ham, and smoked fish—because it inhibits the growth of the bacterium *Clostridium botulinum,* which causes botulism, a form of food poisoning that's often fatal.

The controversy centers on whether nitrite poses a cancer hazard to humans in the quantities consumed. The Food and Drug Administration and the USDA have permitted the use of lowered amounts of nitrite but have not banned it, mainly because no substitute has been developed that matches its preservative effects. While research on alternatives continues, many scientists consider any risks posed by nitrite to be minimal, and preferable to the risks of doing without it in cured meats.

Adding ascorbic acid or a derivative to cured meats lets manufacturers use less nitrite and still preserve their product. In addition, phosphates and/or citrates are sometimes added to aid in the curing process.

Like nitrite, salt is a traditional curing ingredient. Most hot dogs are high in sodium. The best-tasting hot dogs have more than 400 milligrams of sodium—one of several unfortunate facts of life about hot dogs.

People with a sensitivity to the flavor enhancer monosodium glutamate should avoid hot dogs with that ingredient.

Nutrition

From a nutritional standpoint, the best hot dog is the one with the highest proportion of protein to fat. Another unfortunate fact about hot dogs: A good-tasting hot dog isn't likely to have a better than fair protein-to-fat ratio.

Poultry hot dogs have a much better protein-to-fat ratio than beef or meat franks.

A beef hot dog averages about 155 calories without the bun. So, if you eat more than one, go easy on dessert. You can do a little better with poultry dogs. Their calorie content averages close to 120.

Flavor

Hot dogs come fully cooked, so when you "cook" a frank you are really just reheating it. Grilling can add a special flavor and crispiness that many people like. Most people heat their franks in boiling water. You could follow a routine recommended by the National Hot Dog and Sausage Council: Place the hot dogs in a pan of boiling water, cover them, remove the pan from the heat, and let it stand for seven minutes. Or you might want to microwave hot dogs for a minute or two (depending on the oven's power and on the number of franks in the batch being heated).

The ideal hot dog is relatively dense, packed full of meat, and has a meaty taste. However, because hot dogs are made from highly processed meats combined with added flavoring and preservatives, the kind of meat used is less important than the overall texture and seasoning of the product. A strong meaty flavor should be balanced by a slight but distinct fat flavor.

As hot dogs are cooked, a layer of protein coagulates on the outside, sealing in the juices. On an ideal hot dog, that "skin" resists slightly when you bite into it. Breaking through this outer layer, your mouth is rewarded with a spurt of meaty juice. The meat at the center is moist and firm, not hard and dry or soft and gummy. The ideal hot dog doesn't crumble into pieces as you chew but holds together, without being doughy.

Recommendations

A hot dog, like all meats, is high in saturated fats. But unlike most meats, it gives a low protein return for the fat you must consume to get it, and it contains a lot of sodium.

No hot dog will bring joy to the heart of a nutritionist or prudent dieter, so buy the franks that taste best to you.

Canned Beans

Beans are the basis for a large number of simple heat-and-eat dishes that can be ready for the table in little more time than it takes to lay out the silverware.

The most common canned bean varieties consist of navy beans, also called, simply, small white beans. But there are also products made from pinto beans, pink beans, and Great Northern beans (a common white bean, two to three times as big as a navy bean but with about the same taste). No matter what the variety, once beans are cooked in sauce, their distinctive characteristics become too submerged for any differences in flavor to come through.

Although not a perfect food, beans are a surprisingly good source of several key nutrients (see pages 220–22). The small amounts of meat, usually bacon, in many canned products help round out beans' plentiful plant protein.

Flavor

Some brands of canned beans have a meaty taste, others lean toward the sweet, spicy, or smoky. These are trivial departures from a balanced bean flavor.

Defects that aren't so trivial include bitter and burned flavors and strong, uncharacteristic spices.

Regardless of the sauce, beans should be moist and moderately firm, about as resistant to the bite as sliced American cheese.

Overall, canned beans tend to be soft and a bit dry—texture problems possibly attributable in part to the canning. A slight metallic flavor may be present in the beans; that seems to be characteristic of canned beans in sauce, be they packaged in cans or glass.

Here's how the types taste:

Pork and Beans This Southern cousin to baked beans should have a meaty flavor related to the pork and pork fat it contains. It could have moderate tomato, smoke, onion, or "brown spice" accents (brown spices come from the cinnamon/clove/allspice family).

Baked Beans A sweet flavor is what you should expect in baked beans.

Barbecue Beans Southwest-style spiciness and barbecue-sauce sweetness are characteristic for this type. Some meat or smoke flavors (or both) are common. Meat flavor is not an infallible clue that meat was in the recipe. Yeast (extract or torula yeast) or hydrolyzed vegetable protein (HVP) can add a "meaty" flavor.

Vegetarian Beans Several companies put out a type called vegetarian. Some brands may suffer from flavors that shouldn't be there—untypical or unbalanced spices and bitter or scorched flavors.

Nutrition

If baked beans were a perfectly balanced food, all the bars on the chart below would be the same length as the one for calories. Some desirable nutrients are found in surplus—protein, fiber, and iron. That's good news if they are in short supply elsewhere in the day's diet. Sodium is also in surplus, a warning sign for those on low-sodium diets. Fat density is low, a good sign for those whose diets already have too much fat.

Beans, even those cooked in a sugary, fatty sauce, are a low-calorie food. A side-dish serving of a half-cup of beans averages only 164 calories. Beans also contain relatively large amounts of vegetable protein, fiber, and iron. As such, they carry a dense load of nutrients for their small load of calories.

The protein in beans is not as complete as that found in meat or dairy foods because the amino acids aren't in the proportions required for human nutrition. But when beans are eaten with meat products, milk, or cheese, the foods complement one another and the bean protein is more completely utilized by the body.

Average Baked Beans
(half-cup servings)

% daily intake		0	25	50
Calories	164			
Protein	8 g.			
Fiber	8 g.			
Calcium	73 mg.			
Iron	3 mg.			
Total fat	2 g.			
Sodium	475 mg.			

Profiles are based on an average woman's daily dietary needs. Recommended amounts for an average man are greater for calories, protein, and fat; for children, lower.

As published in a **January 1989** report.

Meat—pork, bacon, even wieners—is an ingredient in some canned beans, but it's there in such negligible amounts that it won't fully complement the bean protein. In fact, the pork and pork fat don't have much of an impact on the fat content of the dish, adding only one to three grams of fat and nine to 27 calories. Unlike meat, beans are practically devoid of fat.

Whereas the fiber in beans is generously supplied, it is mostly soluble fiber, the type that breaks down in digestion, unlike the insoluble fiber found in some grain products, such as wheat bran. Beans' fiber is the sort that's abundant in prunes, pears, oranges, apples, cauliflower, zucchini, sweet potatoes, and corn and oat bran. It adds bulk and thickness to the contents of the stomach, which may help dieters control their appetites, and it slows the absorption of sugars from the small intestine, which may be of some benefit to diabetics.

Soluble fiber is not the type that has been recommended by some experts as important in reducing the risk of colon cancer. That's insoluble fiber (cellulose and lignin), which is abundant in grains. Although a half-cup of beans can provide the daily requirement of soluble fiber, you should still eat breads and cereals to get their insoluble fiber.

A half-cup of beans provides one-sixth of the recommended day's ration of iron, an excellent showing for this mineral, which is likely to be in short supply in many people's diets.

Like many other prepared foods, canned beans are heavily salted. Most yield 450 to 500 milligrams of sodium in a half-cup serving. That would use up a major portion of the day's allotment for someone on a severely sodium-restricted diet.

In addition to all other nutrients, beans contain complex carbohydrates called oligosaccharides. Since humans do not have enzymes to digest these carbohydrates, they pass into the lower intestine. There they are acted on by nonharmful bacteria that are normally present in the colon, with gas production as the end result.

Not all people suffer those consequences of eating beans. You can minimize the problem if you rinse the beans thoroughly before cooking them in the recipe. That leaches out the oligosaccharides. Of course, you're pouring some protein and other nutrients down the drain, but the trade-off in comfort might be worth it.

Recommendations

Eat beans: They're inexpensive, easy to fix, and a good source of several key nutrients. They are good in a weight-loss regimen because they are low in calories and very filling. You can always dress up a can of beans with catsup, Worcestershire sauce, or wieners.

Ratings of Canned Beans

Listed by types; within types, listed in order of estimated overall sensory quality as shown by the sensory index.
As published in a January 1989 report.

Pork and beans

Product	Sensory index	Cost	Calories	Sodium, mg	Sensory comments
Bush's Best Deluxe	Very good	15¢	164	504	Meaty and smoky with brown-spice notes. Soft beans with little flavor.
Campbell's Home Style	Very good	15	154	504	Meaty and smoky with brown-spice notes. Little bean flavor.
Hunt's Big John Beans 'n Fixin's	Very good	30	194	519	Vinegar-sour smell; oniony flavor; meaty and smoky with brown-spice notes. Little bean flavor.
Town House (Safeway)	Good	15	151	624	Meaty.
Campbell's	Good	15	149	407	Soft beans with little flavor.
Van Camp's Beanee Weenee	Good	45	189	486	Vienna-sausage flavor dominates. Smoky, low sweetness. Soft wieners, soft beans with little flavor.

(Sensory index scale: Poor, Fair, Good, Very good, Excellent)

(Per serving: Cost, Calories, Sodium, mg)

Ratings of Canned Beans (cont'd)

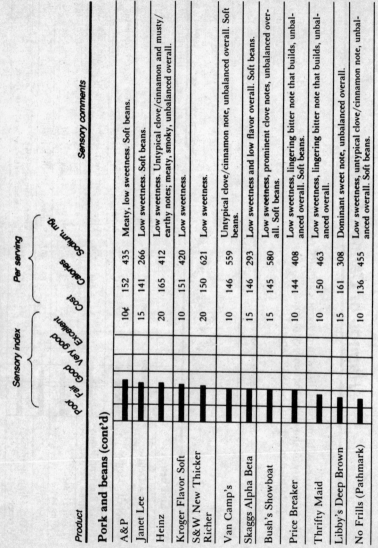

Product	Sensory index Poor / Fair / Good / Very good / Excellent		Cost	Calories	Sodium, mg	Sensory comments
Pork and beans (cont'd)						
A&P			10¢ 152		435	Meaty, low sweetness. Soft beans.
Janet Lee			15 141		266	Low sweetness. Soft beans.
Heinz			20 165		412	Low sweetness. Untypical clove/cinnamon and musty/earthy notes; meaty, smoky, unbalanced overall.
Kroger Flavor Soft			10 151		420	Low sweetness.
S&W New Thicker Richer			20 150		621	Low sweetness.
Van Camp's			10 146		559	Untypical clove/cinnamon note, unbalanced overall. Soft beans.
Skaggs Alpha Beta			15 146		293	Low sweetness and low flavor overall. Soft beans.
Bush's Showboat			15 145		580	Low sweetness, prominent clove notes, unbalanced overall. Soft beans.
Price Breaker			10 144		408	Low sweetness, lingering bitter note that builds, unbalanced overall. Soft beans.
Thrifty Maid			10 150		463	Low sweetness, lingering bitter note that builds, unbalanced overall.
Libby's Deep Brown			15 161		308	Dominant sweet note, unbalanced overall.
No Frills (Pathmark)			10 136		455	Low sweetness, untypical clove/cinnamon note, unbalanced overall. Soft beans.

Baked beans

Product					Notes
Van Camp's (bacon)		20	182	557	Meaty, smoky.
Bush's Best		15	177	531	Meaty, smoky. Soft beans.
The Allens		15	177	450	Meaty and smoky with mild brown-spice notes. Soft beans.
Thrifty Maid		15	171	474	Meaty and smoky with mild brown-spice notes. Soft beans.
Hanover		25	184	486	Meaty, smoky. Soft beans.
Campbell's Old Fashioned		15	165	623	Mildly meaty. Soft beans.
S&W Maple Sugar		20	170	473	Mildly meaty. Beany.
Van Camp's		20	181	347	Mildly meaty, prominent black pepper and sweet notes, unbalanced overall.
B&M New England Style		25	180	476	Smoky, mildly meaty; prominent acrid/scorched/burned and sweet notes; unbalanced overall.
S&W All Natural		25	172	514	Mildly meaty; somewhat bitter; prominent salty, acrid/scorched notes; unbalanced overall.
Kroger Country Style		15	177	477	No meatiness; prominent acrid/burned-molasses notes; unbalanced overall. Beany, variable bean firmness.
B&M Brick Oven (can)		25	175	410	Low sweetness; mildly meaty; prominent acrid/scorched/burned notes; unbalanced overall. Soft beans.
B&M Brick Oven (jar)		25	186	415	Mildly meaty; prominent acrid/scorched notes. Variable bean firmness.

Ratings of Canned Beans (cont'd)

Product	Sensory index	Cost	Calories	Sodium, mg	Sensory comments
Barbecue beans					
S&W New Texas Style	Good	15¢	155	582	Tomatoey, meaty, smoky, spicy, low sweetness. Soft beans.
Hanover	Good	25	190	279	Meaty and smoky with brown-spice notes, vinegar-sour smell. Soft beans with little flavor.
B&M Sweet Smoky Flavor	Good	30	193	570	Meaty and smoky with brown-spice notes. Soft beans with little flavor.
Campbell's	Good	20	156	660	Tomatoey, meaty, and smoky with spicy notes; low sweetness. Soft beans.
S&W Smokey Ranch	Fair	20	148	476	Meaty, peppery, low sweetness. Soft beans with little flavor.
Ranch Style	Fair	15	149	556	Meaty, peppery, low sweetness. Soft beans with little flavor.
Kroger	Poor	15	152	489	No meatiness; slightly spicy with prominent untypical cinnamon note; unbalanced overall.

Per serving: Calories, Sodium, mg

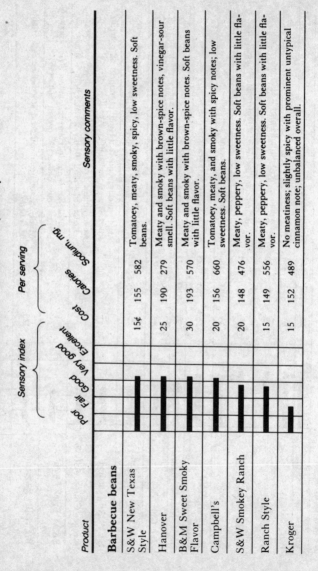

Vegetarian beans

Libby's Deep Brown		15	161	340	Tomatoey. Soft beans.
Heinz		15	147	528	Tomatoey; untypical clove/cinnamon notes; low sweetness; unbalanced overall. Soft beans.
B&M New Brick Oven		30	190	425	Low tomato notes; slightly spicy; prominent acrid/scorched/burned notes; unbalanced overall.
A&P		10	165	481	Tomatoey; low sweetness, unbalanced overall. Soft beans with a lingering bitterness that builds.
Van Camp's		15	150	523	Slightly tomatoey; slightly spicy with untypical clove notes; unbalanced overall. Soft beans.

Quick 'n' Spicy Beans

This recipe blends the flavors of beans, pork, onion, and tomato, with only a mild spiciness. If you like more zing, try adding additional garlic, chili powder, or cloves. For a vegetarian version that contains less sodium, try substituting one-half to one pound of sliced, fresh mushrooms for the pork and sauté the onion and mushrooms in one tablespoon vegetable oil.

> ¼ lb. salt pork, cubed
> 1 medium-size onion, chopped
> ½ tsp. ground mustard
> ¼ tsp. freshly ground black pepper
> 2 tsp. Worcestershire sauce
> ½ cup tomato puree
> 2 tbsp. molasses
> 3 tbsp. dark brown sugar
> ¼ cup water
> 5½ to 6 cups (3 cans) small white beans, drained

Using a heavy-duty four-quart pot, lightly brown the salt pork. Add the chopped onions and sauté till translucent. Add mustard, pepper, Worcestershire sauce, tomato puree. Stir well and simmer about three minutes. Add molasses, brown sugar, and water. Simmer for five minutes. Add the beans, stirring gently to mix well without breaking them. Simmer on low heat for about 30 minutes. Yield: 13 half-cup servings.

Salad Dressings

Supermarket shelves are jammed with bottles of Russian, Thousand Island, Italian, Green Goddess, Roquefort, French, Blue Cheese, and Taco salad dressings, and more. If a bottled product strikes you as not fresh enough, you can pick up a jar of refrigerated dressing over in the fresh-vegetable or dairy section. You can mix your own dressing with a packet of salad-dressing herbs and oil and vinegar. If you have a special dietary need, there are low-sodium or low-calorie products.

Flavors

French and Italian dressings, the most popular varieties, are vinaigrettes—sauces based on oil and vinegar, plus herbs and spices that give each dressing its special character. With a French dressing, those extras are typically salt, pepper, mustard, and garlic or onion; with an Italian dressing, they're a bolder array that includes basil, oregano, and garlic.

In America, however, the classic recipes have gone through some changes. "French" dressings usually contain tomato, which alters the flavor and color. And "Italian" dressings often come in "creamy" versions that may or may not contain dairy products.

The recipes on pages 231–32 were developed by Consumers Union as a yardstick for testing purposes. They include aromas and flavors at intensities considered ideal.

The French dressing has a moderate but not biting flavor and aroma of vinegar and onion, as well as a slight sourness and a hint of bitterness. The flavors are well blended, so that no one of them dominates. The dressing is devoid of gumminess. A commercial dressing should meet those standards, but few do.

Other qualities in a dressing are, within broad limits, a matter of personal preference. You may, after all, prefer a touch of extra sweetness or a stronger taste of oil.

Most commercial French dressings fall into a broad middle class. Among the common failings are a deficiency in onion or garlic flavor, a touch too much vinegar, or an unblended character. Diet dressings, too, may have a poor overall blend of flavor, among other things.

The recipe for Italian dressing is of the classic variety. It has a moderate level of the flavors and aromas of garlic and Italian herbs, a mild bite of vinegar, and a touch of sourness. A good commercial Italian dressing should have a similar taste.

A "creamy" Italian dressing should taste as if cream or mayonnaise has been added, with a creamy texture, moderate dairy flavors and aromas, and some mayonnaise taste.

Another variation on Italian dressing is a plainish vinaigrette compounded of red-wine vinegar and oil.

A so-so commercial Italian dressing suffers from such defects as a trace of excess sourness, too little onion or garlic, or a lack of basil and oregano.

Nutrition

There's not much nutrition in a dressing; such nutrients as a salad provides come mostly from the greens. Not surprisingly, only a minority of the dressings carry nutrition labeling. Some labels note sodium content, others don't.

Even information that *is* presented needs interpretation. Manufacturers are free to pick any serving size as a standard of measurement; most choose a one-tablespoon serving. But an average serving of dressing is apt to be several times that much, especially with the thicker dressings.

Salad dressing's chief contributions to the daily diet are fat and calories. The fat is generally from vegetable oil, and most of it is unsaturated. The oil supplies most of the calories. The typical calorie content of commercial dressings is nearly 100 calories per tablespoon (including the homemade recipes). Products with 40 calories or less term themselves reduced- or low-calorie dressings.

To be low in calories, a dressing must be made with little or no oil. Since oil is a key ingredient, low-calorie products, not surprisingly, resort to some fancy food technology to make up for the lack, often with lackluster results. Nevertheless, some reduced- and low-calorie products taste fine, especially among the Italian products.

A number of dressings provide a good dose of sodium, especially if you use several tablespoonsful as a serving. In general, Italian dressing tends to be rather high in sodium. For people on low-sodium diets, there are tasty alternatives, at least among Italian dressings.

Two Homemade Salad Dressings

One advantage of making your own salad dressing is that you can control the amount of sugar or salt it contains, or otherwise adjust the ingredients to suit your taste.

Each of the following recipes yields one cup.

Homestyle French Dressing

¾ cup salad oil
2 tbsp. water
2 tbsp. white vinegar
1 tsp. dry mustard
1 tsp. sugar
½ tsp. salt
½ tsp. white pepper
1 tbsp. ketchup
2 tsp. finely chopped onion

After measuring out the oil and setting it aside, mix the water and vinegar in a cup and put that aside as well. Now combine the mustard, sugar, salt, pepper, and ketchup in a small bowl. Into that bowl, pour about a tablespoonful of the oil and then about one-half tablespoon of the water-vinegar mixture, beating with a wire whisk until the mixture is smooth and creamy. Continue beating while adding small amounts of the oil and the water-vinegar mixture alternately. Stir in the onion. Refrigerate any leftover dressing.

Classic Italian Dressing

½ tsp. basil
½ tsp. oregano
¾ tsp. salt
½ tsp. sugar
¼ tsp. pepper
¼ tsp. crushed garlic (1 medium clove)
3 tbsp. red-wine vinegar
1 tbsp. water
¾ cup olive oil

Crumble the basil and oregano in the palm of your hand to release maximum flavor, then drop the crushed herbs into a jar, along with the salt, sugar, pepper, garlic, vinegar, and water. Cap the jar tightly and shake well. Now add the oil and shake again. Store the dressing in the refrigerator, but serve it at room temperature.

Lowfat Vegetable Oils

In an effort to eat less saturated fat, many people have switched from butter or lard to vegetable oils in cooking.

All vegetable oils contain some saturated fat, however. Indeed, tropical oils such as coconut and palm-kernel oil contain a lot of it.

If vegetable oils are not all alike, you might ask, what kind is *lowest* in saturated fat? The answer is, canola oil. Canola, sold by Procter & Gamble under the *Puritan* brand, has been on the market since 1986. It comes from rapeseed, a major Canadian crop. Although widely sold in Canada, canola oil took a while to catch on in the United States. For one thing, its original name—LEAR oil, for low erucic acid rapeseed oil—wasn't very appetizing. In 1988, the FDA authorized the use of its common name, canola. And with the help of an endorsement by the American College of Nutrition (which calls canola oil "an excellent choice to help meet . . . dietary recommendations for reducing saturated fat and cholesterol intake"), Procter & Gamble has promoted it heavily.

Consumers Union's tests comparing *Puritan* canola oil with two other top-selling vegetable oils—*Wesson,* made from soybeans, and *Mazola* corn oil—showed that *Puritan* has the lowest saturated fatty acid content at 7 percent. *Mazola* and *Wesson* have 14 and 15 percent, respectively. The three oils are similar in cost.

All three are mild in taste. The CU testers found that canola oil has a "clean" taste, with "slight fragrant green (cut-grass)" hints. It has a very slight oily feel in the mouth, and there are no off-tastes.

If you're seeking to modify your saturated-fat intake, you may find *Puritan* canola oil a helpful, healthful choice.

Pasta Salads

Food companies have come out with packaged salad-bar-style pasta salads you can make at home. *Mueller's Salad Bar Pasta, Betty Crocker Suddenly Salad,* and *Lipton Cool Side Salads* all contain dried pasta, along with herbs, spices, and dried vegetables. *The Betty Crocker* and *Lipton* add a bit of Parmesan cheese.

The mixes save you the bother of mincing vegetables and mixing a dressing. Otherwise, they don't save much time or money. Typically, all you do is boil the pasta and vegetables, then drain and rinse them. Mix the seasoning with some oil and water and toss with the pasta. The *Betty Crocker* mix packs the pasta and vegetables in a mesh bag, so you don't even need a colander to drain the pasta (although you may wish you'd used one when you try to get all the vegetables out of the bag).

As for each brand's Italian version, the *Mueller's* tastes the best. It has a heavy onion/garlic flavor, with a strong note of pepper and a good proportion of sauce to pasta. The *Betty Crocker* mix, judged good, tastes mostly of dehydrated vegetables. Even though the mix contains cheese, you may not easily detect its flavor. *Lipton,* the worst of the lot, has an intense garlic/onion flavor with a dehydrated, sulfury character.

A pasta salad made with fresh vegetables and your own mix of herbs and spices should taste better than any of these products.

Nutritionally, the three salads are more alike than different. All make a nutritious side dish. Calorie for calorie, the *Lipton* mix carries the greatest amount of desirable nutrients. The *Mueller's* has the most sodium: 400 milligrams per serving, compared with about 325 milligrams for the others.

Snacks

Chocolate Bars

Candy isn't just kids' stuff anymore. Adults buy more than half of it these days, and what they buy, mostly, is chocolate candy. Not necessarily the familiar *Hershey* bar of childhood, but fancier stuff, with a fancier price.

Those chocolate mavens aren't just your urban habitués of fancy-food boutiques, looking for yet another little luxury. Supermarkets across the land carry specialty brands like *Tobler, Lindt,* and *Droste* right alongside the *Nestlé's Crunch, Whitman's Milk Chocolate,* and *Hershey's Mr. Goodbar.*

Do you buy something superior when you peel off bills for a *Tobler* or a *Perugina* instead of spending loose change for a *Hershey* or a *Nestlé*? To find out, CU evaluated more than four dozen brands and varieties of chocolate bar—dark bittersweet chocolates, milk chocolates, white chocolates, and chocolates with added nuts, fruits, or crisped rice. The selection included imports from Switzerland, the Netherlands, Germany, Belgium, and Italy, as well as a broad range of domestic bars.

The results of the taste tests may throw the chocolate mavens into disarray. The high-priced brands weren't necessarily the best. And when it came to milk chocolates and chocolates with nuts or fruits, a number of moderately priced American brands did better than the imports.

Flavor

One food taster characterizes high-quality chocolate as "complicated, sophisticated . . . not child's play." Indeed, chocolate terminology can be like the rarefied language of the connoisseurs of fine wines.

But there are certain family resemblances from one brand of chocolate to the next. All chocolate has some "chocolate impact," varying from slight-to-moderate (white chocolate) to intense (dark and milk preparations). There are also hints of the nutty/woody character typical of the cacao from which chocolate is made. The flavor of any additions (fruit, caramel, or nuts) should be, at most, slight.

Other criteria, of course, depend on the particular kind of chocolate being sampled.

Dark Chocolate   This is the type of chocolate most prized by the chocolate connoisseur for its intensity. The best is very firm, with a brittleness that makes a piece snap off cleanly when you break it. It also melts very quickly and is only moderately creamy. It is slightly to moderately sweet, with a touch of sourness and bitterness as well. You shouldn't be able to taste distinct flavors of cocoa or milk.

Chocolate makers seem to be of several minds about sweetness. In the majority of products, bitterness is at least as strong as the sweetness level. (Bitterness is a relative term. No candy is anywhere near as harsh as, say, unsweetened baking chocolate.)

Milk Chocolate   American chocolate makers have long specialized in this type, as opposed to the darker kind. And until only a few years ago, Americans seemed to prefer the lighter, sweeter taste of milk chocolate. One chocolatier commented, in an article on chocolate trends: "We've historically been a milk-chocolate country because we were raised on *Hershey* bars."

In the best milk chocolate, the chocolate impact is intense, but slightly less so than in dark chocolate. The milky notes almost equal the chocolate impact. Slight sourness and slight flavors of cooked milk, caramel, or butterfat are okay; the taste of processed milk isn't. An excellent milk chocolate will also be slightly lower than dark chocolate in sourness, bitterness, snap, firmness, and speed of melting, but higher in sweetness and creaminess.

White Chocolate Strictly speaking, this isn't chocolate at all; it's made from sugar, milk powder, and cocoa butter. That butter, a main ingredient, theoretically contains no chocolate flavors once it has been pressed from the chocolate liquor. However, it is possible to detect some chocolate essence in some brands: Some makers actually add chocolate liquor.

The best white chocolate is very sweet, with only the slightest sour and bitter notes. Its texture is like that of an excellent milk chocolate; it has only a slight-to-moderate chocolate impact and slight milk character. There should be no cocoa flavor in a white chocolate.

Chocolate Bars Plus If you like a bit of crunch in your candy, you can get a chocolate bar with fruit, nuts, or crisped rice mixed in. There should be a proper wedding of the flavor and texture of the chocolate and what's mixed into it.

What's in a Chocolate Bar?

Chemically speaking, chocolate is quite complex.

Calories The best way for dieters to deal with chocolate is to avoid it. All chocolate—whether dark, milk, or white—is similarly fattening, about 150 calories per ounce.

Cocoa Mass It's possible to determine how much cocoa is used in a bar. Dark bars typically contain the most—anywhere from about 13 to as much as 25 percent. Milk chocolate is generally lower in cocoa content, as are most bars containing fruits, nuts, and the like. White chocolate contains only traces of cocoa.

Alkaloids Like coffee and tea, chocolate contains caffeine, a relatively mild, somewhat addictive stimulant. A bit of caffeine can provide a psychological lift and a wide-awake feeling. But too much—or even any, if you're sensitive to it—can induce unpleasant side effects.

Healthy adults are apt to feel stimulative effects after consuming 150 to 250 milligrams of caffeine, roughly the amount in a cup or two of brewed coffee. Some people can expect to suffer "coffee nerves," more formally called caffeinism or chronic caffeine intoxication, at intakes ranging from 200 to 750 milligrams a day.

Only chocoholics or the caffeine-sensitive are apt to have any problems with chocolate's caffeine content. You'd have to consume six to eight ounces of dark chocolate—or at least a pound or two of milk chocolate—to get the caffeine of one to two cups of coffee. White chocolate's caffeine is negligible.

Two other alkaloids, theophylline and theobromine, are closely related to caffeine. (All three are known chemically as methylxanthines.) Tea contains theophylline, but chocolate doesn't. Chocolate does contain a fair measure of theobromine, a very weak stimulant of the central nervous system. It's unlikely that most people will suffer any effects from the theobromine in chocolate bars.

Recommendations

Occasionally, you may come across a chocolate bar with a whitish or grayish film on the surface. The discoloration, called "bloom," can occur if chocolate is exposed to warmth; fat or sugar then migrates to the surface of the bar. Fat bloom is greasy and can be rubbed off; sugar bloom is crystalline. Bloom doesn't affect flavor or make chocolate unsafe. Don't worry about it.

Chocolate-Chip Cookies

Packaged chocolate-chip cookies aren't particularly expensive or particularly voluptuous. For years, they have been a standard snack or dessert in a brown-bag lunch and a child's lunchbox.

People who wanted a softer, sweeter, more chocolaty treat baked their own, most likely following the recipe immortalized on the *Nestlé* chocolate-chip package. That cookie was first devised by a woman named Ruth Wakefield in 1931, when she chopped a *Nestlé* candy bar into some cookie dough. That original cookie perhaps also qualifies as the first "gourmet" chocolate-chip cookie.

Today, the gourmet cookie—whether homemade, served up at a specialized cookie boutique, or fresh-baked at the supermarket— commands most of the attention and much of the money to be made in cookies. Wally Amos, literally now a *Famous Amos*, may have been the first to spot the possibilities of designer baked goods. His cookies, initially brought to market about 15 years ago, are among the most conspicuous on the gourmet cookie shelf of a store.

But competitors have come crowding in. And cookie bakeries built into supermarkets have become commonplace.

Oddly enough, the rise of the specialized cookie boutique and its rich fare (indeed, a trend toward all sorts of premium-priced sweets) coincides with a heightened concern for fitness and nutrition. Food magazines report that desserts and nutrition are their readers' two favorite topics. People are eating fewer desserts than before—but when they do indulge, they apparently go whole hog.

Some deep thinkers see a lesson in all this. They trace the popularity of food splurges to an era of high prices and diminishing expectations. The rich dessert, then, represents consolation in a world of contracting opportunities. A dollar or more may be a fancy price for a single cookie, but it's still a pretty small-caliber extravagance. And you can afford to indulge your waistline if you don't do it too often. Still, at those prices it's evident that the fancy cookie is a grown-up's morsel, not a kid's snack.

If you try out a number of cookbook recipes, you will probably have trouble coming up with an ideal chocolate-chip cookie. Not even the classic recipe on the back of the *Nestlé* chocolate-chip package produces consistently outstanding results.

But if you modify the *Nestlé* recipe, sooner or later you'll find an ideal combination of baking times, temperatures, and mixing procedures. Consumers Union testers did just that and came up with the following recipe, which is practically perfect.

The Practically Perfect Chocolate-Chip Cookie

This practically perfect cookie provides an intense jolt of chocolate aroma and flavor, with just a hint of vanilla and tastes and smells of milk and butter. The chips have the moderate "cocoa bitterness" typical of true chocolate, combined with come-hither tenderness. They melt with silky smoothness. The cookie smacks moderately of sweetness and caramel, with traces of salt, vanilla, and dairy flavors. It provides a double texture—a crisp edge, with a moderately firm, chewy center—and leaves a faint mouthcoating after each bite.

This recipe makes 40 medium-size cookies.

2¼ cups flour
1 level tsp. baking soda
1 level tsp. salt
¾ cup white sugar
¾ cup dark-brown sugar, packed
2 sticks (½ lb.) sweet butter, at room temperature
1 teaspoon vanilla extract
2 large eggs
One 12-oz. package *Nestlé* semisweet chocolate chips

Preheat the oven to 375° F.

Mix the flour, baking soda, and salt in a bowl and set aside.

Use a stand-type electric mixer to mix the two sugars briefly at low speed. Add the butter in small gobbets, mixing first at low speed and then at high. Beat the mix until it's pale, light, and very fluffy.

Add the vanilla at the mixer's lowest speed, then beat at high speed for a few seconds. Add the eggs, again at the lowest speed, switching to high speed for the final second or so. The eggs should be well beaten in, and the mix should look creamed, not curdled.

Add the flour, baking soda, and salt, one-half cup at a time, mixing at low speed for about one minute, then at high speed for a few seconds.

Scrape down the bowl's sides with a spatula, add the chocolate chips, and mix at low speed for about 10 seconds. If need be, scrape the bowl's sides again and mix for a few more seconds.

Put tablespoonfuls of the mix on an ungreased cookie sheet. Bake until the cookies are pale golden brown (nine minutes in an electric oven, 10 to 11 minutes in a gas one). Remove and let them cool on a rack.

Cookie Nutrition

You'd better enjoy eating that cookie; its nutritional benefits are close to nil. The main yield of a cookie, of course, is calories. Chocolate-chip cookies average close to 140 calories per ounce. Cookies are mainly carbohydrate, with slight to moderate amounts of fat and very little protein. There are minor differences between packaged supermarket cookies and boutique or homemade ones. Packaged sweets tend to use relatively inexpensive vegetable oils. Homemade or boutique cookies apparently use butter and have many more chips, making them slightly higher in saturated fats; they're also a bit higher in protein.

All these cookies contain sodium, but the amounts are of interest mainly to people on a severely sodium-restricted diet. At 55 to 125 milligrams per ounce, most brands would yield quite a bit of sodium to someone who ate three or four cookies.

Popcorn

As snack foods go, popcorn is fairly nutritious—low in calories, reasonably high in fiber. And it's cheaper than most snacks for munching. Without oil or added butter, a three-cup serving can cost as little as three cents.

Proper popping depends a lot on the corn kernels. The corn has to contain enough moisture to puff up the starches when heated, within a hull that's thick enough to contain steam yet brittle enough to explode. Corn grown for popping is bred to expand a lot when popped and to leave behind few unpopped kernels. (See page 312 for information about popcorn-popping equipment.)

Varieties

Popcorn sold for use in a microwave oven used to be frozen, to retard spoilage of the cooking oil that such popcorn is packaged with. The frozen varieties have now been largely replaced by shelf-stable varieties, any of which will retain its "pop" even longer if it's stored in the freezer. However, a few brands of frozen popcorn still exist.

The microwave products on supermarket shelves come in numerous varieties, including "natural," "butter," and other flavors. Natural flavor more or less means plain, unbuttered popcorn, though some natural products come with *added* "natural flavor"—an essence of corn, presumably. Any added flavoring is contained in the product's oil, a solidified mass packed with the corn in the disposable microwaving package—typically a bag. The usual recipe: partially hydrogenated soybean oil, salt, and occasionally preservatives and artificial color.

Of course, many nonmicrowave brands still exist.

The flavor of an excellent popcorn is rather delicate—a slight to moderate baked-corn flavor, a whiff of toasted grain, a hint of heated oil (if it's cooked in oil or if it's a microwave brand). Saltiness may be the most obvious taste (a moderate level is allowed). If a butter flavor is present, it should suggest a dairy origin, not a chemist's beaker. Other off-notes include a burned taste or the "cardboardy" taste of oil on its way to rancidity.

Popcorn should be crisp but not tough. It should shear off cleanly and compress easily as you chew, but not pack the teeth too much. Once chewed, it should be easy to swallow, leaving few crumbled bits in the mouth.

The way you cook popcorn probably affects taste more than the brand. Microwave popcorns are better than the corns cooked in hot oil, and those are better than the same products cooked by the hot-air method.

By and large, popcorn popped in hot oil is less crisp and a little tougher than microwave popcorn—telltale signs of too much moisture in the cooking. Apparently, microwave cooking allows moisture to escape better than hot-oil poppery.

Hot-air popping perhaps allows moisture to escape too well. It makes the corn pop into the biggest blossoms, but they tend to be tougher and less crisp than kernels popped either in a microwave oven or in hot oil. With popcorn, bigger (and fluffier) is not necessarily better. Hot-air-popped corn also tends to leave more particles stuck in your teeth.

Varieties that come in their own pan pose problems of a different sort. They are among the most troublesome to make because you have to keep the pan moving in a vigorous motion on the stove (and you still end up with burned corn at the bottom).

Inevitably, not all the kernels pop successfully. Down at the bottom of the bowl or the bag one finds unpopped and partly popped kernels. Microwaving generally leaves a bit more unpopped corn than other methods.

If you decide on buying bagged, prepopped popcorn, you can expect a lack of crispiness and an overly chewy texture.

Natural Versus Butter Varieties The names of three famous Americans—Orville Redenbacher, Paul Newman, and Betty Crocker—topped the Ratings. Specifically, the microwave, natural-flavor versions of *Newman's Own, Betty Crocker Pop Secret,* and *Orville Redenbacher's Gourmet* came out on top by a small margin. In fact, most "natural" microwave brands are likely to be very good. One element of quality seems to be the presence of some oil. Without oil, the kernels tend to scorch before the corn is fully popped, resulting in a slightly burned flavor.

Butter flavoring generally detracts from the taste, although most of the "butter" varieties are good. To get a butter flavor, manufacturers can add small amounts of flavor components, such as diacetyl, that can be obtained from butter or synthesized in the laboratory. Even products that use natural butter extract don't taste as though they use much of it, and the other products have the imitation butter flavor typical of some movie-theater popcorn.

Nutrition

The nutritional virtues of popcorn have more to do with what it lacks than what it has. Most snack foods contain a great deal of fat or sugar. Popcorn doesn't. Its calories come from corn starch—a complex carbohydrate—and whatever oil it's cooked in. A three-cup serving of plain, air-popped popcorn has, on average, about 75 calories. A three-cup serving of popcorn cooked in two tablespoons of oil contains about twice the calories.

Popcorn is a bit more nutritious than some other snack foods, and it's a lot lower in calories than most. Still, it's just a snack, not a meal. It has little usable protein and no vitamins or minerals in appreciable quantities. It does have a little dietary fiber, two to four grams per serving, comparable to the amount found in an equal weight of shredded wheat cereal.

Microwave brands, except the salt-free varieties, contain added salt. Most are in the range of 200 milligrams of sodium per serving, about the equivalent of two large pinches of table salt.

Cost

You pay a considerable premium for the convenience of microwave popcorn. A typical price for a three-cup serving is about 25 cents, versus 12 cents for oil-popped corn (including the price of the oil) and 5 cents for air-popped corn.

One factor that can affect the price per serving is the size of the popped kernels. Other things being equal, popping with air tends to puff a bigger bloom of popcorn out of each kernel, so it takes fewer kernels to make three cups. A typical serving of air-popped corn weighs about two-thirds of an ounce, whereas most microwave and hot-oil varieties weigh a full ounce, plus or minus a small fraction.

Recommendations

If you like popcorn and own a microwave oven, you're in luck. The taste and texture of microwave products tend to be very good.

If texture is paramount, pass up hot-air poppers. They tend to make the popcorn less crisp and a little tough. If calories are critical, however, you may be more inclined to put up with that foamed plastic-like texture.

Ratings of Popcorn

Listed by types or popping method; within types or methods,
listed in order of sensory quality.
As published in a **June 1989** report.

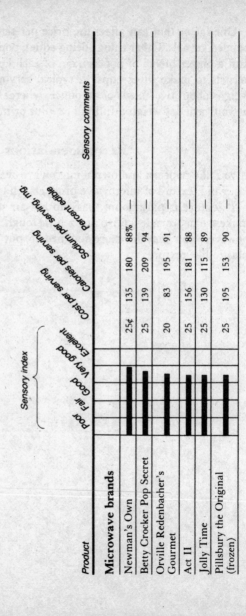

Product	Sensory index	Cost per serving	Calories per serving	Sodium per serving, mg	Percent edible	Sensory comments
Microwave brands						
Newman's Own		25¢	135	180	88%	—
Betty Crocker Pop Secret		25	139	209	94	—
Orville Redenbacher's Gourmet		20	83	195	91	—
Act II		25	156	181	88	—
Jolly Time		25	130	115	89	—
Pillsbury the Original (frozen)		25	195	153	90	—

Sensory index: Poor, Fair, Good, Very good, Excellent

Product		Value 1	Value 2	Value 3	Value 4	Comments
A&P		15	150	150	90	—
Kroger		20	150	150	90	Very slight burned flavor.
Pillsbury the Original		30	210	380	85	—
Planters Premium Select		25	140	226	89	—
TV Time Gourmet		20	173	188	87	Very slight burned flavor.
Town House		20	150	150	88	—
Act I (frozen)		20	137	198	90	—
Jiffy Pop		35	141	228	92	—
Safeway's Town House (butter)		20	150	150	88	Little to no butter flavor.
Act II (butter)		30	110	158	86	Little to no butter flavor.
Kroger (butter)		20	150	150	89	Little to no butter flavor.
Orville Redenbacher's Gourmet (frozen)		15	105	233	93	—
Betty Crocker Pop Secret (butter)		25	140	250	90	Little to no butter flavor.
Newman's Own (butter)		30	135	180	88	Little to no butter flavor.
Planters Premium Select (butter)		30	140	200	93	No oil flavor; slight butter flavor (partly imitation).
Pillsbury (butter)		35	210	380	87	No oil flavor; slight butter flavor (mostly imitation).
Orville Redenbacher's Gourmet (butter)		25	132	172	93	No oil flavor; slight butter flavor (mostly imitation).

Ratings of Popcorn (cont'd)

Microwave brands (cont'd)

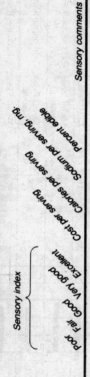

Product	Sensory index (Poor · Fair · Good · Very good · Excellent)	Cost per serving	Calories per serving	Sodium per serving, mg	percent edible	Sensory comments
Orville Redenbacher's Gourmet (salt-free, butter)		25¢	134	3	92	Slight butter flavor (mostly imitation); a bit low in corn, grain flavors.
Jolly Time (butter)		20	130	115	88	Little to no butter flavor.
TV Time Gourmet (butter)		20	169	82	87	Little to no butter flavor; very slight burned flavor.
Act I (frozen, butter)		20	150	198	87	Little to no butter flavor.
A&P (butter)		15	150	150	88	Little to no butter flavor; slight burned flavor.
Betty Crocker Pop Secret (salt-free, butter)		25	140	0	89	Little to no butter flavor.
Jiffy Pop (butter)		35	142	181	89	No oil flavor; slight butter flavor (mostly imitation).
Weight Watchers		30	73	1	78	Very slightly tough; no oil flavor; slight burned flavor; not salty.

Hot-oil-popped

Safeway's Town House Yellow	10	182	1	87	Moderately crisp.
Jolly Time American's Best Yellow	10	133	1	98	—
Jolly Time Yellow Hulless	10	152	2	93	—
TV Time Yello-Pearl	10	141	1	93	—
Planters Premium Select	15	131	1	97	—
Newman's Own	15	135	1	97	—
Orville Redenbacher's Gourmet Original	15	127	2	98	—
Orville Redenbacher's Gourmet Hot Air	15	138	1	96	Low in crispness, slightly tough; stuck in teeth a bit more than others.

Hot-air-popped

Safeway's Town House Yellow	5	97	1	87	A little more crisp and less tough than others.
Jolly Time Yellow Hulless	5	81	1	92	A bit less tough than others.
Jolly Time American's Best Yellow	5	72	1	96	—
Newman's Own	5	71	1	97	—

Ratings of Popcorn (cont'd)

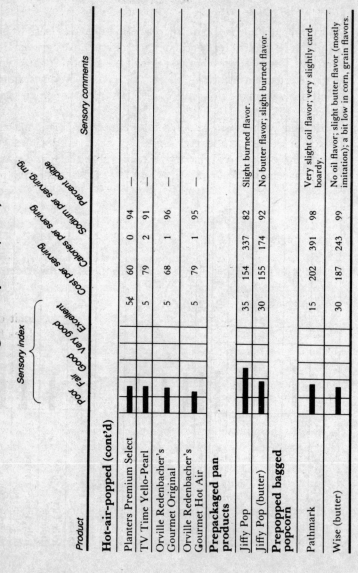

Product	Sensory index (Poor · Fair · Good · Very good · Excellent)	Cost per serving	Calories per serving	Sodium per serving, mg	Percent edible	Sensory comments
Hot-air-popped (cont'd)						
Planters Premium Select		5¢	60	0	94	—
TV Time Yello-Pearl		5	79	2	91	—
Orville Redenbacher's Gourmet Original		5	68	1	96	—
Orville Redenbacher's Gourmet Hot Air		5	79	1	95	—
Prepackaged pan products						
Jiffy Pop		35	154	337	82	Slight burned flavor.
Jiffy Pop (butter)		30	155	174	92	No butter flavor; slight burned flavor.
Prepopped bagged popcorn						
Pathmark		15	202	391	98	Very slight oil flavor; very slightly cardboardy.
Wise (butter)		30	187	243	99	No oil flavor; slight butter flavor (mostly imitation); a bit low in corn, grain flavors.

Ice Cream

Government standards require ice cream to have at least 10 percent butterfat (8 percent for chocolate), ice milk to have between 2 and 7 percent. The sweetener must be one of the natural sugars, typically corn sweetener, corn syrup, or sugar syrup. A product cannot call itself ice cream or ice milk if it uses aspartame, an artificial sweetener.

Beyond government-imposed minimums, ice-cream makers are free to increase the butterfat content as much as they like. Within limits, there's a direct relationship between butterfat and rich taste.

The ice-cream trade calls products that exceed 18 percent butterfat "superpremium." Those brands further enhance the sensation of luxury by limiting "overrun"—the introduction of air into the mix during processing. The result is ice cream that feels dense and substantial when it melts in your mouth.

Too little overrun, though, can be too much of a good thing. Ice cream with no pumped-in air would be a thick, solidly frozen mass, not very refreshing to eat. Even the superpremiums have at least 20 percent overrun.

Cheaper, airier ice cream may approach the legal limit of 100 percent overrun. That means a portion of ice cream has been fluffed up to almost twice the volume of its solid ingredients.

Low overrun is no guarantee of high quality. Even if it were, you can't generally tell how much air is in an ice cream from its label. But if you're interested, you can make your own check. Weigh the package on a scale in the produce department or at home; the more it exceeds the minimum 2.25 pounds for a half-gallon, the lower the overrun. (Allow about two ounces for the weight of the packaging.)

"Unnatural" Ingredients

Some other ingredients, alien to a homemade ice cream, may turn up in commercial products. Stabilizers are noted on labels as vegetable gums (guar, locust or carob bean, cellulose). They improve smoothness, minimize growth of ice crystals, and help keep the ice cream from melting rapidly. Emulsifiers (mono- and diglycerides, lecithin, and carrageenan) help ice cream hold its smooth emulsion and make it easier to whip air into the mix. Both sorts of additive in effect embalm ice cream so that it can languish in a store's freezer without betraying its age. They also let manufacturers mimic butterfat's textural advantages with cheaper ingredients.

Labels on one or another product also disclose other unhomey ingredients. Polysorbate 80 is an artificial emulsifer. Natural colors have been extracted from other foods; artificial and "FD&C" colors originate in a chemistry laboratory. If a dye called FD&C Yellow #5 is used, the label must name it specifically; some people are allergic to it.

Then come flavorings, disclosed on the front of the container but not very prominently—and not much more clearly in the ingredients list. A naturally flavored vanilla ice cream (labeled merely "vanilla") will contain pureed vanilla beans or vanilla extract. A naturally flavored product that also contains a small amount of artificial flavoring (often vanillin) is "vanilla flavored." Where the flavoring is wholly or mostly fake, the label reads "artificial vanilla" or "artificially flavored vanilla." The regulations permit labels to soft-pedal "flavored" or "artificial"—those words need be only half the height of the type that says "vanilla."

Many in the ice-cream trade defend chemical or processed stabilizers and emulsifers as necessities. It's interesting to note that the makers of *Breyers, Häagen-Dazs,* and *Frusen Glädjé* get along nicely without any of them.

Nutrition

Ice cream certainly is not a diet food. But as desserts go, it's not all that fattening. With the calories comes a respectable scoop of nutrition.

Consider: A slice of iced yellow cake will cost you 240 calories; a wedge of apple pie, 410 calories. Have two scoops (one-half cup) of a nonpremium ice cream instead, and you get away with about 150 calories, on average. A premium ice cream averages 245 calories a serving. Even if every calorie counts, you don't necessarily gain anything with an ice milk: The product runs between 110 and 115 calories in a two-scoop portion.

Like other dairy products, ice cream and ice milk contain substantial amounts of protein. A double scoop offers about one-quarter to one-third the protein of an eight-ounce glass of whole or lowfat (1 percent) milk. Yet the average ice cream has about the same calories as the whole milk, and ice milk has roughly the same calories as lowfat milk.

Butterfat is the source of half the calories in ice cream. That fat runs some seven to eight grams a serving, and it's mainly saturated. If you're watching your fat intake, you'd be better off with ice milk, which has only about three grams of fat per serving.

After fat, carbohydrates (generally sugars) are the chief source of calories in ice cream. Milk and other dairy products contain sugar naturally, but much of ice cream's total sugars have been added.

Sodium is a natural part of milk, although a number of manufacturers add a bit extra, especially to their chocolate products. Vanilla and strawberry ice creams average 60 milligrams per serving, as does ice milk. Chocolate runs a little higher.

Flavor

Trained tasters assess ice cream's "coldness" (not actual temperature but a sensory impression that can be affected by an ice cream's specific ingredients). They also evaluate fluffiness or density, the presence of ice crystals, ease of melting, foaminess, graininess, viscosity, and residual mouthcoating.

Overall, ice creams should be smooth and creamy, although allowing for chunks of fruit in fruit-flavored ice cream or chocolate chips, for example.

The following criteria apply to the three most popular flavors of ice cream:

Vanilla   A vanilla ice cream should be pleasantly sweet, with a creamy, dairy flavor, a delicate vanilla bouquet, and an agreeable aftertaste. All the ingredients should be balanced.

Chocolate   To earn top marks, the ice cream must have pronounced chocolate and cocoa flavors and be reasonably sweet, without harshness, bitterness, or any fake flavor notes. Some hint of milk, cream, or butter may come through.

Strawberry   The ideal ice cream has a marked flavor of the fresh fruit. Dairy flavors are also apparent, since strawberries taste fairly mild. All flavors are balanced, without harshness or artificial notes suggesting candy or chewing gum. As for the weight of strawberries that end up in a given package, it's probably a matter of potluck.

Homemade Ice Cream

With homemade ice cream, even vanilla doesn't have to be plain vanilla. You can make a dessert that's as rich and creamy as your waistline will allow, and you control the ingredients.

The following recipe makes slightly more than a quart.

   1 large egg
   ⅔ cup sugar
   1 tsp. vanilla extract
   1 cup heavy cream
   2 cups half-and-half

In a mixing bowl, combine the egg, sugar, and vanilla. Mix with an electric mixer at medium speed for one minute. Add the cream and half-and-half; mix on low speed for three minutes. Immediately pour into the ice-cream maker and process.

This mixture will yield an ice cream that can hold its own against all but the best store-bought varieties. It contains 200 calories per half-cup serving.

If you prefer a smoother, richer ice cream and don't mind going to a little more trouble, try this recipe, adapted from the Donvier *ice-cream maker's instruction book:*

3 eggs
2 cups milk
1 cup sugar
2 cups heavy cream
2 tsp. vanilla extract

In a large saucepan, beat together the eggs and milk. Add the sugar and cook over low heat, stirring constantly, for about 10 minutes or until the mixture is thickened. Don't let it boil, or the eggs will curdle. The mixture is thick enough when it coats the back of a spoon smoothly. Cool, then stir in the cream and vanilla. It's best to cover and refrigerate the mixture overnight before churning it in an ice-cream maker. This ice cream has 250 calories per half-cup serving.

Ice-Cream Bars

The same ingredients that make an ice-cream bar taste good also make it fattening: lots of butterfat and cocoa butter, lots of sugar. Coconut oil, a tropical oil high in saturated fat, is used in the coating to help keep the chocolate shell from falling off. Clearly, these are not desserts or snacks for the calorie-conscious or for those worried about dietary fats.

Or are they? It all depends on how you look at these products. If you're trying to limit your daily fat intake to the recommended maximum of 30 percent of all calories, you should aim to eat no more than 67 grams of fat, evenly divided among saturated, monounsaturated, and polyunsaturated fats.

One superpremium ice-cream bar contains 20 to 31 grams of fat, most of it saturated and all of it loaded with calories. To the one out of 10 Americans who eats ice cream every day, all that fat makes the 30 percent goal just about impossible to achieve. To the once-a-month splurger, however, the extra fat and the extra few hundred calories may not matter.

Hoping to appeal to the nutrition-conscious, frozen-novelty makers offer many products that sound more wholesome than ice-cream bars. In addition to ice-milk bars, they make frozen yogurt bars, pudding bars, and *Tofutti* bars. Such products, however, are nearly as rich as ice-cream bars. They have fewer calories mainly because they're on the small side.

There are several attributes worth considering when judging an ice-cream bar:

Thickness of the Coating   A thin coating doesn't add much flavor. A thick coating of chocolate may taste good, but it's more likely to fall off in pieces when you bite into it. Solution: Keep plate, napkin, or wrapper handy.

How Quickly the Coating Melts in the Mouth   The sooner the chocolate starts to melt on your tongue, the faster the taste comes through. Like butter, a fast-melting chocolate delivers a sharp burst of flavor. Slower coatings, like some margarines, yield less taste.

Intensity of the Flavors   Vanilla should be well balanced, as in vanilla ice cream. The intensity of the chocolate in chocolate ice cream ought to approximate the intensity of an ordinary milk-chocolate bar. So should the chocolate in the coating, unless the coating is specified as "dark." A dark coating could approach the intensity of semisweet baking chocolate. The cream flavor should be somewhere between whole milk and cream. A diet product can be less creamy.

Sweetness An ice-cream bar should taste sweet, at about the level of four to six teaspoons of sugar dissolved in a cup of water.

Other Flavors A bit of the flavor of butterscotch or roasted cocoa beans is all right. There shouldn't be noticeable saltiness or the off-flavor called "freezer taste"—the sometimes stale flavor of a food that has been stored too long in the freezer. The taste, closely related to "package taste," can also occur when ice cream has been thawed and refrozen.

Bitterness The ideal chocolate ice cream should have little or none of this attribute. But you'd expect some bitterness in dark chocolate coatings.

Iciness Sherbet feels icy to the tongue; ice cream shouldn't. A poor-quality ice-cream bar can have a coarse, icy texture. That flaw is often associated with improper storage; ice crystals form when ice cream has been allowed to thaw and refreeze.

Recommendations

Ice-cream image is one thing and quality is another; designer ice creams don't always come out on top. When comparing equally rated products, price is a reasonable tie-breaker.

However good ice cream, ice milk, or an ice cream bar may be, it won't stay that way forever. Quality starts to decline after one to four months following manufacture, even at temperatures below zero. When noticeable ice crystals form, the product has started to deteriorate. You could avoid elderly products if packages carried a manufacturing date. As matters stand, you can't tell what the dates on many packages mean.

To enjoy ice cream or an ice cream bar at its best, buy in small quantities. Have the container packed separately or in the same bag as other frozen foods. Get it home fast, wrap it in plastic, and store it in the coldest part of your freezer.

Ratings of Ice Cream Bars

Products are listed in order of sensory score; products rated equally are listed alphabetically.
As published in an **August 1989** report.

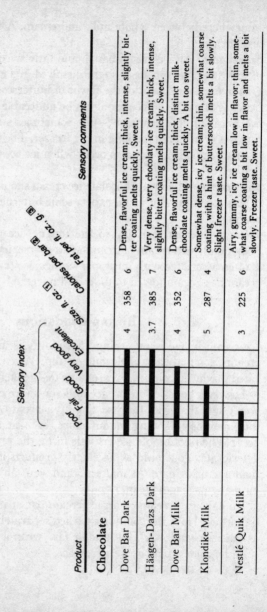

Product	Sensory index Poor / Fair / Good / Very good / Excellent	Size, fl. oz. [1]	Calories per bar [2]	Fat per fl. oz., g. [3]	Sensory comments
Chocolate					
Dove Bar Dark	Excellent	4	358	6	Dense, flavorful ice cream; thick, intense, slightly bitter coating melts quickly. Sweet.
Häagen-Dazs Dark	Excellent	3.7	385	7	Very dense, very chocolaty ice cream; thick, intense, slightly bitter coating melts quickly. Sweet.
Dove Bar Milk	Very good	4	352	6	Dense, flavorful ice cream; thick, distinct milk-chocolate coating melts quickly. A bit too sweet.
Klondike Milk	Good	5	287	4	Somewhat dense, icy ice cream; thin, somewhat coarse coating with a hint of butterscotch melts a bit slowly. Slight freezer taste. Sweet.
Nestlé Quik Milk	Fair	3	225	6	Airy, gummy, icy ice cream low in flavor; thin, somewhat coarse coating a bit low in flavor and melts a bit slowly. Freezer taste. Sweet.

258

Vanilla

Dove Bar Milk	4	342	5	Dense flavorful ice cream; thick, smooth, distinct milk-chocolate coating melts quickly. Very sweet.
Häagen-Dazs Dark	3.7	377	7	Very dense, flavorful ice cream; thick, smooth, slightly bitter, intense coating melts quickly. Sweet.
Häagen-Dazs Milk	3.7	319	6	Very dense, flavorful ice cream; thick, smooth, distinct milk-chocolate coating melts quickly. Very sweet.
Dove Bar Dark	4	353	6	Dense, flavorful ice cream; thick, smooth, slightly bitter, intense coating melts quickly and falls off in pieces. Sweet.
Dreyer's Dark	4	295	5	Dense, slightly icy, flavorful ice cream; very thick, slightly bitter, intense coating melts quickly. Sweet.
Polar Bar Milk	3.5	234	5	Somewhat dense, slightly icy, flavorful ice cream; somewhat thick coating. Sweet.
Klondike Milk	5	294	4	Dense, slightly icy, flavorful ice cream; somewhat thick coating with a hint of butterscotch but a bit low in chocolate flavor, melts a bit slowly. Sweet.
Nestlé Milk	3.7	286	5	Dense, slightly icy, flavorful ice cream; thick coating with a hint of caramel melts quickly. Very sweet.
Häagen-Dazs Milk with Almonds	3.7	377	8	Very dense, flavorful ice cream; thick coating melts quickly. Almonds have intense roasted flavor but leave particles behind. Very sweet.
Eskimo Pie Original Dark	2.3	182	6	Somewhat dense, slightly icy ice cream a bit low in flavor; thick, slightly bitter, intense coating. Sweet.
Baskin Robbins Dark	3.5	310	6	Somewhat dense, slightly icy and gummy ice cream a bit low in dairy flavor; thick, slightly bitter, intense coating melts quickly. Slight freezer taste. Sweet.

Ratings of Ice Cream Bars (cont'd)

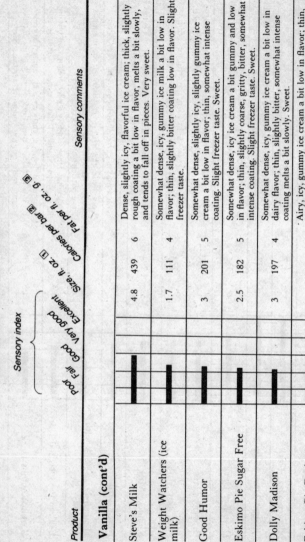

Product	Sensory index (Poor / Fair / Good / Very good / Excellent)	Size, fl. oz. [1]	Calories per bar [2]	Fat per bar, fl. oz., g [3]	Sensory comments
Vanilla (cont'd)					
Steve's Milk		4.8	439	6	Dense, slightly icy, flavorful ice cream; thick, slightly rough coating a bit low in flavor, melts a bit slowly, and tends to fall off in pieces. Very sweet.
Weight Watchers (ice milk)		1.7	111	4	Somewhat dense, icy, gummy ice milk a bit low in flavor; thin, slightly bitter coating low in flavor. Slight freezer taste.
Good Humor		3	201	5	Somewhat dense, slightly icy, slightly gummy ice cream a bit low in flavor; thin, somewhat intense coating. Slight freezer taste. Sweet.
Eskimo Pie Sugar Free		2.5	182	5	Somewhat dense, icy ice cream a bit gummy and low in flavor; thin, slightly coarse, gritty, bitter, somewhat intense coating. Slight freezer taste. Sweet.
Dolly Madison		3	197	4	Somewhat dense, icy, gummy ice cream a bit low in dairy flavor; thin, slightly bitter, somewhat intense coating melts a bit slowly. Sweet.
Eskimo Pie Dark		3	209	5	Airy, icy, gummy ice cream a bit low in flavor; thin, slightly bitter, slightly rough, somewhat intense coating. Slight freezer taste. Sweet.

Freezer Pleezer	▮	2.5	147	4	Airy, icy, gummy ice cream a bit low in flavor; thin, somewhat intense coating melts a bit slowly. Slight freezer taste. Somewhat sweet.
Nestlé Crunch Milk	▮	3	190	4	Somewhat dense, icy, gummy ice cream a bit low in flavor; thin, somewhat intense coating melts a bit slowly. Slight freezer taste. Sweet.
A&P	▮	2.5	151	4	Somewhat dense, icy, gummy ice cream a bit low in flavor; thin coating a bit low in flavor. Slight freezer taste. Sweet.
Pathmark	▮	2.5	151	4	Airy, very icy, slightly gummy ice cream a bit low in flavor; thin coating with low flavor. Slight freezer taste. Somewhat sweet.
A&P (ice milk)	▮	2.5	131	3	Airy, very icy, gummy, slightly salty ice milk a bit low in flavor; thin coating a bit low in flavor, melts a bit slowly. Freezer taste. Sweet.

1 Ice cream is measured by volume, in fluid ounces. Because of varying amounts of air pumped into ice cream during processing (known as overrun), this measurement is not a good guide to the weight of the ice cream.

2 As measured by CU. The ingredients that make some ice-cream bars taste better than others are, sadly, the ones that add the most calories.

3 The fat comes mostly from the cream, but also from coconut oil and cocoa butter used in the coating. All three contain highly saturated fats.

Microwave Cake Mixes

Cake mixes formulated for baking in a microwave oven have been improving. Even so, microwave cakes still aren't a match for a conventional cake mix baked in a conventional oven.

The yellow and one of the chocolate versions of *Pillsbury Microwave Cake Mixes* bake more evenly and have a finer crumb, or texture, than *Betty Crocker MicroRave* mixes. The *Betty Crocker* cakes emerge from the oven looking rumpled, with a texture more like cornbread than cake.

Sampled plain, without frosting, the *Pillsbury* yellow cake is bland with a very slight off-note reminiscent of Play-Doh. The *MicroRave* yellow cake is very sweet, with strong butterscotch and vanilla flavors. Of the two chocolate cakes, the *Pillsbury* tastes more chocolaty.

According to the packages, MicroRave claims to serve six, *Pillsbury* eight. It's more realistic to count on four servings from the *MicroRave* mix, six from the *Pillsbury*. On that basis, cake with frosting provides 400 to 450 calories per serving.

3

Fast-Cooking Appliances

Midsize Microwave Ovens

More U.S. households own microwave ovens than own toaster ovens, VCRs, or food processors. Increasingly, people are looking to buy their second microwave.

For the replacement market, manufacturers pitch expensive, full-featured models. These boast such niceties as "jet defrost," "cook 'n watch," "minute plus," and "micro popper." Features like browning elements, "dual wave" energy distribution, and turntables are supposed to compensate for any deficiencies of microwave cooking.

Also supposed to make up for those deficiencies is the microwave/convection oven, sometimes promoted as the microwave oven's successor. This hybrid offers a microwave's speed and a regular oven's skill at browning and baking (see page 292).

A midsize microwave oven offers as much speed and almost as much capacity as a larger oven yet takes up less room on the counter.

Depending on how you use your microwave oven, you may want to consider a cheaper, more basic model, or one with a particular feature you fancy, or a smaller, more compact unit (see page 282).

Performance

The size of a microwave oven is a rough guide to its heating speed—the larger the oven, the faster it's likely to cook. That's because a larger model has generally a more powerful magnetron, the part that generates the invisible, high-energy cooking waves. Full-size microwave ovens generally have 700 or 750 watts in magnetron power; midsize ovens range from 600 to 700 watts. Compact or subcompact ovens have only about 500 watts.

How well a microwave oven cooks is just as important as how fast it cooks. Microwave ovens still can't produce a browned, roasted meat loaf the way a regular oven can. Still, a microwaved meat loaf can turn out very well, especially if assisted by the oven's temperature probe. But you may still have to experiment to get good results. For example, some ovens force you to change the power setting because the temperature probe shuts the oven off before the meat is done.

The majority of ovens handle most cooking chores well, including reheating leftovers, a common job for the microwave oven.

Defrosting

Defrosting frozen foods is another common chore for the microwave oven, and manufacturers have responded with "jet defrost," "auto defrost," and "weight defrost." Any microwave oven—even one without a fancy defrost feature—can do a good job if you take the trouble to monitor the progress of defrosting and turn the food periodically.

"Assisted defrost" features vary, but most involve built-in prompting or programming. Such features take some of the work out of defrosting by lowering or cycling the power as the food thaws, minimizing the ovens' tendency to start cooking areas of the food that are no longer icy. Even with assisted defrost and a turntable, however, you still have to turn most foods for even thawing.

Some defrost features go by the weight of the food. You program the weight and the type of food, and the oven defrosts for a preprogrammed period of time. With others, you set the time, and the oven automatically changes the power level over the time period.

A mode available on some models, called "defrost/cook," lets you go from frozen to cooked food in one process. The oven starts in its defrost cycle when the food is icy, pauses, and then goes into the cooking program you've selected.

Some defrost features have built-in pauses, with a beep to let you know it's time to turn the food; that's a helpful reminder. Results are often improved if the food stands a bit after defrosting, and so some models beep after a "hold" time at the end of the defrost.

The models that do the best job of defrosting deliver uniformly thawed food. The best models are also the slowest, taking 20 minutes or so to thaw an average meat loaf. The fastest models take less than 10 minutes with the meat loaf but may leave icy or cold parts.

Microwave Popcorn

Microwave ovens seem to have turned an old-fashioned snack into a national pastime (see pages 242–44). The best popcorn maker is one that leaves the fewest unpopped kernels without burning any popped ones. The timing is tricky. The longer you wait for the kernels to finish popping, the more you risk burning the corn.

Despite the popularity of microwave ovens for popping popcorn, these machines aren't likely to win any awards for their popping performance. In fact, if you are accustomed to popping corn in a hot-air or oil popper, or in a pan on top of the range, you will probably be disappointed by the amount of unpopped kernels in microwaved popcorn.

Furthermore, results are inconsistent. Consumers Union's tests—with bagged microwave popcorn and regular popcorn in a plastic container—usually yielded nearly opposite results in any one oven.

Most manufacturers caution you not to overcook popcorn, something that's easy to do if you're trying to get more kernels to pop. Overcooked popcorn can char or catch fire. The best precaution is to follow the popcorn package instructions; if a range of cooking times is given, use the minimum time.

In the event of a fire, it's important to keep the oven door closed, then disconnect the power at the outlet. With the door closed, the fire will use up its limited oxygen supply and die out. Afterward, don't use the oven until it's been checked over by a service technician.

A Rundown of Oven Features

Most people use a microwave oven for simple chores such as reheating coffee, cooking a frozen dinner, or thawing leftovers. For such jobs, you may need only a small oven (see pages 284–85). But in any oven you do need some basic features:

- A minimum of five power levels gives you sufficient flexibility to cook most foods.
- High-power default means you program the power level only when you want other than the highest power available.
- Automatic short cook is a convenient feature that provides one-button operation for short, specified cooking times.
- A direct-entry control pad is easier to use than pushing a button while the numbers on a display count up to the time you want.
- A large, bright control display panel is desirable.
- An oven window you can easily see through helps you check on the progress of a dish.
- The light bulb should be easy to change.
- The instruction book should be clearly written and logically arranged.

If you expect to use an oven for cooking elaborate dishes, or dinners from scratch, you probably need a midsize oven with the basics noted above, plus some extras:

- A temperature probe shuts the oven off when food reaches the programmed temperature.

- "Assisted defrost" provides built-in power cycling and prompting to simplify defrosting.
- If there are cooking stages, the oven's controls will be able to "remember" and perform more than one specific set of commands for power, time, or temperature.
- A built-in set of preprogrammed recipes give you specific, built-in settings keyed to certain foods. Some models have user-programmable recipes that let you enter your own specific settings into the oven's memory for later use.
- A shelf inside the oven is handy for cooking more than one dish at a time. But you may want to forgo a shelf for a turntable, which tends to improve evenness of cooking.

Safety

In the early days of microwave ovens, safety concerns focused on the microwaves themselves. For years ovens have been well within the U.S. Bureau of Radiological Health's standard for microwave-radiation leakage (though prudence still dictates not standing close when an oven is in use). Meanwhile, safety concerns about microwave cooking are shifting to the food cooked in these appliances and the wraps and packaging materials the food is cooked in.

An outbreak of listeriosis, a potentially deadly form of food poisoning, in the United Kingdom, may have been linked to the failure of microwave ovens to heat commercially prepared, precooked dinners thoroughly. Consumers Union's counterpart organization in Britain, the Consumers' Association, reported that microwave heating of the refrigerated meals, widely sold in Britain, may be too uneven to kill any bacteria present from poor sanitation or handling.

In the United States, concern has focused more on chicken, since chicken, particularly in the Northeast, can be contaminated with salmonella. The U.S. Department of Agriculture recommends cooking whole birds to an internal temperature of at least 180 degrees. But a bird that's hot inside may still be fairly cool on the skin, where salmonella bacteria are found. That's why it's important to follow directions for "stand time" after cooking. After the chicken has been standing the recommended 10 to 20 minutes, depending on the cut, heat concentrated inside radiates outward until the skin is hot, too. Stuffing for chicken or turkey should be cooked separately, not in the bird, to minimize opportunities for bacterial growth. (That's true of conventional cooking, too.)

Other foods that can cause problems when undercooked include pork, because of trichinosis, and fish, because of parasite larvae.

Since microwave heating is uneven, home canning in a microwave oven is especially dangerous. Proper canning requires foods to be heated for a specified time and to a specified temperature throughout the food, lest you risk contamination with deadly botulism toxin.

When covering dishes to be cooked in the microwave, it's important to avoid letting plastic wrap touch foods, particularly fatty ones. Some plastic wraps contain plasticizers that can leach chemicals into foods. Higher temperatures and longer cooking times increase the potential for leaching, or migration.

Chemicals may migrate into foods from commercial packaging, too. The U.S. Food and Drug Administration, after receiving consumer complaints in 1988 about off-tastes in microwaveable fish and popcorn, began to investigate that.

When the FDA originally approved the use of various plastics and laminates in microwaveable-food packaging, it presumed those materials would be in contact with the food only at low, warming temperatures. Convenience-food manufacturers, however, soon developed "heat susceptors"—metalized portions of packaging that concentrate heat to brown and crisp food or to pop corn. Heat susceptors raise temperatures as high as 400° to 500°F. At those temperatures (or at the longer cooking times you'd set in a conventional oven for a food in a "dual-ovenable" tray), chemicals may migrate from the packaging into the food.

The FDA recommends that consumers follow the manufacturer's cooking directions.

Some other cautions:

Don't try deep-fat frying. Microwave ovens don't allow control over the temperature of the oil, which can spatter or boil over even when it's not overheated. And if moisture were to reach the oil while your hand is inside the oven, the popping oil would have a close-range target. Some manufacturers won't honor their warranty if you use their microwave oven for deep-fat frying.

Let steam escape from covered dishes. When you cover a dish with plastic wrap before microwaving, punch a couple of holes in the wrap or leave a corner open so steam can escape. A tight seal could allow steam to build up, with painful consequences when you remove the food from the oven.

Don't leave the oven unattended when you're microwaving popcorn. If you microwave popcorn too long, there's the chance of a fire. Heat can build up if the package includes a heat susceptor, which acts as a kind of internal hot plate. Handle the package and whatever it's rested on carefully.

Don't heat up baby bottles. The milk inside can become scalding while the bottle remains only warm. Also, a buildup of steam in the liner could cause an explosion when the bottle is shaken.

Train children in microwave basics. Be sure they know them before they use the oven unsupervised. And it's a good idea—worth repeating—to insist that anyone stay a few feet from a microwave oven when it's operating.

Recommendations

A midsize microwave oven cooks nearly as fast as a large microwave and provides enough room inside for most foods. Yet midsize ovens are still small enough to be mounted under a cabinet or to sit on the kitchen counter without taking up an excessive amount of space.

Microwave ovens' track record for repairs is much better than that of other electronic products, such as VCRs and CD players. Only one in 20 microwave ovens purchased since 1985 has ever needed a repair, according to a 1988 Consumers Union survey.

The survey was based on consumers' experiences with nearly 22,000 midsize microwave ovens, all bought new from 1985 to 1988, most with electronic touch controls. The data enabled the calculation of Repair Indexes for 14 brands.

Brands at the top of the chart had a much better repair record than those at the bottom, as measured by the percentage of respondents whose ovens needed at least one repair. Differences of less than three points aren't meaningful. Since appliances tend to need more fixing as they age, the data were adjusted for differences in age among models of different brands.

Note that the data apply only to brands—individual models may fare better or worse than the brand as a whole. And the data are historical in nature, indicating only how reliable a brand has been in the past. A brand's past doesn't inevitably predict a model's future. Still, you can improve your odds of getting a reliable oven by choosing from brands near the top of the chart.

Repair Index of Microwave Ovens by Brand

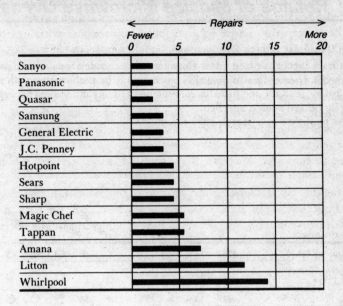

Ratings of Midsize Microwave Ovens

Listed in order of estimated quality based on performance, convenience, and features. Except as noted under Comments, most models would rank about the same when estimated quality is based mainly on performance with no regard for features and little for convenience. Quality differences between closely ranked models are slight.

As published in a **March 1989** report.

Brand and model	Price	Size (H × W × D), in.	Capacity, cu. ft.	Power, watts	Performance Speed	Performance Reheating	Performance Defrost assistance
Litton LP16610	$260	12 × 23¾ × 14	.9	700	⊙	⊙	◑
General Electric JEM31H	225	11½ × 23½ × 12½	.9	700	◑	○	⊙
J.C. Penney 5537	249	13 × 20¾ × 13½	1.0	650	◑	◑	⊙
Quasar MQ6698W	250	11¾ × 23½ × 12¾	.9	700	◑	⊙	◑
General Electric JEM30WH	225	11¼ × 23¾ × 12½	.8	600	◑	○	◑
Amana M86P	189	12½ × 20¾ × 12½	.8	600	○	⊙	○
Samsung MW5710	169	12½ × 20¾ × 13½	.9	600	○	⊙	○
Hotpoint REM30F	200	11¼ × 24 × 12½	.8	600	○	◑	○
J.C. Penney 5545	179	13 × 23 × 15½	1.0	600	○	◑	○
Sharp R4P80	280	12½ × 20¾ × 16	1.0	600	○	○	○
Tappan 562897	177	12¼ × 23 × 13	.8	650	◑	○	○
Whirlpool MW3601XS	240	12 × 22½ × 13	.8	650	◑	○	◒
Sharp R4A70	200	12½ × 20½ × 15½	1.0	600	○	◑	○
Frigidaire MC890L	240	12¼ × 23 × 12¾	.8	700	◑	○	○
Panasonic NN5808A	215	11¾ × 20¼ × 14½	.8	600	○	◑	⊙

Better ⟵⟶ Worse

		Convenience											
Popping corn	Space efficiency	Display prompts	Display clarity	Control panel	Number pad	Instruction manual	Noise	Door opening	Window visibility	Advantages	Disadvantages	Comments
◐	○	⊙	⊙	⊙	◑	◐	○	◐	◑	E,F,I,J	c	A,B,C
◐	◑	⊙	◐	◑	⊙	◑	◑	○	○	E,F	i	C,D,F
◐	◑	○	○	○	◑	◐	○	○	◑	A,F	f	J
◐	◑	○	◑	○	◐[1]	○	○	○	◑	E,G,I	g,i	D,K
◐	○	⊙	○	○	○	⊙	○	◐	○	E,F	e,k	C,F
◐	○	○	◑	◐	◐	◐	○	○	◑	A,E,I	h,l	B
◐	○	◐	◑	◐	◑	◑	○	◐	◑	A,E,F,I	l	B,C
◐	○	⊙	◑	◑	○	⊙	○	◑	○	—	e,m	C,F,L
◐	○	◑	○	◐	◐	◑	○	○	○	A,D,F	f,l	I
◐	◑	◐	○	○	◑	○	○	○	◑	D,E,F,G	g	G
◐	○	⊙	◑	◐	◐	◐	○	○	◑	E,H	g,m	E
◑	○	○	◑	◑	◐	⊙	◐	○	○	—	g,m	D,F
◐	◑	○	○	○	●[1]	◐	○	○	◑	C,D,E,F	g,n,o	—
◐	○	⊙	◐	○	◐	○	○	○	◑	E,H	g,m	E,M
○	◑	○	◐	○	◐[1]	○	◑	○	◑	G,H	g	D,N

Ratings of Midsize Microwave Ovens (cont'd)

Brand and model	Price	Size (H × W × D), in.	Capacity, cu. ft.	Power, watts	Speed	Reheating	Defrost assistance
White-Westinghouse KM485L	$225	12¼ × 23 × 12½	.8	700	◐	○	○
Panasonic NN5508A	189	11½ × 20¼ × 14¼	.8	600	○	○	◉
Litton 1439C	200	11¾ × 21¾ × 13	.8	650	◐	◐	◐
Sears Kenmore Cat. No. 88627	189	11¾ × 21¾ × 13¼	.8	650	○	○	◐
Goldstar ER654S	199	13 × 21¾ × 15½[2]	1.0	650	◐	◐	◐
Sanyo EM380[1]	249	11¾ × 21¾ × 13½	.9	650	○	◐	◐
Magic Chef M1510P	177	13¼ × 20½ × 14¼	.8	600	◐	○	◐

[1] Number pad uses count-up system.

[2] Vents on top of oven; requires additional inch or so of clearance.

[3] Manufacturer warns against popping corn, but gives instructions on how to do it.

Specifications and Features

All have: • At least five power levels, a sufficient number for any cooking task. • Oven on-times of four to seven seconds per cycle at lowest setting, seven to 19 seconds at medium. • Touch pads that provide audible signals when programmed. • Displays that show time of day when oven isn't in use. • Interior light that goes on when oven is operating and window in door for viewing food. • Weights between 32 and 46 lbs.

Except as noted, all: • Can be used as kitchen timers. • Draw between 1,100 and 1,360 watts. • Have reduced power settings that cycle from 18 to 22 percent of the time at the lowest setting, and 53 to 60 percent at medium setting.

• Make a good two-pound meat loaf, using temperature probe if provided, in 25 to 35 minutes. • Operate on high power unless otherwise instructed. • Have a defrost setting that varies power level. • Have provision for keeping minor spills in oven from running onto counter or floor.

Key to Advantages

A—Percentage of full power at low setting— 12 percent—judged best.

B—Turntable is recessed into oven floor; switch is provided to use oven without turntable rotating. Indicator shows when turntable is on or off.

C—Makes very good meat loaf in only 20 minutes.

D—Oven can accommodate an average-size turkey without touching the walls or ceiling.

E—Oven has built-in programs for cooking or

Popping corn	Space efficiency	Convenience								Advantages	Disadvantages	Comments
		Display prompts	Display clarity	Control panel	Number pad	Instruction manual	Noise	Door opening	Window visibility			
◐	○	○	◐	●	●	○	○	○	◐	E	d, g	—
○	◐	○	○	○	◐①	○	○	○	◐	E	g, k	D, O
◐	○	◐	◐	●	◐	○	◐	⊙	◐	F	e, m	A, H
◐	○	●	◐	○	◐	●	○	◐	○	F	b, g, j	D, J
◐③	◐	○	○	○	◐	●	○	○	○	G, H	a, f	—
◐	○	◐	○	○	◐①	○	◐	○	●	E, H	b, e, g, j	D, P
◐	◐	○	◐	●	◐	○	◐	◐	●	B, E	e, g, m	B, C

reheating; some ovens require entering weight of food.

F—Has control for quickly entering fixed, short cooking time at high power. Multiple pushes of pad increase time with some.

G—Has sensor-controlled cooking or reheating.

H—Has control for increasing or decreasing the degree of "doneness" with automatic cooking.

I—Has memory for one or more user-programmed recipes.

J—"Micro-popper" feature allows popping corn with a single touch of a pad; oven shuts off when popping is done. Feature worked well.

Key to Disadvantages

a—Doesn't do well in cooking microwaveable pizza and brownies because metal turntable causes bottom of foods to be under-cooked. Turntable has high lip; placing food to utilize maximum available space judged awkward.

b—Energy distribution when baking potatoes is worse than it is with other models; overall energy distribution is somewhat worse than others.

c—Does not defrost doughnuts as uniformly as most other models.

d—When oven display is used as a kitchen timer, oven light and blower operate.

e—Percentage on at lowest reduced power setting is relatively high, above 30 percent.

f—Percentage on at medium power setting is relatively high, about 63 percent.

g—Requires service personnel to change interior light bulb.

h—Although light bulb is accessible, manufacturer warns that it is not "customer serviceable."

i—Oven draws 1,460 watts, more likely than most others to overload a branch circuit.

Ratings of Midsize Microwave Ovens (cont'd)

j—Setting power levels above 10 percent requires punching two digits.

k—Manufacturer does not provide recipe book with oven, a slight disadvantage.

l—Full power level must be programmed for each use.

m—Lacks defrost setting that automatically varies power.

n—Cannot be used as a kitchen timer.

o—Cooking time can be set only to the nearest 10 seconds; somewhat less precise than other models where precision is to nearest second.

Key to Comments

A—Flat ceramic interior bottom easily cleaned but has no tray or lip to keep spills from running out of oven.

B—Meat loaf made using temperature probe not as good as that made by estimating cooking time.

C—Making good meat loaf using manufacturer's recommended setting takes about 40 minutes; somewhat longer than most others. Except for the *Magic Chef,* all can be set at a higher level, which should cut time.

D—Manufacturer's defrosting instructions include turning the food for uniform defrosting.

E—Separate on/off switch must be pushed to operate oven and turn it off; most other ovens do not require switching.

F—Manufacturer has free hotline to provide extensive consumer information.

G—This model would have ranked considerably lower if basic performance was the primary criterion and features were not considered.

H—This model would have ranked somewhat higher if basic performance was the primary criterion and features were not considered.

I—According to manufacturer, a later designation for *5545* was *Cat. No. 8630683A.*

J—Although this model was discontinued and is no longer available, the information has been retained to permit comparisons.

K—Replaced by MQ6699W.

L—Replaced by REM30XG.

M—Replaced by MC890E.

N—Replaced by NN5809A.

O—Replaced by NN5509A.

P—Replaced by EM370T.

Features of Midsize Microwave Ovens

Brand and model	Price	Cooking stages	Sensor	Turntable	Delay start	Defrost assistance	Defrost/cook	Preprogrammed recipes	User-programmable recipes	Temperature probe	Other features
Amana											
M84T	$190	3	—	—	—	✓	✓	—	—	—	A
M86P	225	4	—	—	✓	✓	✓	✓	✓	✓	A
Frigidaire											
MC830L	184	1	—	—	—	—	—	—	—	—	F,G,H
MC850L	194	1	—	—	—	—	✓	—	—	—	G,H
MC870L	209	2	—	—	—	✓	✓	—	—	✓	G,H
MC890L	279	2	—	—	—	✓	✓	✓	✓	✓	G,H
General Electric											
JEM20H [1]	204	2	—	—	—	—	✓	✓	—	—	H
JEM22H	234	2	—	—	—	—	✓	✓	—	✓	H
JEM30WH	234	2	—	—	—	✓	✓	✓	—	✓	A,C,G,H
JEM31H	244	2	—	—	—	✓	✓	✓	—	✓	A,C,I
Goldstar											
ER653MA	300	3	—	✓	✓	✓	—	—	—	—	—
ER654M	300	3	—	✓	✓	✓	✓	—	—	—	—
ER654S	320	3	✓	✓	✓	✓	✓	—	—	—	—
Hotpoint											
REM10F	169	1	—	—	—	—	—	—	—	—	E,I
REM30F	194	2	—	—	✓	—	—	—	—	✓	C,I
J.C. Penney											
5545 [2]	210	3	—	—	✓	✓	✓	—	—	—	A
5537 [3]	230	3	—	—	✓	✓	✓	—	—	—	A
Litton											
1437 [3]	—	2	—	—	—	—	✓	—	—	✓	G,H
1439C	250	2	—	—	—	—	✓	—	—	—	A,G,H
1455 [3]	—	2	—	—	—	—	✓	—	—	✓	G,H
1465 [3]	—	2	—	—	✓	✓	—	—	—	✓	G,H
LP16610	300	2	—	—	✓	✓	✓	✓	✓	✓	A,C,G,H
Magic Chef											
M1510P	219	2	—	✓	—	✓	✓	✓	—	✓	—

Features of Midsize Microwave Ovens (cont'd)

Brand and model	Price	Cooking stages	Sensor	Turntable	Delay start	Defrost assistance	Defrost/cook	Preprogrammed recipes	User-programmable recipes	Temperature probe	Other features
Panasonic											
⌐NN5368A	$199	2	—	✓	✓	✓	—	—	—	—	—
└NN5508A	219	3	—	✓	✓	✓	✓	—	—	—	—
NN5808A	249	3	✓	✓	✓	✓	✓	—	—	—	—
Quasar											
MQ6658W	210	2	—	—	✓	✓	✓	✓	✓	—	H
MQ6668W	220	3	—	—	✓	✓	✓	✓	✓	—	H
MQ6678W	240	3	—	—	✓	✓	✓	✓	✓	✓	H
MQ6698W	280	3	✓	—	✓	✓	✓	✓	✓	—	H
Samsung											
MW5510	206	4	—	—	✓	✓	—	✓	—	—	A
MW5710	216	4	—	—	✓	✓	—	✓	✓	✓	A
Sanyo											
EM355 ③	180	1	—	—	—	✓	—	—	—	—	H
EM363 ③	190	2	—	—	—	✓	✓	✓	—	—	H
EM364 ③	190	3	—	—	✓	✓	✓	✓	—	✓	H
EM380 ③	250	3	✓	—	✓	✓	✓	✓	✓	✓	G, H
Sears											
Cat. No. 88425	250	2	—	—	✓	—	—	—	—	—	A, B, J
Cat. No. 88426	250	2	—	—	✓	—	—	—	—	—	A, B, G, J
Cat. No. 88627 ③	290	4	—	—	✓	✓	✓	✓	—	✓	A, B, J
Cat. No. 89628	300	4	—	✓	✓	✓	✓	✓	—	✓	A, B, G, J
Sharp											
R4E80	210	2	—	✓	—	✓	—	—	—	—	A
R4A70	230	3	—	✓	✓	✓	—	✓	—	—	A
R4A80	240	3	✓	✓	✓	✓	—	—	—	—	A
R4P80	270	3	✓	✓	✓	✓	—	—	—	—	A
R4H80	300	3	✓	✓	✓	✓	—	—	—	✓	A

Brand and model	Price	Cooking stages	Sensor	Turntable	Delay start	Defrost assistance	Defrost/cook	Preprogrammed recipes	User-programmable recipes	Temperature probe	Other features
Tappan											
561246	$164	1	—	—	—	—	—	—	—	—	F,H
562278	189	3	—	—	—	✓	✓	—	—	—	H
562478	209	3	—	—	—	✓	✓	—	—	✓	H
562897	259	2	—	—	—	✓	✓	✓	✓	✓	H
Whirlpool											
MW3200XS	170	1	—	—	—	—	—	—	—	—	F,H
MW3500XS	210	4	—	—	—	✓	✓	✓	✓	✓	D,H
MW3600XS	230	6	—	—	✓	✓	✓	✓	✓	✓	H,H
MW3601XS	230	6	—	—	—	✓	✓	✓	✓	✓	C,H
White-Westinghouse											
KM484K	184	1	—	—	—	—	—	—	—	—	F,H
KM485L	194	3	—	—	—	✓	✓	—	—	—	H
KM487L	209	3	—	—	—	✓	✓	—	—	✓	H

[1] When a manufacturer has more than one basic design, models that are similar are bracketed.

[2] According to manufacturer, a later designation for *5545* is *Cat. No. 8630683A.*

[3] Model was discontinued at the time of original publication in *Consumer Reports.* The information has been retained here, however, to permit comparisons.

Key to Other Features

A—Each press of a command button gives a short period of high-power cooking.

B—Has 100 power levels.

C—Unit comes with shelf.

D—Braille adapter kit available as option.

E—Has mechanical controls, with continuously variable power levels and a 35-minute timer.

F—Has mechanical controls, with five power levels and a 30- or 35-minute timer.

G—Cabinet in white, *GE JEM30WH, Litton LP16610, Whirlpool MW360IXS;* in silver, *Sanyo EM380, Sears 88426* and *88628;* in taupe, *Litton 1437, 1439, 1455, 1465;* in gray, all *Frigidaires.*

H—Hardware for under-cabinet mounting is optional.

I—Hardware for under-cabinet mounting is included.

J—Hardware for wall mounting is included.

Small Microwave Ovens

You can probably get by with a small microwave if you just want a fast, convenient way to defrost frozen foods, warm leftovers, and make popcorn. A small oven is best suited, too, for a kitchen with limited space.

The smallest, plainest ovens look like little more than a cabinet with a mechanical dial timer. They're often only a bit larger and a bit more expensive than a toaster oven.

But features common on larger microwave ovens—electronic touchpad controls, automatic defrost assistance, and multistage cooking—show up even on some small ovens.

Size

Manufacturers classify their small microwave ovens as either compact or subcompact. But what one maker considers compact another might deem something else. Further, the cavities of ovens with similar external dimensions can actually be quite different, and ovens with the same nominal capacity can vary greatly in what they'll actually hold. Some ovens are so small that they can't hold a 10-inch plate, a six-pound chicken, or a large TV dinner. Those models have a capacity of about 0.3 cubic feet. Ovens just slightly larger—0.4 cubic feet—can easily fit these items.

A turntable, which saves you the trouble of rotating a dish so that it cooks more evenly, usually diminishes the usable space by about one-third. But thoughtful design can compensate. If the oven's turntable is mounted flush with the oven floor and can be switched off, that makes the entire interior usable. However, a turntable made of plastic can be marred if a container overheats.

Just as in a larger microwave oven, a small unit's speed depends largely on the power of the magnetron, the part that generates the high-energy waves that do the cooking. In small ovens, the power is usually only 400 to 500 watts (there are a few 600-watt models).

Note that many cookbooks and convenience-food package instructions are written solely for the more powerful ovens. With a small oven, you'll have to extend the time or adjust the power level.

Controls

Although easy to use, ovens with mechanical controls lack many features provided by electronic controls, such as multistage cooking, variable-power defrost, a time-of-day clock, and a kitchen timer. A few don't even have an audible beep to tell you the food is ready. The dial on some allows only 15 minutes, too short for many tasks.

More important, mechanical timers are imprecise, and may miss the mark by as much as 20 or 30 seconds—and seconds count in microwave cooking.

Electronic controls are better. Whereas on larger, top-of-the-line models, such controls can be quite complex, on small models, programming and other electronic options are simpler. To begin a typical program, you press a pad labeled "Time" or "Cook" and then enter the appropriate time. The power level is automatically set to high unless you program it otherwise.

Larger ovens than these often allow for several cooking stages, each at a different time and power setting. Most small models allow two. That's handy if you want to go directly from, say, Defrost to Cook.

The displays on a few models take you through the programming routine step by step with prompts—a panel flashing "Time cook," for example, or spelling out "Power" next to the chosen setting.

Although manufacturers try to equate versatility with the number of power levels they give their models, five well-spaced settings are enough for even the most advanced oven.

Performance

Product literature, even for small ovens, is full of photographs depicting rib roasts, Cornish game hens, and soufflés. But people are more apt to use a microwave oven to defrost hamburger, heat pizza, cook frozen entrées, and bake things like potatoes.

Defrosting

Any microwave can adequately thaw frozen food if you pay attention and turn the food periodically. An automatic defrost mode can eliminate some of the guesswork and labor. With most ovens, it works by automatically lowering the power level over the thawing period. With some, it works for a preprogrammed period based on an item's weight. Either way, it prevents part of the food from cooking while other parts are still icy.

There are big differences in how well a small oven will defrost a pound of ground chuck.

As in many aspects of microwave cooking, you may have to experiment some to find the best way to defrost. The manufacturer's own instructions won't always yield the best results.

Reheating Pizza

Leftover pizza is a particularly tough food to heat because it tends to sizzle at the tip and crust edge while remaining cool in the middle.

Most models leave the center quite a bit cooler than the tip or crust. You may be able to improve the result by using a lower power level for a longer time.

Making Popcorn

The best ovens will make the fluffiest popcorn and leave the fewest kernels unpopped or burned. Placing the popcorn bag on an inverted glass pie plate sometimes improves results.

Baking

With few exceptions, small ovens can bake potatoes and brownies reasonably well. Some models bake potatoes better and quicker than others, but with experimentation, you should get good results in any oven.

Safety

The same cautions and considerations apply to a small microwave as to a midsize one. (See page 269 for a rundown on safety.)

Recommendations

The best small microwaves will cost about $150 after the usual discount from list price. You should consider one of them only if space is truly at a premium.

Many midsize models cost only a little more but provide much more for the money. They're roomy enough for most foods you're apt to prepare. They're faster. And they provide more features.

Ratings of Small Microwave Ovens

Listed by types; within types, listed in order of estimated quality, based mainly on performance and convenience. Closely ranked models differed little in quality.

As published in a **November 1989** report.

◉ ◓ ○ ◒ ●
Better ⟷ Worse

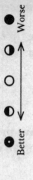

Brand and model	Price	Size (H × W × D), in.	Capacity, cu. ft.	Weight, lbs.	Power, watts	Speed	Reheating	Defrosting	Popping corn	Baking brownies	Instruction manual	Noise	Door opening	Window visibility	Advantages	Disadvantages	Comments
J.C. Penney Cat. No. 863-2853	$140	11¼ × 19¾ × 13¼	0.7 [1]	34	500	○	◓	◓	◓	○	◉	○	○	○	E, F, G, J	m	—
Whirlpool MW1501	167	10½ × 19¼ × 13¼	0.5	31	500	◓	◓	◓	◓	○	◉	◉	◒	○	A, G, I, L, M	—	—
General Electric JE48	126	9¾ × 18 × 13¾	0.4	31	500	○	○	○	○	◓	◉	○	◓	○	E, I, K	j	—
Sharp R-3A80	181	11½ × 18¼ × 13¾	0.7 [1]	28	500	○	◉	◉	○	◒	○	○	○	◓	G, I, L	e, i, j	*C*
Hotpoint REM4F	160	11¼ × 19¾ × 13½	0.6	37	500	○	◒	◓	○	◒	◉	○	◓	◓	E, G, J	j	—
Sears Kenmore 88214	120	9¾ × 18 × 14¾	0.5	29	500	○	◓	◓	○	○	◉	◓	◓	◒	I	n	*C*
General Electric JEM4WH	160	11¼ × 19¾ × 13½	0.6	36	500	○	○	○	○	○	◉	○	◓	◒	E, I, J	j	*B*

Emerson AT738	147	12¾ × 18½ × 14	0.7 [1]	30	530	◓	◓	◓	◒	○	◓	◒	○	●	F, G, H, L	e, k	—
Tappan 56-2077	135	10¾ × 19¼ × 13½	0.5	33	500	○	○	○	○	◓	◓	○	○	◓	F, G, L	e	—
Admiral MA5C-6	189	12¾ × 20½ × 15	0.6	41	600	◓	○	◓	○	○	◓	◓	○	◒	B, L	k	—
Welbilt MR-73T	160	12¼ × 18¼ × 13½	0.7 [1]	35	500	◓	○	◓	◒	◒	◓	◓	○	○	F, G, H, L	e, j	—
Magic Chef M5E-10	189	12¾ × 20½ × 15	0.6 [1]	41	600	◓	◒	◓	◓	◒	◓	◓	○	○	B, C, L	b, k	*A*
White-Westinghouse KM-159K	180	10¾ × 19¼ × 13½	0.5	33	500	○	◒	◒	◓	◓	◓	○	○	◓	F, G, L	e	—
Panasonic NN-4368A	124	9½ × 18 × 13½	0.4	25	500	○	○	◓	○	○	○	○	○	◒	—	h, i, o	*C*
Sears Kenmore 88219	105	9¾ × 17 × 13	0.4	27	450	○	○	◒	○	●	◉	○	○	●	I, L	e, l	*C*
Models with mechanical controls																	
Sharp R-3F50	128	10¾ × 17¾ × 14¼	0.6 [1]	26	500	○	◒	○	○	◓	○	◒	○	◓	—	e	—
Sharp R-1M50	99	13¼ × 13½ × 13½	0.5 [1]	24	400	◒	○	◒	◒	○	○	○	◓	◓	D	c, e, p	—
Goldstar ER3553	89	9¾ × 17 × 13¼	0.4	25	500	○	●	◒	◓	◒	○	○	○	●	—	c, d, p	—
Samsung MW2170U	91	9¼ × 18¼ × 13¼	0.4	24	500	◒	◒	○	○	○	○	◒	○	●	—	c, e, f	—

Ratings of Small Microwave Ovens (cont'd)

The following models have very limited capacity and are therefore judged unusable for many tasks

Brand and model	Price	Size (H × W × D) in.	Capacity, cu. ft.	Weight, lbs.	Power, watts	Speed	Reheating	Defrosting	Popping corn	Baking brownies	Instruction manual	Noise	Door opening	Window visibility	Advantages	Disadvantages	Comments
General Electric JE3	$94	9¾ × 16 × 11¾	0.3	23	475	◑	○	○	○	●	○	○	○	○	E	a, p	—
Samsung MW1010	68	9¾ × 16 × 11¾	0.3	23	450	○	◑	○	○	○	○	○	◑	—	—	a, e, o, p	—
Emerson AR301	84	9¾ × 15¾ × 12¾	0.3	21	400	◑	●	◑	○	○	○	○	◑	—	—	a, e, g, p	C

1 Includes turntable.

Specifications and Features

All: • Are countertop models (kits for mounting units beneath cabinets are available for some units. See features table on pages 290–91. • Have a door that is hinged on the left. • Draw 840–1,190 watts. *Except as noted, all:* • Have interior light that goes on when door is opened or oven is running. • Need professional servicing to replace light bulb. • Have a glass tray or ceramic floor. • Have a provision to keep spills inside the oven from leaking out. • Can hold a six-pound roasting chicken, one 7 × 10¾-inch frozen dinner, or a 10-inch dinner plate.

Except as noted, all models with electronic controls: • Do not require power level to be programmed when cooking at full power. • Have a well-lit display and control panel, with numbers arranged telephone-style. • Have a timer that can be set to the nearest second. • Have a reduced power setting that cycles at about 20 percent of full power at lowest level.

Key to Advantages

A—Keypad beep can be shut off.
B—Comfortably accommodates 12-inch plate.
C—Turntable is recessed into oven floor; can be switched on or off (but see Disadvantage b).
D—Takes up least amount of counter space of any model; controls mounted above door instead of to side.
E—Light bulb is easily replaced by user.

F—Percentage of power at lowest setting is less than 20 percent.

G—Comes with cookbook or instruction guide with many recipes.

H—Start touchpad is particularly prominent.

I—Start and Stop touchpads are well positioned and prominent.

J—Electronic display has mode indicators and extensive prompts to make programming easier.

K—Display has mode indicators and some prompts.

L—Display has mode indicators.

M—Keypad beep volume is adjustable.

Key to Disadvantages

a—Severely limited floor space; won't hold a typical dinner plate, large frozen dinner, or six-pound chicken.

b—Plastic turntable could be damaged by overheated food (but see Advantage C).

c—No beep to signal end of cycle.

d—No interior light.

e—Light doesn't go on when door is opened.

f—Most imprecise of mechanical timers; cooking time can be miscalculated by as much as 30 seconds.

g—Poorly marked timer control; numbers are far from dial and marked in five-minute intervals.

h—User must program power when cooking at highest setting.

i—Liquid-crystal display is darker and more difficult to see than other electronic readouts.

j—Number pads arranged in two sequential rows, judged somewhat inconvenient.

k—Number pads arranged in alternating rows or single column, judged inconvenient.

l—"Count-up" method of setting time, with minimum setting of 15 seconds,

less convenient and precise than direct-entry method.

m—Confusing control panel and markings.

n—Setting power levels above 10 percent requires punching two digits.

o—No recipe book included; instruction manual has limited cooking ideas.

p—Maximum time setting only 15 minutes, too short for many tasks.

Key to Comments

A—Flat interior floor is easily cleaned but has no lip to keep spills from leaking out.

B—Users with poor vision might prefer wood-grain version (model *JEM4H*) because its control-panel color contrasts better with the control markings.

C—Although this model was discontinued and is no longer available, the information has been retained to permit comparisons.

Features of Small Microwave Ovens

As published in a November 1989 report.

Brand and model	Power levels	Cooking stages	Quick-set cooking	Turntable	Time-of-day clock	Variable-power defrost	Delay start	Removable glass tray	Exterior finish [1]	Other features	Similar models
J.C. Penney 863-2853	10	3	—	✓	✓	✓	✓	✓	WG	B,C	—
Whirlpool MW1501	10	2	—	—	✓	✓	—	✓	W	D	MW1000XS, $139, a; MW12000XS, $169, b; MW1500XS, $189, e
General Electric JE4	5	1	—	✓	—	✓	✓	✓	WG	D	JE42, $104, a; JE45, $124, b
Sharp R-3A80	5	2	✓	✓	✓	✓	—	✓	WG	B,C,D	—
Hotpoint REM4F	10	2	—	✓	—	✓	✓	✓	WG	E	REM2F, $144, b
Sears Kenmore 88214	100	1	✓	—	—	✓	✓	✓	G	A,D	—
General Electric JEM4WH	10	2	—	✓	—	✓	✓	✓	W	D	JEM4H, $160, c; JEM2G, $154, b
Emerson AT738	10	2	—	✓	✓	✓	✓	✓	WG	—	—
Tappan 56-2077	10	2	—	✓	✓	✓	✓	✓	B	—	56-1007, $119, a; 56-1037, $119, b
Admiral MA5C-6	10	1	—	✓	—	✓	✓	✓	W	—	MA5C-3, $149, b
Welbilt MR-73T	9	2	—	✓	—	✓	✓	✓	W	—	MR72, $149, b

Model										
Magic Chef M5E-10	10	1	—	✓	✓	—	—	—	W	—	M5E1, a, d
White-Westinghouse KM-159K	10	2	—	—	✓	✓	✓	✓	B	—	—
Panasonic NN-4368A	6	2	—	✓	✓	✓	✓	WG	D	—
Sears Kenmore 88219	3	2	—	—	—	✓	B	—	—
Sharp R-3F50	2	1	—	✓	✓	—	✓	W	D	R-3M80, $169, c
Sharp R-1M50	1	1	—	✓	—	—	W	—	—
Goldstar ER3553	1	1	—	—	✓	B	—	—
Samsung MW217OU	2	1	—	—	✓	W	D	—
General Electric JE3	1	1	—	—	✓	B	—	—
Samsung MW1010	1	1	—	—	✓	W	—	—
Emerson AR301	2	1	—	—	✓	W	D	—

1 Cabinet colors include the traditional simulated wood grain (WG), white (W), beige (B), and gray (G).

Key to Other Features

A—Child lock-out feature.

B—Special reheat mode to warm specific foods.

C—Touch pad is coded to cook or defrost certain foods by entry or weight.

D—Hardware for under-cabinet mounting is optional.

E—Hardware for under-cabinet mounting is included.

Key to Similar Models

a—Mechanical controls, 15-minute timer, single power level, no clock or other electronic features.

b—Mechanical controls, 30- to 35-minute timer, two or more power levels, no clock or other electronic features.

c—Only one power level.

d—No turntable.

e—Wood-grain finish.

Microwave/Convection Ovens

Like an ordinary microwave oven, a combination oven makes short work of heating leftovers and thawing frozen food. And like a traditional range oven, it can brown food on the outside—something an ordinary microwave oven can't do.

A combination oven can be set to cook with microwaves only, convection heat only, or a combination of the two. It's the convection heat mode that makes the food crisp and brown on the outside. Microwaves don't heat food directly. The energy penetrates the food, agitating molecules of moisture and generating heat that cooks from within.

In convection cooking, a fan circulates hot air to brown what microwaves alone leave pale. But some combination designs have no fan, relying on the natural circulation of heat to brown the food— "microwave/thermal" cooking as opposed to "microwave/convection" cooking. The no-fan design is apt to be less effective overall.

The power of the microwave magnetron is stated in watts. Power varies from model to model, which causes considerable confusion when trying to work with microwave recipes. Usually (but not always), the higher the wattage, the faster the cooking.

When used in the heat-only mode, combination ovens function much like a regular electric oven (and just like a convection oven, an appliance fad of a few years back). Most can be set for a full range of temperatures, from 200° to 450°F.

Most microwave/convection ovens can be programmed to cook first with microwaves, then with convection heat, or vice versa. But "combination cooking" generally means the oven cycles back and forth between microwave and convection cooking.

To make such cooking easier, manufacturers have devised various combination "programs." With one, for example, you tap Micro-Bake and the time, and the machine does the rest. Another design gives you two choices: Combi-High, which cycles between 375° and 30 percent power; and Combi-Low, which gives you 350° and 10 percent power. Others offer more choice—and thus can be more complicated to figure out.

The speed of microwave cooking along with the roasting or browning provided by convection heat makes the combination mode especially good at cooking meat and poultry dishes and casseroles.

Instruction Books

A great deal of new equipment requires considerable study and experience before you feel comfortable using it. With microwave cooking, you certainly need a lot of know-how if you intend to do more than simply reheat food. Combination cooking requires even more proficiency. That's why instructions and recipe books are so important.

The literature that comes with combination ovens leaves much to be desired. You have to search long and hard through both the use-and-care booklet and the cookbook to find out which accessories and utensils to use and what time, power, and temperature to set.

In a good cookbook, recipes are well organized, with many tables for easy reference. There should be alternative methods given— meatballs made in microwave or convection mode, for example.

Controls

Easy-to-use controls can help you master a complex and unfamiliar technology, especially when you don't perform a task often enough to memorize the procedure.

Here are other ways manufacturers try to make it easier for you to wade through the technology.

Built-in Directions

Some ovens come with a list of common instructions attached to the oven or a wipeable card with such instructions ("To cook with sensor: 1. Touch Sensor Cook. 2. Enter desired Sensor setting.").

Automatic Defrosting

Most of the ovens have some preprogrammed means to help thaw frozen foods evenly. Those aids include automatic lowering or cycling of oven power as well as pauses or beeps to remind you to turn the food. With some, you program the weight of the food into the operation.

Temperature Probe

Some models add a temperature probe to the equation. It works for all modes of cooking. You insert the probe into the food the way you would a meat thermometer. When the food reaches the preset temperature, the oven shuts off or switches to a "hold warm" cycle.

Moisture Sensor

This microwaving feature takes the guesswork out of setting the time and power level. You simply punch in the proper setting (reheat, beef stew, potatoes). The food (which must be covered) gives off moisture as it's cooking; when the sensor detects a certain amount of moisture, the cooking stops. A top-of-the-line feature that adds $40 or $50 to the price of the oven, a moisture sensor is well worth having.

Automatic Cooking Programs

Some models have combination programs that compute temperature, power, and cooking time for half a dozen foods. You key in the food's code; the machine does the rest. Unfortunately, these systems don't always turn out a superior product. You'll find that manual settings consistently give better results.

Safety

The same cautions and considerations apply to a microwave/convection oven as to an ordinary microwave. See page 269 for a rundown on safety.

Recommendations

If you already own a microwave oven and are happy with it, don't rush to buy a microwave/convection model. Although the addition of hot air remedies many of the flaws of microwave cooking, those flaws show up only when you use the microwave to cook, not just to heat up foods. Most people use microwaves to reheat or defrost foods, not to cook recipes from scratch.

Combination ovens are also more complex than microwave ovens;

you'll need to study and learn new cooking techniques. In addition, these ovens take up a lot of counter space. Despite their outside dimensions, however, they're too small inside to make a very good auxiliary oven for holiday baking.

The ovens get hot in their heat modes, so they're harder to clean than ordinary microwave ovens. The heat can find its way out into the kitchen, too—a consideration on hot days.

For broiling and baking, especially in quantity, your regular oven can probably do better.

Despite those drawbacks, a combination oven may still make sense if you have so far avoided buying a microwave oven, or if you find a small, simple microwave insufficient for your cooking needs. A microwave/convection oven can bake bread and biscuits that rise and turn brown on the outside. Hamburgers cooked with convection heat are a big improvement over their microwaved counterparts. Poultry and meat loaf come out evenly cooked on the inside and nicely browned on top.

The microwave/convection may perform better than the microwave/thermal design. Buy a model that has a moisture sensor.

Guide to the Ratings

1. Brand and model. Most have a fan to circulate the hot air.

2. Power. The wattage of the magnetron, as stated by manufacturer. More power usually (but not always) cooks faster.

3. Dimensions. Height, width, and depth. Protrusions are included in the measurements. Note that these ovens have vents at the back, so they can't stand flush against the wall. Some also have vents on top, which require clearance.

4. Exterior. Simulated wood (*S*) is still very popular, but white (*W*) and gray (*G*) can be found, too.

5. Speed. The slowest oven here takes about 45 percent longer than the fastest. Note that where the food is placed in the oven can affect heating speed.

6. Reheating. The more evenly the food heats, the higher the score. Models that have a moisture sensor do very well, even if you vary the amounts of foods on the plate.

7. Space efficiency. Based on the ratio of usable capacity to overall size. Turntables are space consuming.

Ratings of Microwave/Convection Ovens

Listed by groups in order of estimated quality, based on cooking, convenience, and features. Except where separated by a bold rule, differences among closely ranked models were slight. See also the Features table on pages 303–6.

As published in a **September 1989** report.

1 Brand and model	Price 2	Power	Dimensions (H × W × D), in. 3	Exterior 4	Claimed capacity, cu. ft.	Usable capacity, cu. ft.	Speed 5
Sharp Carousel II R9H80	$539	700	14¾ × 24¾ × 18	G	1.5	0.9	◒
General Electric JET342G001	434	700	15¼ × 24 × 18½	S	1.4	1.4	◒
Montgomery Ward 8288	330	650	15 × 22 × 19¾	S	1.3	1.3	◒
Whirlpool MC8991XTO	422	700	15 × 22 × 19¾	W	1.3	1.3	◒
Panasonic Dimension 4 NN9807	580	700	15½ × 24 × 18½	S	1.4	0.9	◒
Panasonic Gemini NN8907 (thermal)	490	700	14¼ × 21¾ × 16¼	W	1.0	0.6	◉
Quasar MQ8798H	479	700	13½ × 23¾ × 16	W	1.1	1.1	○
Amana RMC 720	380	700	14¼ × 21¾ × 16¼	S	1.0	1.0	○
Samsung Multi Chef MW6790C	375	650	14 × 22¼ × 18	S	1.0	0.9	◐
Goldstar ER930C	430	650	14¼ × 21¾ × 16	S	0.9	0.5	○
Tappan Micro-Bake 565897 (thermal)	399	700	15½ × 23½ × 17¼	S	1.3	1.1	◉
J.C. Penney Cat. No. 863-2879	360	650	14¼ × 21¾ × 16	S	0.9	0.5	○

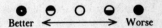

Better ←————————→ Worse

Defrosting	Reheating	Instructions, recipes	Ease of use	Space efficiency	Noise	Advantages	Disadvantages	Comments
	6			**7**				
◐	◉	○	◐	○	○	A, B, C, K, M, N, O	t, cc	D, F, K
◐	◉	◐	◐	◐	●	G, M, Q, S, T, U, W, X	k, x, z	N, O, R
◐	◉	○	◐	◐	○	A, B, D, K, L, M, N	cc	F, K
○	◉	○	○	◐	○	D, E, H, K, M, O, R	y, cc, ee	L
○	◉	◐	○	○	●	G, M, Q, R, T, X	a, t, z, aa, cc	N
◉	◉	◐	○	○	○	G, S, X	a, m, t, u, z, bb, cc, ii	I, M, U
◐	◉	○	◐	◐	●	A, G, O, P, R, T	a, q, r, cc	—
○	◐	◐	◐	◐	●	A, K, S, T, X	b, t, v	O, V
◐	○	○	◉	○	○	B, G, J, K, U, W	o, p, r, ff	E, O, T
◐	◐	◐	◐	◐	◐	B, I, J, O, U	j, s, t, u	F, H
○	○	○	○	○	◐	A, F, M, O, T, U, V	p, bb, dd, ee, gg, ii	E, G, N, O
◐	◐	●	◐	◐	◐	B, I, J, O, U	j, s, t, u	F, H

Ratings of Microwave/Convection Ovens (cont'd)

1 Brand and model	Price 2	Power	Dimensions (H × W × D), in. 3	Exterior 4	Claimed capacity, cu. ft.	Usable capacity, cu. ft.	Speed 5
Sears Kenmore 88963	450	750	15¾ × 24¼ × 19¼	G	1.3	1.3	◓
Brother Hi Speed MF3200	649	650	15 × 21¾ × 19¾	W	0.9	0.5	○
Magic Chef M71C10	439	600	15 × 21¾ × 19¾	S	0.9	0.5	◓

Specifications and Features

All: • Are countertop models. (Built-in or under-cabinet kits are optional for some; see Features table on pages 303–6). • Can hold a six-pound roasting chicken. • Draw 1,345–1,688 watts. • Weigh 46–66 pounds. • Were fairly quiet at full microwave power. • Broil at 450–500° F. • Have door with screened window that swings open to the left. • Have interior light that goes on when oven is operating. • Have provision for keeping minor spills from leaking onto the counter. • Make audible signal when cooking is finished. • Show time of day on electronic display when oven is not in use.

Except as noted, all: • Have electronic touch pad that beeps as it is programmed. • Have at least five microwave power levels. • Can be programmed for up to 99 minutes and 99 seconds for microwave, heat, and combination cooking. • Can preheat to selected temperature and hold that temperature for at least 30 minutes. • Were fairly quiet when cooking with heat only. • Have four basic combination-cooking programs with one microwave power level and varying oven temperatures. • Have one broil setting. • Have minimum temperature setting of 200°. • Hold two 8¾-inch luncheon plates or one 11¾ × 7½ × 1¾-inch glass baking dish.

• Hold five to nine quarter-pound hamburgers on pan or rack or five to nine bread slices on tray, turntable, or floor. • Have push-button door release. • Have stainless-steel interior. • Have interior light that goes on when door is opened. • Come with use-and-care booklet and recipe book that cover all three modes of cooking. • Function as timer.

Key to Advantages

A—Two-step programming for full-power cooking.

B—Specific temperature settings on touch pads made programming of oven heat very easy.

C—100° F minimum oven-temperature setting.

D—150° minimum oven-temperature setting.

E—Can be programmed for up to 199 minutes and 99 seconds in heat and combination modes.

F—Can be programmed for up to four hours in heat mode.

G—Can be programmed for up to nine hours and 99 minutes in heat and combination modes.

H—Large, easy-to-read characters in electronic display.

Defrosting	Reheating	Instructions, recipes	Ease of use	Space efficiency	Noise	Advantages	Disadvantages	Comments
			6		7			
⊖	•	○	●	○	○	H, K, U	c, j, l, n, p, q, r, cc	J, O
○	⊖	○	⊖	⊖	○	C, J, N, O	a, d, f, h, i, j, s, t, u, w, cc	A, C, J, P, Q, S
○	⊖	⊖	⊖	⊖	○	H, K, N	a, d, e, f, g, s, t, u, cc, ee, hh	B, J, P, Q, S

I—Display alternates between oven temperature or power level and time countdown.

J—Took less time than most to bake biscuits.

K—Took less time than most to defrost meat.

L—Took less time than most to combination-cook six-pound chicken.

M—Held a 12½-pound turkey easily.

N—Took less time than most to combination-cook meat loaf.

O—Took less time than most to broil hamburgers.

P—Oven floor can hold 12 bread slices.

Q—Broil area can hold 16 quarter-pound burgers.

R—Oven-width rack slides out and locks in position.

S—Oven-width broil pan slides out and locks in position.

T—Quieter than most in heat mode.

U—Oven door has handle.

V—Nonstick interior finish is easy to wipe.

W—The word "hot" flashes in display when door is opened after preheating.

X—Cookbook judged better than most.

Key to Disadvantages

a—Has count-up buttons for setting time, judged less convenient than full keypad.

b—Keypads don't beep when pressed.

c—Programming power levels above 9 percent requires touching two keypads.

d—Cooking time can be set only to nearest 10 seconds, rather than to nearest second.

e—Has only three microwave power levels.

f—Doesn't beep when preheat temperature has been reached; displays a small symbol.

g—300° F minimum oven-temperature setting.

h—No setting between 100° and 320° F.

i—Confusing power-level symbols in display.

j—Kitchen timer less convenient to set than most.

k—Code for programming moisture sensor not on oven itself; user must refer to instructions.

l—Ceramic oven tray must be removed for convection-only cooking.

m—Turntable must be removed for heat-only cooking.

n—Changing quantities when using programmed recipe feature confusing.

o—Broil pan lacks drain insert.

p—Broil pan must be removed to turn food.

q—Broil pan must be purchased separately.

r—No pan for baking; small baking sheet must be purchased separately.

Ratings of Microwave/Convection Ovens (cont'd)

s—Small turntable holds only four bread slices.

t—Holds only one eight-and-a-quarter-inch luncheon plate.

u—Can't hold 11¾ × 7½ × 1¾-inch baking dish.

v—11¾ × 7½ × 1¾-inch baking dish fits only one way.

w—Took longer than others to defrost ground chuck using automatic defrost.

x—Took longer than others to combination-cook six-pound chicken.

y—Took longer than others to combination-cook meat loaf.

z—Took longer than most to bake biscuits.

aa—Took longer than others to bake bread and broil hamburgers.

bb—For best results when baking bread, top of loaf must be shielded with aluminum foil partway through baking.

cc—Must be taken to shop to replace interior light.

dd—Oven has exposed element on floor; easy to spill on and difficult to clean under.

ee—Oven can't cook in stages.

ff—Oven can't cook in stages in convection or combination modes.

gg—No automatic preheat for broil.

hh—No kitchen timer.

ii—Poor view through oven window.

Key to Comments

A—Push buttons instead of keypad controls.

B—Light does not turn on when door is opened.

C—Oven fan turns on when door is opened.

D—Temperature probe didn't operate properly during convection cooking in one sample.

E—250°F minimum oven-temperature setting.

F—Holds preheat oven temperature for 15 minutes.

G—Combination cooking is preprogrammed for microwave power level and oven temperature, depending on selected cooking time.

H—Has two basic preprogrammed combination-cooking settings, each with different microwave power level and oven temperature.

I—Has five basic preprogrammed combination-cooking settings; microwave power levels and oven temperatures vary from setting to setting.

J—Microwave power level is preprogrammed for basic combination cooking; user can change oven temperature.

K—Has two basic preprogrammed combination-cooking settings; user can change oven temperature but not microwave power level.

L—Has one basic preprogrammed combination-cooking setting; user can change both oven temperature and microwave power level.

M—Has no rack; oven pan can be used for baking and broiling.

N—Broil pan can be used to bake some foods.

O—Has oven-width rack, which can't slide out.

P—Oven can be set so turntable doesn't revolve.

Q—Splash trivet that fits over turntable prevents juices from cooking, but juices are inaccessible for basting.

R—Oven floor can hold 16 bread slices, but all don't cook well when microwaving.

S—Continuous-clean finish on rear oven wall; other walls are stainless steel.

T—Door handle stiff on the sample tested.

U—Replaced by model *NN8858,* $490.

V—Although this model was discontinued and is no longer available, the information has been retained to permit comparisons.

Guide to the Features

1. Number of cooking stages. A stage is a set of commands: time and power-level or time and oven-temperature. Two or more stages allow the flexibility of sequential cooking. All but the *Magic Chef, Samsung, Tappan,* and *Whirlpool* allow you to set an automated cooking sequence of different modes—for example, heat-only followed by microwave-only.

2. Number of racks. Most come with a rack or two. If there's a turntable or tray, the rack generally stands on that.

3. Turntable. Since microwave ovens don't distribute energy with absolute uniformity, many foods need turning now and then. A turntable makes that convenient, but at the cost of usable capacity.

4. Broil pan. Helpful for making hamburgers. Typically, it includes a drain insert that allows juices to drip down into the pan. Most can double as baking pans.

5. Guide card. A plasticized card with abbreviated instructions for frequent tasks. It saves you the bother of referring to the instruction book.

6. Guide on oven. Printed instructions that help you program the cooking—again, saving you the bother of referring to the instructions.

7. Moisture sensor. Allows automated microwave cooking without the need to set power level or cooking time. This useful feature measures moisture escaping from the food (which must be covered for the sensor to work properly). When the sensor detects a certain moisture level, it shuts off the oven. It's especially helpful for warming leftovers.

8. Temperature probe. You insert the slim probe into the food; when the inside of the food reaches the set temperature, the oven signals and shuts itself off or cycles into a keep-warm phase. (For best results, insert the probe at an angle.)

9. Audible preheat signal. Cooking with heat sometimes requires preheating the oven. This feature beeps when it's time to place the food in the oven.

10. Delay start. Lets you program an oven to turn itself on at a future time. Unimportant for microwave use, where cooking is fast anyway. Note that many foods shouldn't be left sitting too long in an oven at room temperature.

11. Defrost assist. To ease defrosting, some ovens can automatically lower or cycle microwave power. Some also pause or beep to remind you to turn the food.

12. Defrost/cook. An automatic two-stage mode. The oven defrosts, then automatically switches to a cooking program. In some cases, this feature increases the number of programmable stages that are available.

13. Keep warm. A separate program to keep food in the oven warm after a cooking program.

14. Mounting hardware. Optional kits allow some ovens to be built in (B) with a trim kit or mounted under a cabinet (C).

Features of Microwave/Convection Ovens

As published in a September 1989 report.

Brand and model	1 Cooking stages	2 Racks	3 Turntable	4 Broil pan	5 Guide card	6 Guide on oven	7 Moisture sensor	8 Temperature probe	9 Audible preheat signal	10 Delay start	11 Defrost assist	12 Defrost/cook	13 Keep warm	14 Mounting hardware	Other features
Sharp Carousel II R9H80	4	2	✓	—	✓	✓	✓	✓	✓	✓	✓	✓	—	B	B,F,H,I,O
General Electric JET 342G001	2	1	—	✓	—	✓	✓	✓	✓	✓	✓	—	—	B	I,N
Montgomery Ward 8288	4	2	—	—	✓	✓	✓	✓	✓	✓	✓	—	—	—	A,I,Q
Whirlpool MC8991XT0	1	2	—	—	✓	✓	✓	✓	✓	✓	✓	✓	—	—	A,D,O,Q
Panasonic Dimension 4 NN9807	3	2	✓	✓	—	✓	✓	—	✓	✓	✓	—	B	—	D,J,K,N
Panasonic Gemini NN8907	3	0	✓	✓	—	✓	✓	—	✓	✓	✓	—	B	—	D,J,K,N
Quasar MQ8798H	3	1	—	✓	—	✓	✓	—	✓	✓	✓	—	B	—	B,J
Amana RMC 720	3	1	—	✓	✓	✓	—	✓	✓	✓	✓	—	B	—	C,Q
Samsung Multi Chef MW6790C	2	1	—	✓	—	—	✓	—	✓	✓	✓	—	—	—	N
Goldstar ER930C	2	2	✓	—	—	—	—	✓	✓	✓	✓	✓	—	—	E
Tappan Micro-Bake 565897	1	1	—	✓	—	—	✓	✓	✓	—	—	—	—	—	—
J.C. Penney Cat. No. 863-2879	2	2	✓	—	—	—	—	✓	✓	✓	✓	✓	—	C	E

Brand and model	Cooking stages 1	Racks 2	Turntable 3	Broil pan 4	Guide card 5	Guide on oven 6	Moisture sensor 7	Temperature probe 8	Audible preheat signal 9	Delay start 10	Defrost assist 11	Defrost/cook 12	Keep warm 13	Mounting hardware 14	Other features
Sears Kenmore 88963	3	1	—	—	✓	✓	—	✓	✓	✓	✓	✓	—	—	A,E,G,P
Brother Hi Speed MF3200	3	1	✓	—	—	—	—	—	✓	✓	✓	✓	—	—	D,H,L,M,R
Magic Chef MC71C10	1	1	✓	—	—	—	—	—	—	—	—	—	B	—	L,R

Key to Other Features

A—Tray for oven floor.

B—Separate reheat sensor setting.

C—Separate, preprogrammed reheat setting.

D—Degree of doneness setting for automatic cooking.

E—Shortcut setting for fixed, short microwave cooking time at full power.

F—Shortcut setting for cooking time at full microwave power; multiple touches of keypad increase the time. Setting also extends time at lower microwave power levels and for convection and combination cooking (but not for automatic cooking programs).

G—Recipes can be programmed in memory. Has 25 preprogrammed recipes.

H—Six automatic cooking programs for a variety of foods.

I—Probe allows automatic cooking of certain foods (primarily meat and poultry).

J—Allows automatic combination cooking of meat and poultry based on weight.

K—Allows automatic combination cooking of certain frozen foods based on weight.

L—Special convection setting leaves turntable stationary.

M—Separate fine-tuning switch in addition to doneness setting for automatic cooking.

N—Two broil settings.

O—Slow-cook feature.

P—Child lock-out feature.

Q—Baking sheet.

R—Splash trivet fits over turntable; insulating mat is used between wire rack and metal pan for combination cooking.

Toaster Ovens and Toaster-Oven Broilers

Toaster ovens or toaster-oven broilers are versatile enough to earn their space on a kitchen counter. Of the two types, toaster-oven broilers are the more common.

Uses

In addition to making toast, a toaster oven can heat a frozen dinner, bake potatoes or a small meat loaf, warm rolls, and do many of the chores a regular oven does, albeit on a smaller scale. A toaster-oven broiler can do those baking chores and broil, too.

Toasting

While toasting bread and rolls is a common use for these appliances, a traditional pop-up toaster is quicker and better for toasting bread.

Toaster ovens and toaster-oven broilers don't do well at toasting bread to an even, medium brown on both sides. For the most part, the bread comes out evenly toasted on top, striped on the bottom. Just about any pop-up toaster can do a better job.

Potatoes

A typical unit should do a fine job with potatoes—nicely done inside, with a crispy skin. Most need an hour to an hour and a quarter to bake a batch of four potatoes.

Frozen Entrées

Results should be acceptable, though pot pies may not brown as evenly as in a conventional oven. Some frozen entrée containers are made principally for microwave-oven use; the direct heat of a toaster oven may cause some melting of the plastic containers.

Cake

Some toaster ovens and toaster-oven broilers aren't large enough to hold a cake pan. And many of these ovens don't provide the kind of even heat required for baking a good layer cake.

Burgers and Steaks

A toaster-oven broiler may handle as many as six quarter-pound burgers at a time or as few as three. A toaster-oven broiler may be able to cook hamburgers medium-brown outside and rare to medium-rare inside. But you can cook even better burgers in an aluminum skillet with a nonstick finish; they will be crisp outside and rare to well done inside, depending on your taste.

Skillet cooking is faster too, taking only eight minutes. Broiling in a full-size electric oven requires about 17 minutes, whereas toaster-oven broilers need from 14 to 20 minutes.

T-bone steaks cooked in an oven broiler are acceptable—but they would be better if the little broilers could crisp the outside of the meat a bit more.

Features and Other Considerations

A toaster oven or a toaster-oven broiler is a small appliance meant for small jobs. It is supposed to save you the trouble of heating a full-size oven (and the kitchen, along with it) just to warm a little bit of food. It should also be easy to clean.

Size and Capacity

Most toaster ovens and toaster-oven broilers occupy a space about 10 by 15 inches. Some can be installed under a kitchen cabinet and so take no counter space at all.

Exterior dimensions vary by only inches here and there. Interior dimensions are another story. Buying a very compact model to save a little counter space could be a foolish economy when you discover that the oven will hold only one frozen entrée or two slices of bread.

Controls

On most models, an easy-to-use temperature control activates the baking or broiling element: The controls are marked much like those on conventional ovens, in 25- or 50-degree increments. There may be a timer that starts and stops the oven. Some models have a table of recommended temperature settings right on the face of the unit, which is very handy.

While a temperature control may be clearly marked and easy to use, it may also be less than precise. You will have to experiment (until you become accustomed to the control) to get the food to come out right, especially when baking.

Signals

Most models have a signal light that indicates when the unit is operating. Some cycle on and off with the cooking element, others stay on continuously. All signal the end of cooking with a click or a chime.

Racks and Pans

The oven should have a removable toasting rack held by grooves or projections along the walls. On some ovens, the rack advances automatically when you open the oven door. That makes access easy and helps prevent burns.

There should also be a metal pan for heating small amounts of food. It's helpful if there is an extension at the front that makes the pan easy to grasp when you're wearing oven mitts.

A toaster-oven broiler has a metal broiling insert—a slotted or perforated rack that allows juices to drip into the pan below. In some models, you can flip the broiler insert over to cook food at a different distance from the element.

Cleaning

A number of models have the kind of continuous-clean surface found in full-size ovens. It's supposed to rid itself of grease and grime at normal cooking temperatures. But the rough, porous surface may eventually need cleaning—a difficult chore because you can't use an abrasive cleaner. A unit with a nonstick interior is the easiest to clean.

Energy Consumption

These appliances draw between 10 and 13½ amps. Using another appliance (especially one that heats up, like an electric fry pan) on the same circuit could blow a fuse or trip a circuit breaker. Baking a batch of potatoes, for example, would cost about five to seven cents. The cost in a well-insulated conventional electric oven would be about the same. Cooking six hamburgers in a toaster-oven broiler would cost only a penny or two. A conventional electric broiler would cost a lot more to run—but you could cook a lot more burgers.

Recommendations

A toaster-oven broiler is more versatile than a toaster oven and may cost no more, especially when you consider the big discounts you can often find for these products. A small toaster-oven broiler can be handy for quick warm-ups when you want crispness rather than the steamy quality that a microwave oven provides. An oven broiler makes adequate toast and does a good job with baked potatoes, toasted muffins, and the like. A skillet on a range top makes a better burger, but a toaster-oven broiler is convenient and does a respectable job.

Popcorn Poppers

The microwave oven has many talents. Among them is its capability as a popcorn machine. Much of the credit goes to microwave bags of popcorn, which make the job easy and require no cleanup.

But not all microwave ovens do a good job with the bags. Those that don't often do better with specially made bowls. The brand of popcorn you use can also spell the difference between failure and success (see page 246).

Of course, micro-popping isn't the only way to puff a kernel.

The electric hot-air popper, the last technological popping innovation, showed up in the late 1970s. The original shape—upright with a spout—still predominates. The appeal of the hot-air popper is convenience—it's easy to use and requires little cleanup. Plus you need no oil for popping, which significantly reduces the popcorn's calories.

The electric appliances made for popping corn in hot oil haven't changed much either. They're short, saucer-shaped, and a nuisance to store. Popcorn made this way still has its fans, despite the necessary cleanup and the additional calories.

An even simpler method of hot-oil popping is popular—the special stove-top popping pan. Finally, there's the plain old pan with a lid.

Popping Successfully

Successful popping depends on using the right combination of heat, moisture, and hull strength. With too much heat, you scorch and burn the kernels. With insufficient heat, the kernels don't pop. Too much moisture in the cooking results in popcorn that is tough and chewy. Not enough moisture in the kernels impedes the popping process. (That's why poorly packaged or stored popcorn produces a lot of duds.)

The bottom line for popping is in the bottom of the bowl—the unpopped kernels. Most poppers consistently pop close to every last kernel. But a few hot-air models do poorly with certain brands of popcorn, leaving lots of duds behind.

Hot-air poppers produce the fluffiest popcorn because constant, all-round heat makes for the greatest expansion of the corn kernel. But the kernel loses a bit of crispness when it's puffed that big.

Most hot-oil models will scorch the bottom layer of popcorn if not turned off at the right time, despite the automatic shutoffs they all have.

Poppers generally have a provision for melting butter. In addition, hot-oil models are designed to disperse the melted butter on the popcorn. Hot-air models use their measuring cup to hold the butter while it melts; then you pour it on.

Range-Top Popping

The special stove-top poppers are aluminum pots with a built-in stirring rod and, typically, a lid divided into flaps.

A range-top pan, even an ordinary two-quart saucepan, will produce fluffy popcorn, similar to the popcorn made in the electric hot-oil poppers. And like the hot-oil appliances, the pans leave few unpopped kernels.

They are also fast. In fact, the pans tie with the fastest of the electric poppers.

Microwave Popping

Micro-popping usually works well, but sometimes it doesn't. The reason may be the oven itself, the brand or grade of popcorn, or the container holding the popcorn. An oven that does well with bags often doesn't do a good job with bowls, and vice versa.

In one test, Consumers Union technologists tried one brand of popcorn, *Orville Redenbacher's Gourmet Original,* and one brand of bowl, the *Rubbermaid 5517* ($11), in five different ovens. The bowl worked best in an oven that had performed poorly with bags in past tests. It left the fewest unpopped kernels and expanded the kernels generously.

During the testing, they discovered one disadvantage to the *Rubbermaid* bowl—the holes in the top of the lid, which serves as a butter melter and dispenser, are too large. When they inverted the lid for use as a bowl, unpopped kernels fell through.

Before they closed the door on microwave popping, they taste-tested popcorn made in a microwave bowl. The texture was comparable to popcorn cooked in hot oil—not quite as good as the microwave type that comes in its own bag.

Comparison of Popping Methods

Here's a summary of the various popcorn popping methods, with their advantages and disadvantages.

Hot Air Poppers

Advantages:

- Safe and easy to use.
- Need little or no cleanup.
- Make popcorn with half the calories of hot-oil methods.
- Youngsters can use this type themselves.

Disadvantages:

- The big, fluffy kernels lack crispness.
- The upright shape is awkward to store.
- Some models require a few minutes' preheating.

Hot-Oil Poppers

Advantages:

- Make tasty popcorn.
- Require less attention than other hot-oil methods (because of their automatic shutoffs).
- The dome becomes a serving bowl.

Disadvantages:

- Cleanup can be messy.
- The dome may not be dishwasher-proof.
- Take up a lot of cabinet space.

Stove-Top Pans

Advantages:

- Efficient at popping all the kernels, and make tasty popcorn.
- Built-in manual stirrer eliminates need for shaking.
- Pan washable in soapy water or in a dishwasher.

Disadvantages:

- Some skill is required to adjust the heat and to know when to remove pan from heat.

Your Own Pan

Recipe: Use enough vegetable oil to cover the bottom of the pan and three corn kernels. Turn heat up to medium and cover the pan.

When the kernels pop, add enough kernels to cover the pan's bottom. Cover and shake the pan occasionally.

Advantages:

- No extra cost and no extra storage needed.
- Makes tasty popcorn, and leaves few kernels unpopped.
- Pan washable in soapy water or in a dishwasher.

Disadvantages:

- Some skill is required to adjust the heat and to know when the popcorn is done.
- Youngsters should be supervised.

Ratings of Corn Poppers

Listed by types; within types, listed in order of estimated quality based primarily on completeness and speed of popping. Bracketed models are essentially similar and are listed alphabetically. As published in a **June 1989** report.

Better ● ◐ ○ ◑ ● Worse

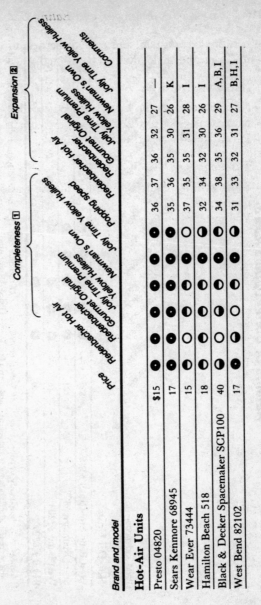

Hot-Air Units

Brand and model	Price	Completeness [1] Redenbacher Hot Air	Gourmet Original	Jolly Time Premium	Yellow Hulless	Newman's Own	Jolly Time Yellow Hulless	Popping speed	Expansion [2] Redenbacher Hot Air	Redenbacher Original	Gourmet Original	Jolly Time Premium	Yellow Hulless	Newman's Own	Jolly Time Yellow Hulless	Comments
Presto 04820	$15	●	●	●	●	●	●	36	37	36	36	32	27			—
Sears Kenmore 68945	17	●	●	●	●	●	●	35	36	35	35	30	26			K
Wear Ever 73444	15	○	◐	◐	○	◐	◐	37	35	35	35	31	28			I
Hamilton Beach 518	18	◐	◐	◐	◐	●	◐	32	34	32	32	30	26			I
Black & Decker Spacemaker SCP100	40	○	○	◐	◐	◐	◐	34	38	35	36	35	29			A,B,I
West Bend 82102	17	●	◐	◐	○	○	◐	31	33	32	31	27				B,H,I

317

Ratings of Corn Poppers (cont'd)

Brand and model	Price	Completeness [1] Redenbacher Hot Air	Gourmet Original	Jolly Time Premium Yellow Hulless	Newman's Own	Jolly Time Yellow Hulless	Popping speed	Expansion [2] Redenbacher Hot Air	Gourmet Original	Jolly Time Premium Yellow Hulless	Newman's Own Yellow Hulless	Comments
Hot-Oil Units												
West Bend Stir Crazy 5346	$27	—	◐	●	●	●	—	32	32	28	20	C, D
Sears Kenmore 6899	21	—	●	●	●	●	—	27	29	25	17	C, E, K
West Bend 82204	16	—	●	●	◐	◐	—	27	29	25	17	E, J
Regal K6727	20	—	●	●	●	◐	—	26	28	25	18	E, F, G, J

[1] A measure of how many unpopped kernels were left after popping with several brands of popcorn. A few models came close to popping every kernel; the most wasteful left scores at the bottom of the bowl.

[2] The number given is the ratio of popped volume to the volume of the kernels. According to our sensory tests, too much expansion may detract from texture—specifically, crispness.

All hot-oil models have: • Detachable cord about two feet long. • Heat-resistant plastic base with nonstick cooking surface. • Transparent plastic cover that serves as a bowl and that has a butter melter and dispenser at top.

Key to Comments

A—Mounts under cabinet; width is 11 inches, height eight inches, depth nine-and-a-half inches.

F—Butter dispenser did not disperse butter as well as others.

G—Manufacturer's instructions call for two-thirds cup of kernels; once popped, that much gourmet popcorn lifted off cover.

H—Essentially similar to *Proctor-Silex* H7340, not tested.

I—Two to three minutes preheating required, done automatically in the

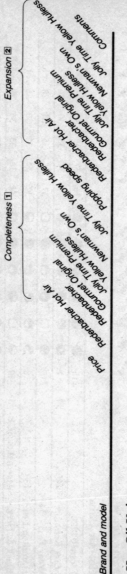

Specifications and Features

All hot-air models have: • Attached cord about two-and-a-half feet long.

Except as noted, all have: • Plastic base and transparent plastic chute. • Measuring cup built into chute. • Cup that serves as a butter melter.

B—Unit discharged many kernels that popped in bowl, causing popped corn to fly out onto floor and countertop.

C—Six-quart capacity.

D—Has metal stirring rod; delivered fluffier popcorn than other hot-oil methods.

E—Tended to scorch bottom layer.

Black & Decker.

J—Four-quart capacity.

K—Although this model was discontinued and is no longer available, the information has been retained to permit comparisons.

Bread Makers

A $300-or-so electric bread maker makes it very easy to bake your own bread.

You simply measure the flour, water, yeast, and other ingredients into the countertop machine. The device mixes and kneads the dough, lets it rise, then bakes it on the spot. A fresh loaf is ready some four hours after you pour in the ingredients.

The *Panasonic Bread Bakery* and the identical *National Bread Bakery* are white chests about the size of a compact microwave oven. They turn out rectangular loaves that are higher than they are wide and that weigh just under a pound. The *Welbilt Bread Machine* looks like the robot R2D2 from the movie *Star Wars;* its loaves are tall and round.

Performance

Consumers Union's testers baked numerous loaves of bread in the machines, using their recipe books and experimenting with cookbook recipes. You can use the machines not only for making basic bread, but also to prepare dough that you remove and reshape into coffee cakes, dinner rolls, and the like to be finished off in a conventional oven. Besides making white bread, the *Welbilt* has settings for French and sweet breads; in each case the loaf adopts the stubby, rounded shape of the *Welbilt*'s baking pan.

Ideally, a loaf of white or whole-wheat bread should have a uniform texture, a fine grain, and an evenly browned, rounded top crust. Too much yeast or too long a rising time results in a loaf with a coarse, open grain and a flattened or sunken top.

Using its own basic bread recipes, the *Panasonic/National* machine produces very nice loaves: light in texture, with evenly browned crusts, rounded on top. But it's important to remove those loaves promptly. If you leave one in for more than a few minutes after an electronic beep tells you the baking cycle is over, the inside becomes overcooked and the crust becomes soggy and overbrowned.

Sometimes bread baked in the *Welbilt* rises too much, hits the lid, and collapses. Sometimes unmixed flour produces a darkened smear on the side of the loaf. Many times the top crust fails to brown. With the *Welbilt* cookbook's white-bread recipe, you get better results if you reduce the water from 10½ to nine ounces and the yeast from two-and-a-quarter teaspoons to one-and-a-half. The resulting bread has a nicer, more even texture than bread from the *Panasonic/National*. However, its top still doesn't brown properly.

One hitch inherent in all these bread makers is that the bread is baked around the kneading blade inside the baking pan. Removing the blade once the bread is done tears the bottom of the loaf.

Avoiding a burn while lifting out the hot baking pan from the *Panasonic/National* requires using oven mitts. But the mitts make it awkward to jiggle the rotor of the kneading blade, which you must do to free the bread from the baking pan.

Bread left in the *Welbilt* doesn't overcook as in the *Panasonic/National*. That's because the *Welbilt* has a cool-down phase after its baking cycle. The cool-down also means that you don't have to handle a hot baking pan.

The *Panasonic/National* has a removable crumb tray underneath the baking pan that catches any spilled ingredients. The *Welbilt* has no crumb tray, and anything that gets spilled outside the pan and inside the baking well is a chore to clean up.

All three machines have a timer that lets you delay the baking process for several hours so the bread can be baked unattended, ready in time for breakfast or dinner.

Recommendations

You're a candidate for an automatic bread maker if you love warm, fresh loaves but have never relished the idea of doing all that kneading and pounding yourself. You're a candidate if you don't mind loaves baked into a shape quite different from what you—and your toaster—are probably used to.

You're a candidate if you have the counter space to devote to the machine permanently. A bread maker, which takes up about one square foot of countertop and 15 inches of headroom, isn't very portable.

Finally, you're a candidate if you are willing to spend $300 or so on a machine that does only one job.

A Fast Stew Cooker

A microwave oven isn't a perfect cooker. Hence the profusion of turntables, browning trays, and other items designed to blend the benefits of traditional baking with those of microwave cookery.

One unusual microwave-oven accessory is *Nordic Ware*'s *Tender Cooker,* $32 at hardware and department stores. It's a pressure cooker meant to combine "old-fashioned, slow-cooked texture and flavor with the speed of space-age microwave cooking." The cooker's capacity is only two-and-a-half quarts, so it's smaller than many conventional pressure cookers. But if the *Tender Cooker* were much larger, it wouldn't fit in many microwave ovens. As it is, the cooker requires an oven compartment at least eight inches high.

The cooker's recipe booklet lists more than 30 entrées. It states that "regular microwave cooking drives moisture from food, making meats and other foods tough and dry. The *Tender Cooker* . . . seals in moisture (and nutrition) by cooking at higher temperatures for shorter periods of time." True enough—for any pressure cooker. The recipe booklet goes on to claim that the cooker will "tenderize beef, pork, and poultry." But stews cooked in the *Tender Cooker* and the glass casserole are much alike, except that the *Tender Cooker* has a significant advantage in speed: it produces stew in about 20 minutes; the glass casserole in about an hour.

If you want stew with that "old-fashioned, slow-cooked texture and flavor," you must use the old-fashioned slow method. The tastiest stews are produced by simmering for hours on a range top.

Index